# More Praise for this Book from Around the World

"A straightforward, concrete, information-packed book from a generous, funny guru. The new chapter on online appeals is worth the price of the book by itself. Fortunately for us, there is much, much more."

*—Karen E. Osborne, president, The Osborne Group, Inc.*

"Mal Warwick is a direct mail genius. And he has generously devoted much of his talents and time to help others raise more money. This book is a classic that every fundraiser must own and read."

*—Harvey McKinnon, president, Harvey McKinnon Associates*

"This book doesn't just offer a uniquely insightful perspective on the familiar turf of writing fundraising letters. Now, in the second edition, it also provides a realistic assessment of the often fantastic world of the Internet and email fundraising. Truths are revealed that will shatter preconceived notions about e-philanthropy. The author places you firmly on the correct path in cyberspace through concrete case studies and provides insightful writing guidance for these new kinds of campaigns."

*—Senny Boone, executive director, Nonprofit Federation of the Direct Marketing Association*

"Just when I had thoroughly memorized the first edition of the bible on my desk, *How To Write Successful Fundraising Letters* by Mal Warwick, here comes Mal's new second edition, which takes fundraising writing squarely into the 21st century—blending the new age with the timeless. It's indispensable."

*—Jennie Thompson, fundraising and communications advisor*

"Mal Warwick's decades of experience lends accessibility and direction to all of us—from novice fundraisers to bold entrepreneurs for social change. This new edition will surely enhance any nonprofit's fundraising effectiveness, including those of us seeking to expand our online revenue."

*—Kelle Louaillier, executive director, Corporate Accountability International*

"While I loved the first edition, this revision has even *more* useful examples to help you reach out, engage, and motivate your donors to give. Now it also includes valuable information for online fundraising letters and strategies."

*—Alice Benson, MBA, CFRE, Lutheran Planned Giving, Metropolitan Washington, D.C.*

"*How to Write Successful Fundraising Letters* sits in a little bookcase by my desk, ready for constant reference. Now the new chapter on writing online appeals prepares me to meet the future with confidence. Thanks again, Mal."

*—Steve Thomas, CFRE, chairman/creative director, Stephen Thomas Ltd.*

"A second edition on fundraising letters could be like a second renewal notice! Not, however, when it comes from Mal Warwick. This updated version looks at all the basics with a fresh eye and includes the newer world of electronic fundraising. In Mal's inimitable fashion there is truly something here for everyone—founded on the basics, the book also contains helpful information and reminders for the veteran who recognizes the need to test and refine. I don't usually like re-runs, but I'm making a definite exception for this one!"

—*Steven P. Miller, director of development and membership, Bread for the World*

"I highly recommend Mal Warwick's book to colleagues as the essential and fundamental source of information and inspiration for creating and writing direct mail."

—*Roberta Zucker Catalinotto, chief development officer, Jewish Community Federation of San Francisco, the Peninsula, Marin, and Sonoma Counties*

"Mal Warwick has done it again. He's taken the seemingly simplest and most obvious of subjects and brought rigour, insight, and fresh thinking to it. Read this book and change, or stay stuck in the past of 'what used to work'."

—*Bernard Ross, director, The Management Centre (United Kingdom)*

"Few things matter more to fundraisers than effortlessly and effectively managing the mail and email appeal process, and no one knows more about this than Mal Warwick. This updated, fully-revised classic will rarely rest on your bookshelf for, being indispensable, it's sure to be mostly found open on your desk, bristling with Post-it notes."

—*Ken Burnett, author of* Relationship Fundraising, *and organizer of SOFII.org, the Showcase of Fundraising Innovation and Inspiration (France)*

"Never underestimate the power of good copy. There is no point doing all that work in targeting, printing, and mailing unless you write brilliant letters—and Mal's book tells you how to write brilliant letters that work. This book is a *must* for anyone who mails or emails fundraising letters to their donors."

—*Sean Triner, cofounder and director, Pareto Fundraising (Australia)*

"Fundraising is an art. Mal Warwick is not only the master of this art, but also of putting this across to fundraisers in the most convincing way. As a fundraiser I have found his book *How to Write Successful Fundraising Letters* most useful and its updated version much more so. Want to remain contemporary and successful? Just don't miss it!"

—*Maj. Gen. Surat Sandhu (Ret.), chair, South Asian Fundraising Group (India)*

"Mal Warwick is the world's leading authority on fundraising by mail, and *How to Write Successful Fundraising Letters* should be read by everyone who seeks success in fundraising. It's easy to read and full of excellent examples. Mal writes about his extensive experience in a practical way, making it easy to translate his insights into practical, day-to-day applications. If you want to put direct mail fundraising techniques to work for you, this is the book to read."

—*Custodio Pereira, founder, Brazilian Association for Fundraising Professionals (ABCR), and director general, Rio Branco Integrated Faculties (Brazil)*

"Mal's style of writing hooks you from the first sentence, and you feel you are trapped by his stories, jokes, and surprises. I find him one of the most entertaining and knowledgeable authors on fundraising. Mal's constant use of vivid and pertinent examples always impresses me. You can tell he has been there, and that his learning comes from real-life experience."

—*Víctor Naranjo, resource development director, area office for Latin America and the Caribbean, Habitat for Humanity International (Costa Rica)*

"Mal Warwick is a great fundraiser! He is constantly ahead of other authors. He knows how to mix different ingredients to get the reader involved. With the right contents, the right techniques, and a bit of 'art,' Mal is able to convince a prospect to give, to give regularly, and to give more and more, until the donor leaves a legacy to your cause. The new chapter on writing online appeals is a great added value to this second edition of the book! Thank you, Mal!"

—*Beatrice Lentati, senior fundraising consultant, Amministratore Unico, Lentati & Partners (Italy)*

"Only Mal Warwick can so generously share all the knowledge he has gained from decades of research into the habits and expectations of direct mail donors. This is a brilliant book! It will help any fundraiser find out what's likely to work in the mail and what isn't."

—*Katherine Yong, manager of resource mobilization and communications, Plan International (Peru)*

"One of the best hands-on books every fundraiser should read. It includes a wide array of practical examples and comprehensive advice on how to communicate effectively with prospects and donors. This is a must-have reference for people working in any culture."

—*Norma Galafassi, director, in2action Fundraising & Communication (Argentina)*

"Mal's a whiz at simplifying fundraising to sensible and practical steps. He has superbly recrafted *How to Write Successful Fundraising Letters* to take account of new challenges in online fundraising by clearly showing what works, why it works, and how you can do it, too."

—*Dr. Sue-Anne Wallace, FAICD MFIA, chief executive officer, Fundraising Institute Australia (Australia)*

**Web Resources**

Visit The Mal Warwick Fundraising Series page on www.josseybass.com and learn more about Mal's other books, find out where Mal is speaking and what he is up to, and download useful resources related to his books.

**About the CD-ROM**

The CD-ROM included with this book contains full-color samples of the type of direct mail packages discussed in Chapters 10 through 19 as well as full-color versions of some of the black-and-white samples displayed in the book. Also included on the CD are full-color samples of the black-and-white online examples shown in Chapter 20 as well as full-color samples of additional e-newsletters and online appeals.

# How to Write Successful Fundraising Letters

## Second Edition

## Mal Warwick

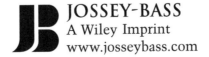
JOSSEY-BASS
A Wiley Imprint
www.josseybass.com

Published by Jossey-Bass
A Wiley Imprint
989 Market Street, San Francisco, CA 94103–1741—www.josseybass.com

Jossey-Bass books and products are available through most bookstores. To contact Jossey-Bass directly call our Customer Care Department within the U.S. at 800-956-7739, outside the U.S. at 317-572-3986, or fax 317-572-4002.

Jossey-Bass also publishes its books in a variety of electronic formats. Some content that appears in print may not be available in electronic books.

**Library of Congress Cataloging-in-Publication Data**

Warwick, Mal.
　　How to write successful fundraising letters/Mal Warwick. —2nd ed.
　　　p. cm.
　　Includes index.
　　　ISBN-13: 978-0-7879-9908-7 (paper/cd)
　　　　1. Direct mail fundraising.　2. Nonprofit organizations—Finance.　I. Title.
　　HV41.2.W378 2008
　　658.15′224—dc22

　　　　　　　　　　　　　　　　　　　　　　　　　　　　　　2007046925

Printed in the United States of America

SECOND EDITION

*PB Printing*　　10 9 8 7 6 5 4 3

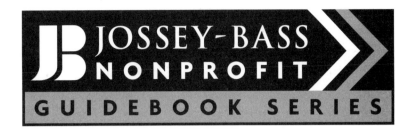

## The Jossey-Bass Nonprofit Guidebook Series

The Jossey-Bass Nonprofit Guidebook Series provides new to experienced nonprofit professionals and volunteers with the essential tools and practical knowledge they need to make a difference in the world. From hands-on workbooks to step-by-step guides on developing a critical skill or learning how to perform an important task or process, our accomplished expert authors provide readers with the information required to be effective in achieving goals, mission, and impact.

**Other Jossey-Bass Titles by Mal Warwick**

Revolution in the Mailbox: Your Guide to Successful Direct Mail Fundraising

Testing, Testing 1, 2, 3: Raise More Money with Direct Mail Tests

Fundraising on the Internet: The ePhilanthropyFoundation.Org Guide to Success Online, Second Edition

Ten Steps to Fundraising Success: Choosing the Right Strategy for Your Organization

The Five Strategies for Fundraising Success: A Mission-Based Guide to Achieving Your Goals

•   •   •

**Other Titles in The Jossey-Bass Nonprofit Guidebook Series**

The Budget-Building Book for Nonprofits: A Step-by-Step Guide for Managers and Boards, Second Edition, *Murray Dropkin, Jim Halpin, and Bill La Touche*

**Coming in the Summer of 2008:**

Strategic Communications for Nonprofits: A Step-by-Step Guide to Working with the Media, *Kathy Bonk, Henry Griggs, Emily Tynes, and Phil Sparks*

Winning Grants: Step by Step, Third Edition, *Mim Carlson, Tori O'Neal McElrath, Alliance for Nonprofit Management*

# Contents

# Preface to the Second Edition

**JUST IN CASE** you're curious about how this second edition is different from the first one, I'll get that out of the way right off the bat:

- There are three wholly new chapters, one on writing e-mail and Internet appeals, the others on building a monthly giving program and on promoting legacy gifts.

- Virtually all the examples are fresh and contemporary. The few exceptions you'll find in this edition strike me as holding up as well today as when I originally selected them.

- This edition includes a CD-ROM featuring all the examples in this book in high-resolution, full-color images.

- I've updated the reading list in Resource H, including online resources as well as newer books.

- I've reviewed every sentence, cutting a word or a sentence here or there or adding some new insight that leapt to mind. In some cases, these insights required an extra sentence, in others a paragraph or more.

## How This Book Is Organized

This second edition is structured in five parts.

Part One begins where the writing of any fundraising appeal should begin: with peering into the mind of the donor. These first five chapters examine the stuff of which successful fundraising is made:

- An appreciation for the broad range of motives that lead people to contribute money to good causes and important institutions

- An understanding of the dynamics in the relationship between the fundraiser and the donor
- Insight into the ways that donors view the fundraising letters they receive
- Knowledge of the characteristics of an effective fundraising letter

To put this understanding into a truly practical context, Part One concludes with a paragraph-by-paragraph tour through a successful appeal.

Part Two looks at the nuts and bolts. We'll approach the task of writing a fundraising letter from a strictly practical, down-to-earth perspective. In successive chapters in this part, we'll cover

- What to do before you sit down to write a fundraising appeal
- The eight steps I recommend following in crafting a fundraising package
- The concrete cardinal rules that determine whether your appeal will be a success (or a dud), along with a self-assessment form that will help you evaluate the likely effectiveness of a fundraising letter in the light of these rules
- The practical guidelines of style and syntax I urge you to follow when you're writing a fundraising appeal—or for that matter, any other prose that's meant to persuade the reader to act

The ten chapters in Part Three take you on a walking tour through the thickets of fundraising, visiting each of the most common types of fundraising letters to examine their unique characteristics and distinctive demands. In the course of Part Three, we'll study letters designed to do the following:

- Recruit a new member or donor
- Welcome a new donor into your organization
- Appeal for a special (additional) gift
- Request a year-end contribution
- Enlist a monthly donor
- Solicit a high-dollar-amount gift
- Persuade a donor to send a bigger gift
- Seek an annual gift
- Thank a donor for a gift
- Promote legacy gifts

Part Four, which consists of a single chapter, is entirely new. It introduces the increasingly lively and timely topic of raising money online—through e-mail appeals, electronic newsletters, and World Wide Web sites.

Part Five is where I invite you to steal my ideas as you might see fit. These resources are for your unregulated use—a bag full of treatments for the dread disease of writer's block:

- Sixty successful outer-envelope teasers

- Fifty-four strong leads for fundraising letters

- Ninety ways to use the word "you" in a fundraising letter

- Sixty-three ways to handle awkward copywriting transitions

- Forty-one powerful ways to end a fundraising letter

- Fifty-eight ways to start a P.S. in a fundraising letter

- Fifteen ways how *not* to get results from your writing

- Books and other resources to help you write successful fundraising letters

## How You Can Use This Book

I'll feel fulfilled as a writer only if you absorb every word in this book with the loving care I invested in it. On a more practical level, however, I'm confident you will find *How to Write Successful Fundraising Letters* useful in at least three additional ways (as some readers of both the first edition and the revised and updated first edition have told me they did):

- As a source of examples and inspiration when a writing task comes due and your mind won't stop thinking about everything other than fundraising

- As a quick-and-easy guide to the distinctive types of fundraising appeals (found in Part Three)

- As a collection of crib sheets (the resources in Part Five) that will help you resolve some of those thorny letter-writing challenges

In any case, please use this book however you see fit. I wrote it for you.

## Acknowledgments

The conventions of the publishing industry conspire to give the impression that one person alone writes a book. While there may be circumstances in which that's true, it's certainly not the case with this book. A number of people played roles in the conception and preparation of each edition of this book.

Stephen Hitchcock, then president of Mal Warwick Associates, first suggested I write this book. Steve's imprint is visible on every page. His fifteen-year-old list of "reasons people give" was the starting point for my work on Chapter One. More important, Steve was my writing mentor for more than a dozen years. Much of what he taught me about writing for results is reflected in the following pages. He reviewed every chapter of the first edition, page by page, painstakingly editing the most challenging parts. Also he played a major role in freeing me from the burdens of the day-to-day management of Mal Warwick Associates so that I was able to undertake the time-consuming project of writing this book.

Almost every appeal included as an example in Chapters Ten through Nineteen was drafted by someone else. Many of these examples were written by my colleagues at Mal Warwick Associates or by the freelance copywriters they employed. I urge you to recognize that I was not the author, so I can't take credit for the power of these appeals. Most of the time, my contribution—if any—was limited to playing the critic. (That's the easy part.)

The central theme of this book is that there are different types of fundraising letters and each type presents unique challenges to the writer. To dramatize the unique aspects of each type of fundraising letter, I lead off the ten chapters in Part Three with illustrations from one nonprofit organization with an extensive and well-organized direct mail fundraising program. I wanted to make clear that a single charity may indeed need to write letters of all the types described in this book. To fill that bill, I turned to Bread for the World, based in Washington, D.C., and a client of Mal Warwick Associates since 1989. I owe special thanks to David Beckmann and his colleagues for their generosity and cooperativeness in granting permission for their materials to be reproduced in this book.

The lists in Part Five represent some of the best work of my colleagues at Mal Warwick Associates over nearly a decade and a half. The original ideas incorporated into the first edition and its revision were suggested by staff involved in almost every phase of the creative and productive process: Stephen Hitchcock, Bill Rehm, Julie Levak, Deborah Agre, Judy Reimann, Marsha Mathews, Lissa Rosenbloom, Julie Weidenbach, Cherie Chavez, Christina Chavez, Sheila Bell, and Ramona Allen. Julie Levak and Deborah Agre won a free lunch at Berkeley's famed Chez Panisse Café for contributing more ideas to the lists than anyone else: seventy-one between the two. (You see? Writing fundraising letters can be fun!)

The freelance copywriting team of Deborah Block and Paul Karps generously took time out from a particularly busy season of their work on bread-and-butter fundraising projects to review the first draft of the original manuscript. They paid particular attention to the case studies. Because of their sharp eyes and extensive knowledge of fundraising letters, they uncovered a great many inconsistencies. Their detailed critique helped me enormously. I'm greatly indebted to them.

The first edition of this book would not have seen the light of day without the help I received from Ina Cooper and Ramona Allen at Mal Warwick Associates. Ina served as production coordinator, and Ramona faced almost daily assignments to scan or transcribe text and prepare seemingly endless rounds of photocopies. The hours they invested in this project may have equaled my own, and I'm very grateful to them.

Two other people went to great lengths to save me from my own excesses in preparing the revised edition. My editor at Jossey-Bass then, Johanna Vondeling, was an unfaltering source of shrewd judgment about the structure and flow of this book. It was much the stronger as a result of her efforts. Her fine editorial eye and sensitivity to style and syntax made this job a great deal easier and more enjoyable for me.

My assistant at Mal Warwick Associates during the preparation of the revised edition, Kimberely Araña, cheerfully endured the deadly combination of my erratic schedule and the many, and often unpredictable, demands on her time that this project occasioned. Her patience, thoroughness, and commonsense organizing skills helped keep me steady through this sometimes unsteadying process.

In preparing this second edition, several staff members of Mal Warwick Associates provided invaluable help. I'm indebted to Erin Ehsani and Kieu Thi Tran for their able assistance in keeping other priority matters from falling through the cracks during this time. I owe special thanks to Hidhe Garcia, who managed the complex and tedious process of procuring examples and securing permission to use them.

The preparation of Chapter Twenty, about writing online appeals, presented me with a special challenge. Although I've been involved in fundraising on the Internet for nearly a decade and a half, I am anything but an expert on its ways and means, much less current on the latest bells and whistles. However, my friends and colleagues Nick Allen of Donordigital and Madeline Stanionis of Watershed are experts. They both graciously took time out of their extremely busy schedules to review my draft and supply me with additional examples, both for Chapter Twenty and for the CD-ROM. Still, if errors remain, please blame me, not them. I'm the guy whose name is on the cover.

I owe a great debt, too, to the many readers of the first edition who encouraged me to think that this book was worth every bit of the time and effort I put into it. I hope you too will find this book to be helpful in your continuing effort to raise money for good causes and enduring institutions. I wish you the very best of luck.

*November 2007*                                                      Mal Warwick
*Berkeley, California*

# About the Author

**MAL WARWICK** has been raising money professionally since 1979 and has gained worldwide recognition as an author, consultant, and trainer. He has written or edited eighteen books, including the standard text *Revolution in the Mailbox, Revised Edition,* as well as the previous editions of this best-selling book.

Mal is founder and chairman of Mal Warwick Associates (Berkeley, California), which specializes in direct mail and online fundraising, and has founded or cofounded three other companies that furnish data processing, telephone fundraising, and online fundraising and marketing services to nonprofits.

Among the hundreds of nonprofits Mal and his colleagues have served over the years are many of the nation's largest and most distinguished charities as well as six Democratic presidential candidates and scores of small, local, and regional organizations. Collectively, Mal and his associates are responsible for raising at least half a billion dollars—largely in the form of small gifts from individuals.

For more than two decades, Mal has been a popular speaker at conferences of the Association of Fundraising Professionals (AFP) and other leading organizations in the philanthropic sector throughout North America. Since 1999, he has spoken at major fundraising conferences all over the globe, teaching the principles and techniques of fundraising to nonprofit executives on six continents and in more than one hundred countries.

Mal is chair of the Resource Alliance (London, UK), which sponsors the annual International Fundraising Congress in The Netherlands and helps build civil society in developing nations. Resource Alliance increases the capacity of nonprofit organizations in those countries to secure the resources they need through accredited courses, conferences and work-shops, awards programs, and consulting services.

He is also editor of *Mal Warwick's Newsletter: Successful Direct Mail, Telephone & Online Fundraising*™, a monthly electronic newsletter with eight thousand subscribers in sixty-seven countries. (Subscriptions are available free of charge at www.malwarwick.com.)

Mal is equally well known as an advocate for socially and environmentally responsible policies and practices in the private sector. He served as chair of the business organization Social Venture Network for four years and is the coauthor (with Ben Cohen, cofounder of Ben & Jerry's) of *Values-Driven Business: How to Change the World, Make Money, and Have Fun.*

A Peace Corps volunteer in Ecuador in the 1960s, he has lived in Berkeley since 1969. You may reach Mal through www.malwarwick.com or by e-mail at mal@malwarwick.com.

# Why You Should Read This Book

**I IMMODESTLY RECOMMEND** that you read this book for a number of reasons:

- If you write fundraising letters for a hospital, a college or university, a museum, a health agency, a human service organization, a public interest advocacy group, or any other nonprofit that needs funds

- If you want to write letters that raise more money for your organization

- If you serve in a leadership role in a nonprofit organization as executive director, development director, or marketing director

- If you are a member of a nonprofit's board of directors and you want to assess the effectiveness of your organization's fundraising appeals

- If you're involved in public relations, advertising, or marketing for a nonprofit organization or institution

- If you want to understand better how fundraising works

- If you want to learn how to write to get results

- If you want to be a more effective writer

If fundraising by mail is a science (a dubious proposition at best), its fuzziest, most inexact, least scientific aspect is writing the letters. There are those in the field who claim fundraising letters can be written by formula, but I'm not one of them. Writing this stuff is tough work because what's effective for one organization may prove counterproductive for another. And what worked last year or last time may not work today.

Though there's no copywriting formula that's worth the paper it's printed on, there are principles and practices of grammar, syntax, word usage, and formatting that need to be respected. Call them rules, if you will. Your rules won't necessarily match my rules, but each of us has to be consistent—and that may mean obsessing over the minutest details. (To get a sense of what I mean by this, take a look at the edited copy reproduced in Exhibit I.1. That's the sort of thing I often do when I take on an editing job.)

**EXHIBIT I.1**

# Editing Example: One Page of a Fundraising Letter

The reality is that for most of us, writing of any sort is a royal pain in the neck. But there are ways to reduce the fuzziness and the pain and to raise the odds that your letters will bring in every nickel you need, and more. Talent helps, but experience counts for a lot too.

Over the years, I've read tens of thousands of fundraising appeals, written or edited thousands of those letters myself, and shared in the creative process as a manager or consultant in thousands of other mailings. All of this experience has given me a front-row seat in a never-ending "copy clinic"—a close-up view of what works and what doesn't (and sometimes even why). This book conveys what I've learned about writing fundraising letters.

In other books I've written, I've explored many of the elements of fundraising. Most (though not all) of this work was about raising money by mail—from choosing mailing lists to working with consultants, from measuring results to designing and producing packages, from strategizing to testing to scheduling. This book isn't about any of those things. It's about writing. My topic here is the effective use of written English in the pursuit of philanthropic gifts.

Over my varied career, I've written newspaper stories, magazine articles, science fiction stories, and comic book scripts; ads for newspapers, magazines, radio, and television; sales letters, brochures, and pamphlets; technical manuals; e-mail promotions and copy for Web sites; speeches for others and speeches for myself—not to mention all those fundraising letters, plus more than a dozen other books about the craft of fundraising. I've written fiction and nonfiction, eulogies and humor, short pieces and long. I've written in three languages and translated from one to another.

Yet despite all this writing, I don't consider myself a particularly gifted writer. I'm no poet; my prose doesn't sing. I've written no unforgettable passage, contributed no timeless witticism to the language. But through long practice and difficult trial and error, I've learned to do one thing moderately well with my writing: get results. And there's just one result I want from this book: to help you write successful fundraising letters.

This book is a guide to the techniques and approaches that have proved successful for me—a tool chest of ideas and examples that will help you sharpen your own writing. If you prefer, look on it as a comprehensive review to help you gain perspective on the challenges you face as a writer of fundraising letters.

And there's one more result I hope to achieve with this book: I want you to enjoy reading it. I've found I do best what I enjoy the most—while those things I approach with deadly seriousness are least likely to turn out well. I suspect you too will find that the more fun you have when you write your fundraising letters, the more money you'll raise.

## Why a Fundraising Letter Is Always More Than Just a Letter

Although the title of this book refers to fundraising letters, you'll see examples that aren't just letters (as well as examples of e-mail and Web site copy that aren't letters in the traditional sense at all). The reasons for this discrepancy are that most people refer to fundraising appeals as letters and that the letter is almost always the most important component of an appeal. But the letter is never the only component of a fundraising package. Many other components of the package are important too. You'll need an envelope for your fundraising letter. And almost all the time you'll need at least two other items as well: a reply device (variously called a response device, coupon, card, form, or something else) and an envelope to mail it back in. Without a reply device and an easy way to return it, most fundraising letters would generate precious few gifts.

Beginners at the craft of writing fundraising letters commonly treat these other components as afterthoughts. I hope after reading this book you won't do so. In fact, you may find you need to devote just as much thought to the reply device and the envelopes—both envelopes—as you do to the letter itself.

## About the Letters Reproduced in This Book

All but one of the before-and-after case studies in Chapters Ten through Nineteen are drawn from the files of EditEXPRESS, a letter-editing service I offered from 1990 to 2000. To judge their value as illustrations, you need to understand how that service worked.

I operated EditEXPRESS as an editor of fundraising appeals, not as a writer of them. I took pains to make as few changes as possible in the letters I was sent to revise. My primary responsibility, as I saw it, was to increase the readability of the appeals. Although the writer or the fundraiser in me may have yearned to introduce new information—or even to take an entirely fresh approach—I usually contented myself by reshaping and rearranging the material I was given. Most of the time, I'm told, that sort of copyediting has been good enough to achieve a significant improvement in results.

I hope you'll find the before-and-after approach of the EditEXPRESS examples to be helpful, as readers of the previous editions have told me they were. However, in this second edition I've added a contemporary example to illustrate each of the eight types of fundraising letter described in Part Three. These examples are drawn from the work of my colleagues at Mal Warwick Associates for our clients during the past year. There are additional examples on the CD-ROM that accompanies this book.

## Why You Can Learn from the Case Studies—Even Though Your Organization Is Different

The causes and institutions represented in this book cover a wide range—from human services to the environment to lobbying against hunger. But what if your organization doesn't happen to fit into one of those categories? Or if it does fit, what if you're convinced it's really too different to benefit from the examples? In fact, you can learn a lot from fundraising letters written by other nonprofit organizations. There are three reasons why I strongly believe this:

1. You can learn how the fundamental rules of writing apply (or don't apply) to the craft of writing fundraising letters. These fundamentals have nothing to do with your cause or your constituency.

2. You can learn how the special techniques of fundraising and direct marketing can be put to work in fundraising letters. These techniques change very little from one cause or constituency to another.

3. You can learn how to improve your fundraising letters if you distance yourself from the everyday needs and details of your organization's work. Often it's much easier to see the forest rather than the trees when you're looking into someone else's forest.

Take my word for that. I've been wandering around in other people's forests for a very long time.

• • •

In a literal sense, I began work on the first edition of this book in 1989. In a larger sense, however, I started the project in 1979 when I founded my direct mail fundraising firm, Mal Warwick Associates, or even in 1949, well over half a century ago, when I wrote my first "fundraising" letter home from summer camp. I've put a lot into this book. I hope you get a lot out of it.

# Part One

# Motivating Your Audience

**THESE FIRST FIVE** chapters examine the stuff of which successful fundraising is made:

- An appreciation for the broad range of motives that lead people to contribute money to good causes and important institutions

- An understanding of the dynamics in the relationship between the fundraiser and the donor

- Insight into the ways that donors view the fundraising letters they receive

- Knowledge of the characteristics of an effective fundraising letter

To put this understanding into a truly practical context, Part One concludes with a paragraph-by-paragraph tour through one successful appeal.

# Chapter 1

# Why People Respond to Fundraising Letters

**IT'S DOWNRIGHT UNNATURAL.** Your fundraising letter must persuade the recipient to take an action that much of humanity thinks peculiar: to give money away.

To accomplish this seemingly unlikely objective, your appeal needs to be built on the psychology of giving. Forget your organization's needs. Instead, focus on the needs, the desires, and the concerns of the people you're writing to. Your job is to motivate them.

Commercial direct marketers frequently say that there are five *great motivators* that explain response: fear, exclusivity, guilt, greed, and anger. But I believe the truth is much more complex: that there are at least two dozen reasons people might respond to your fundraising letter. Any one of the twenty-four might suggest a theme or hook for your letter, and it's likely that several of these reasons help motivate each gift.

## 1. People send money because you ask them to

Public opinion surveys and other research repeatedly confirm this most basic fact of donor motivation. "I was asked" is the most frequently cited reason for giving. And the research confirms that donors want to be asked. Focus group research also reveals that donors typically underestimate the number of appeals they receive from the organizations they support. These facts help explain why responsive donors are repeatedly asked for additional gifts in nearly every successful direct mail fundraising program. When you write an appeal, keep these realities in mind. Don't allow your reticence about asking for money make you sound apologetic in your letter.

## 2. People send money because they have money available to give away

The overwhelming majority of individual gifts to nonprofit organizations and institutions are small contributions made from disposable (or discretionary) income. This is the money left over in the family checking account after the month's mortgage, taxes, insurance, credit cards, and grocery bills have been paid. Unless you're appealing for a major gift, a bequest, or a multiyear pledge, your target is this modest pool of available money.

For most families, dependent on a year-round stream of wage or salary income, the pool of disposable income is replenished every two weeks or every month. That's why most organizations appeal frequently and for small gifts. If your appeal is persuasive, your organization may join the ranks of that select group of nonprofits that receive gifts from a donor's household in a given month. If you're less than persuasive or if competing charities have stronger arguments—or if the family just doesn't have money to spare that month—you won't get a gift.

For example, if you write me a letter seeking a charitable gift, you may succeed in tapping into the $100 or $200 I'll probably have "left over" for charity during the month your letter arrives. If your appeal is persuasive, I might send you $25 or $50—$100 tops—because I decide to add you to the short list of nonprofits I'll support that month.

Now you may have the mistaken impression that as a businessman, a snappy dresser, and an all-around generous fellow, I have a lot of money. You may even be aware I've occasionally made much larger gifts to local charities. But you're unlikely to receive more than $50 because that's all I have available right now. Those few larger gifts I gave didn't come from my disposable income stream. They came from other sources (such as an investment windfall, a tax refund, or an inheritance) and required a lot of planning on my part.

## 3. People send money because they're in the habit of sending money by mail

Charity is habit forming; giving by mail is a special variety of this benign affliction. When I became involved in direct mail fundraising in the late 1970s, I was told that only about one in four adult Americans was *mail responsive*—that is, susceptible to offers or appeals by mail. By the turn of the century, according to the Simmons Market Research Bureau, two out of every three adults were buying goods or services by mail or phone every year. Many purchases involved telemarketing—but there's no doubt Americans are now more mail responsive.

Surveys also reflect the growing importance of direct mail appeals in the fundraising process. Research shows that fundraising letters are the top source of new gifts to charity in America.

## 4. People send money because they support organizations like yours

Your donors aren't yours alone, no matter what you think. Because they have special interests, hobbies, and distinctive beliefs, they may support several similar organizations. A dog owner, for example, may contribute to half a dozen organizations that have some connection to dogs: a humane society, an animal rights group, an organization that trains Seeing Eye dogs, a wildlife protection group. A person who sees himself as an environmentalist might be found on the membership rolls of five or six ecology-related groups: one dedicated to land conservation, another to protecting the wilderness, a third to saving endangered species or the rain forest, and so on. There are patterns in people's lives. Your appeal is most likely to bear fruit when it fits squarely into one of those patterns.

## 5. People send money because their gifts will make a difference

Donors want to be convinced that their investment in your enterprise—their charitable gifts—will achieve some worthy aim. That's why so many donors express concern about high fundraising and administrative costs. It's also why successful appeals for funds often quantify the impact of a gift: $35 to buy a school uniform, $40 for a stethoscope, $7 to feed a child for a day. Donors want to feel good about their gifts.

Your donors are striving to be effective human beings. You help them by demonstrating just how effective they really are.

## 6. People send money because gifts will accomplish something right now

Urgency is a necessary element in a fundraising letter. Implicitly or explicitly, every successful appeal has a deadline: the end of the year, the opening of the school, the deadline for the matching grant, the limited pressrun on the book available as a premium. But the strong attraction in circumstances such as these is best illustrated when no such urgent conditions apply. If the money I send you this week won't make a difference right away, shouldn't I send money to some other charity that has asked for my support and urgently needs it?

## 7. People send money because you recognize them for their gifts

You appeal to donors' egos—or to their desire to heighten their public image—when you offer to recognize their gifts in an open and tangible way: a listing in your newsletter; a plaque, certificate, lapel pin, or house sign; a screen credit in a video production; a press release. If your fundraising program can provide appropriate and tasteful recognition, you're likely to boost response to your appeals by highlighting the opportunities for recognition in your letter or newsletter. Even if donors choose not to be listed in print or mentioned in public, they may be gratified to learn that you value their contributions enough to make the offer.

## 8. People send money because you give them something tangible in return

Premiums come in all sizes, shapes, and flavors: bumper strips, gold tie tacks, coffee-table books, membership cards, even (in one case I know) a pint of ice cream.

Sometimes premiums (such as name stickers or bookmarks) are enclosed with the appeal; these so-called front-end premiums (or freemiums) boost response more often than not and are frequently cost effective, at least in the short run. In other cases, back-end premiums are promised in an appeal "as a token of our deep appreciation" when donors respond by sending gifts of at least a certain amount. Either way, premiums appeal to the innate acquisitiveness that persists in the human race.

## 9. People send money because you enable them to "do something" about a critical problem, if only to protest or take a stand

Today we are bombarded by information about the world's problems through a wide variety of channels. Although we may isolate ourselves inside triple-locked homes, build walls around suburbs, and post guards at gateposts, we can't escape knowing about misery, injustice, and wasted human potential. Often we feel powerless in the face of this grim reality. Charity offers us a way to respond—by helping to heal the sick or balm troubled souls, imprint our values on a new generation, or feed the hungry. Your appeal will trigger a gift if it brings to life the feelings that move us to act, even knowing that action is never enough.

If you offer hope in a world drowning in troubles, your donors will seize it like the life jacket it really is.

## 10. People send money because you give them a chance to associate with a famous or worthy person

There are numerous ways that the identity, personality, or achievements of an individual might be highlighted in a fundraising appeal. For example, that person may be the signer of the letter, the organization's founder or executive director, the honorary chair of a fundraising drive, a patron saint, a political candidate, an honoree at a special event—or simply one of the organization's members or clients. If the signer's character or accomplishments evoke admiration or even simply a past personal connection, your donors may be moved to send gifts in response. The opportunity to associate with someone who is well known or highly esteemed may offer donors a way to affirm their noblest inclinations—or compensate for what they believe to be their shortcomings.

## 11. People send money because you allow them to get back at the corrupt or the unjust

There are too few outlets for the anger and frustration we feel on witnessing injustice and corruption in society. Both our moral sense and the secular law hold most of us in check, preventing expressions of violence or vocal fury that might allow us to let off steam. For many, contributing to nonprofit causes or institutions is a socially acceptable way to strike back. Whether your organization is a public interest group committed to fighting corruption in government or a religious charity devoted to revealing divine justice, it may help donors channel their most sordid feelings into a demonstration of their best instincts.

## 12. People send money because you give them the opportunity to "belong"—as a member, friend, or supporter—and thus you help them fight loneliness

Your most fundamental task as a fundraiser is to build relationships with your donors. That's why so many organizations use membership programs, giving clubs, and monthly gift societies. The process of solicitation itself can help build healthy relationships. Shut-ins, for example, or elderly people with distant family and few friends may eagerly anticipate the letters you send. Most of us are social animals, forever seeking companionship.

## 13. People send money because you enable them to offer their opinions

The act of sending a gift to some nonprofit organizations might itself constitute a way to speak out. Consider, for example, the American Civil Liberties Union or the Republican National Committee or the Human Rights Campaign; support for these groups makes an obvious statement about a donor's views. But almost any charity can offer donors an opportunity to state an opinion by including in an appeal an involvement device such as a membership survey, a petition, or a greeting card that might later be sent to a friend or family member. Although most donors may ignore the chance to offer suggestions, they may regard the invitation to do so as a strong sign of your respect and concern for them.

## 14. People send money because you provide them with access to inside information

Even if your organization or agency isn't an institution of higher education or a research foundation, you still hold knowledge many donors crave. Nonprofit organizations are often on the front lines of everyday, hands-on research, gathering important data day after day from clients, visitors, or program participants. Their staff members are likely to be specialists, and often experts, in their fields.

Every nonprofit possesses information that is not widely known to the public and that donors may perceive as valuable. A loyal supporter may be vitally interested in the health and well-being of your executive director (who was ill lately), the progress of a project you launched last year (after a spectacular start), or what your field staff learned last month (three months after the hurricane).

Disseminating inside information, which is intrinsically valuable and thus constitutes a gift from you, also helps build strong fundraising relationships by involving your donors in the intimate details of your organization.

## 15. People send money because you help them learn about a complex and interesting problem or issue

In most advanced industrial nations, the citizens think it is largely government's responsibility to provide funding for education, health care, and the arts. In contrast, the traditional American response has been to meet important needs such as these principally through private, voluntary action. Nonprofit organizations in the United States tackle issues or problems that society otherwise ignores or undervalues. Don't think just of the private schools and colleges, nonprofit hospitals, museums, and symphony orchestras. Think about Mothers Against Drunk Driving, Disabled American Veterans, Planned Parenthood, the Nature Conservancy, and the hundreds of thousands of other organizations like them that are far less well known. Often these organizations are on the front lines of research or public debate on the most challenging, the most controversial, the most engaging issues. If that's true of your organization, the emphasis you place in your appeal on your special knowledge may help motivate donors to give.

Your donors may even perceive the appeal itself as a benefit. As research frequently reveals, donors regard the letters they receive from charities as a source of special knowledge. I believe that helps explain why long letters containing hard facts and intriguing ideas often outpull more emotional appeals.

## 16. People send money because you help them preserve their worldview by validating cherished values and beliefs

The very act of giving affirms a donor's dedication to a charity's worthy aims. Donors support your organization's work because you act on their behalf, pursuing your mission with time and effort they could never bring to bear themselves. In this passionate pursuit, you act out their values and beliefs—the deep-seated convictions that lead them to join in your mission. But you must constantly remind them of the connection.

If your organization's mission is congruent with widely shared values and beliefs—a commitment to piety, for example, or saving dolphins or promoting efficiency in government—you face an obvious marketing opportunity. But if your nonprofit is dedicated to an unpopular cause, such as prisoners' rights, you possess a similar (if unenviable) advantage: for that small number of donors willing to take a stand on an issue that others reject, the values and beliefs that make the act of giving a form of personal affirmation suggest to the fundraiser a language both may speak.

## 17. People send money because you allow them to gain personal connections with other individuals who are passionately involved in some meaningful dimension of life

A charity is an intentional community of sorts—a cooperative venture, an institutional expression of a shared creed or common hopes. Your job as a fundraiser is to strengthen the bonds that tie your community together.

Your greatest asset may be the heroic members of your field staff, who daily risk their lives to right the world's wrongs, or simply a particular person within your community whom donors may regard as an inspiring example: a selfless, dedicated staff member; a passionately committed trustee; a model client or beloved beneficiary of your work. If you bring such people to life through your fundraising appeals, you enable your donors to live vicariously through them—and that can be a meaningful and rewarding experience for donors, as well as profitable for your organization.

## 18. People send money because you give them the chance to release emotional tension caused by a life-threatening situation, a critical emergency, or an ethical dilemma

The charitable impulse is often precipitated by special circumstances that cause pain, fear, or even embarrassment. Consider the enduring popularity of memorial gifts to commemorate the passing of friends or loved ones or the spontaneous outpouring of gifts to aid crime victims or the families of kidnapped children. People want to help relieve pain and suffering, if only because they share these feelings. And they want to respond to grave emergencies, if only because they fear death. Your appeal for funds may afford them an opportunity to ease their affliction.

## 19. People send money because they are afraid

Fear motivates. The American public has been subjected to billions of fundraising letters expressly conceived to evoke fear. Fear of death. Fear of poor people or foreigners. Fear of Social Security benefit cuts. Fear of higher taxes. Fear of Democrats or Republicans, liberals or reactionaries. No Pollyannish view of human motivation can erase the evidence that vast sums of money have been raised by such appeals. Fear sells. Yet I believe with all my heart that it's often unseemly, at times ethically questionable—and ultimately counterproductive—to use this obvious stratagem.

Consider the would-be prophet who predicts Armageddon next year. Who will heed the prophet when next year has come and gone and the world is still in one piece? A fundraiser who builds the case for giving on the worst-case scenario may be building on quicksand.

## 20. People send money because you allow them to relieve their guilt about an ethical, political, or personal transgression, whether real or imagined

Guilt undeniably plays a role in prompting some gifts. Think of the $1 or $2 cash contribution mailed in response to direct mail packages containing name stickers or greeting cards, the belated membership renewals that follow a long series of increasingly insistent demands, or the millions of small gifts sent every year in response to photographs of skeletal children. Our complex society allows few of us the luxury of acting out of purely ethical motives. Compromise is woven through the fabric of our daily lives. The fact is that none of us is likely to feel guilt-free at any time. Sometimes giving to charity, like throwing coins into the poor box in an earlier era, will help release the pressure.

Yet I believe guilt is highly overrated as a motivator. Rarely will donors who are moved primarily by guilt prove loyal over the years, and larger gifts from them are relatively rare. As a fundraising strategy, guilt may be just as counterproductive in the long run as fear.

## 21. People send money because you give them tax benefits

No list of motivating factors for charitable giving is complete without at least passing reference to tax benefits. Without question, the charitable tax deduction has played a major role in stimulating many large gifts and legacy gifts, because the benefits to the donor are substantial. (This is particularly true of gifts of artwork or other forms of appreciated property to such institutions as museums, because the tax laws are specifically structured to encourage such gifts.) However, many small donors mistakenly believe they too gain a great advantage from the tax deductibility of their gifts. That's why it's always advisable when requesting a gift to inform the donor that it may be deductible: this information may not help, but it can't hurt.

Still, it's dangerous to construct an appeal exclusively on the basis of tax benefits, even an appeal to buy into a tax-reduction program such as a charitable remainder trust. Experts in planned giving advise that *donative intent*—the desire to help, to do good, to make a difference—is usually of far greater importance than any financial considerations. And there are lots of tax-reduction schemes available to well-to-do people from institutions with no charitable purpose whatsoever.

## 22. People send money because they feel it's their duty

Many of our religious traditions teach us that it's wrong to live life without observing our duty to others to relieve their pain, enlarge their opportunities, or brighten their lives. There is also a secular belief, widely shared in the United States, that as citizens in a democracy, we have an obligation to help make things better for our fellow citizens. Those who benefit from military training may acquire a heightened sense of duty.

Not every nonprofit organization can appeal explicitly to donors' sense of duty (though many charities can do so). But duty may nonetheless play a role in inspiring the gifts any nonprofit receives, for duty by its very nature is self-activating.

## 23. People send money because they believe it's a blessing to do so

The Christian belief that "it is more blessed to give than to receive" is deeply ingrained in Western civilization and far from limited to practicing Christians. In the Jewish concept of *mitzvah*, for example, many Americans find justification for believing that doing good is its own reward. Clearly—at least in our idealized vision of ourselves—we Americans celebrate the notion of charity. Our self-image as "nice people" derives in no small part from our generous response to charitable appeals.

## 24. People send money because they want to "give something back"

Despite the growing gap between rich and poor in America—or more properly, because of it—the U.S. economy has spawned millions of millionaires, not to mention tens of millions of individuals who earn annual six-figure salaries. Huge amounts of cash slosh around in the melting pot that is American society. Although most of that money buys ever-larger homes and cars and increasingly contrived luxury goods, more each year is finding its way into the coffers of the nation's one million nonprofit organizations. Why? Because many of those well-to-do people are motivated to share their good fortune with their communities or society at large. "Giving something back" is frequently cited by major donors as a principal reason for their gifts, and unquestionably it helps account for the generosity of tens of millions of less-prosperous donors.

• • •

Now that we've got a handle on two dozen of the reasons donors might respond to that fundraising letter you're writing, let's take a look at the dynamics at work when they find your letter in their mailbox.

# Chapter 2

# How a Fundraising Letter Is Like a Personal Visit

**MOST OF US** who write letters to raise funds—or to sell products or services, for that matter—have a one-word answer to the question "How do you know whether that will work?" *Test*.

A German professor of direct marketing named Siegfried Vögele has two answers. He's just as firmly committed as any of us to the rigors of head-to-head testing to determine which of two or more variations in copy, design, or content will secure the best response. But Vögele also cites chapter and verse from a realm of research that uses such devices as eye-motion cameras and machines that measure subtle changes in skin chemistry. This research, conducted over many years, has given him profound and detailed knowledge of the ways human beings react when they hold direct mail materials in their hands.

Many of us guess about these things; we have insights or hunches. Siegfried Vögele often *knows*.

Vögele has been practicing and teaching his craft in Germany since the 1970s. In 1980, he caused a sensation at the all-European direct marketing conference and has taught his Dialogue Method throughout Europe ever since. He asserts that a direct mail letter works when it successfully involves readers in a silent dialogue with the signer. Thousands of marketers have attended his seminars, and articles based on his eye-motion research have made their way to America. His *Handbook of Direct Mail*, published in German in 1984, has been translated into Italian, French, and English. In other words, the story's getting out. (Resource H provides details about his book.)

This chapter sets out the essence of Vögele's Dialogue Method as it applies to writing direct mail letters—and I'll carry the translation one step further into the realm of fundraising.

## What Happens in a Personal Fundraising Visit?

The doorbell rings. You trudge to the front door, switch on the porch light, and squint through the peephole.

Standing at your door is a young woman, nineteen or maybe twenty years old, scruffily dressed, a clipboard tightly gripped in one hand, and an eager smile pasted on her face. You may be thinking, "Is this another of those annoying canvassers? Do I have to write another check for twenty or twenty-five bucks to get her to leave? What group does she represent, and why are they bothering me? Am I really going to let this little pest inside my home?"

Nevertheless, you open the door, greet the young woman, and listen to her long enough to hear that she is representing a charity called [fill-in-the-blank]. Not only that, but she says something about what [fill-in-the-blank] is doing that relates directly to things you care about. Besides, she's a beguiling young person who appears to have a bright future. You sigh, open the door a little wider, and (still reluctant) let her into the house.

Now, perched on the edge of your living room couch, the young canvasser launches into her pitch for [fill-in-the-blank]. You're not listening closely, but you get the gist of it. Every so often you nod, smile, or gesture. Encouraged, she plunges ahead, keeping her eyes on you all the while she speaks, emphasizing this or that or the other thing as you demonstrate more interest (or less) by the way you nod your head, fold or uncross your arms, or even occasionally ask a question or venture a comment. There are lots of questions on your mind, but you pose few of them, not wanting to drag out this unwanted conversation. And although you don't understand or agree with everything the fundraiser says, when you frown, shrug, or lift your eyebrows in a questioning way, she slips in a quick answer or makes a reassuring statement, then quickly rushes on to the next point. All this goes on for a few minutes until the fundraiser says something that really catches your attention.

Fully engaged for the moment, you make a casual reference to an experience related to what she has just said and—just to be polite—you ask her a pointed question. With a rush, she launches into a detailed answer. It's interesting for a few seconds, but then your eyes start glazing over. Noticing your disengagement, the young woman makes some comment about the lateness of the hour and immediately makes her pitch: "So, can I count on you for a gift of $50 tonight to help [fill-in-the-blank]?"

Fifty dollars is far too much, so you demur, settling for $25 instead. (Truth to tell, you're just as interested in getting her to leave you alone as you are in helping [fill-in-the-blank].) The canvasser gratefully volunteers to wait while you retrieve your checkbook. She accepts your gift with effusive thanks and departs, leaving behind a thin sheaf of papers with the latest developments at [fill-in-the-blank] and a promise that soon you'll be hearing from this group again so you'll know how your gift has been used.

Now, what has just happened here?

1. The canvasser got your attention by ringing your doorbell. You weren't expecting her, and as far as you're concerned, the evening would've been just as pleasant, if not more so, if she'd never shown up.

2. The moment you set eyes on her, barely conscious questions started welling up in your head in quick order: you wondered who she was and why she'd come and what she wanted you to do—and you answered most of those questions for yourself as quickly as they popped into your mind because the answers were obvious.

3. The young woman was representing an organization that's working on an issue you care a lot about. If she'd asked your help for some other cause or to address some other issue, you might just as well have smiled as politely as you were able and wished her better luck with the neighbors.

4. Her manner or her appearance—combined with something about your own mood and circumstances—induced you to let her into your home. You weren't planning to do so; it just happened. And you invited her in even though you knew perfectly well she was going to ask you for money.

5. Once inside, the young woman delivered her pitch, watching your body language all the while and answering every question you raised as responsively as she could, some more fully than others.

6. Something she said triggered a strong reaction in you—enough to provoke a comment of your own and a substantive question. Right away, the fundraiser gave you all the details you asked for and more.

7. As soon as she sensed your patience waning, she moved quickly to ask for a gift. She knew perfectly well you support the work of [fill-in-the-blank]. Her challenge was to make you admit it.

8. You declined to contribute the full amount she requested but did agree to give something. Since you had taken up so much of her time, it seemed the least you could do. Anyway, [fill-in-the-blank] does such valuable work!

9. The canvasser didn't just take your money and run. She thanked you for your support, reassured you it would make a big difference, and promised you would hear again soon from [fill-in-the-blank].

In short, you started the evening with absolutely no intention of giving a cent to [fill-in-the-blank]—or any other group for that matter, let alone a check for $25. You've done so anyway, and you feel pretty good about it!

Now let's consider a similar scene—one in which the appeal for funds comes by mail rather than in person. By comparing these two experiences, we'll gain important insight into Vögele's Dialogue Method.

## How People Decide Whether to Open Fundraising Letters

You've just gotten home from a tough day at the office. You toss the mail into a heap on the coffee table, grab something to drink from the refrigerator, and collapse into the easy chair, flicking on the TV with the remote control with one hand and pulling the wastebasket close to your chair with the other. Now, one or two deep breaths later, barely paying attention in the flickering glow of the television screen, you retrieve a handful of mail and begin the daily ritual.

Plunk! Into the wastebasket goes the fourth duplicate copy of that clothing catalogue. Plunk! Again, in one smooth, unhesitating motion: another credit card offer. And again and again: that health charity that reminds you of things you want to forget, a packet of discount coupons from a store you wouldn't visit if your life depended on it, a promise of untold wealth from Publishers Clearing House, a picture of pathetic little children. Now you come to the gas and electric bill—and something else that may be worth a glance: an envelope from [fill-in-the-blank], the people who do all that good stuff about whatchamacallit. At least they spelled your name right (unlike the catalogue merchant and the senders of some of the other pieces of mail). You know whom it's from because the organization's name and address are right there in the upper-left-hand corner and, besides, there's a photo on the envelope that looks a lot like whatchamacallit. Anyway, it looks familiar.

Chances are that this is another fundraising appeal from [fill-in-the-blank]—but you never know for sure until you look inside. Maybe the group has something interesting to say, even if it is a solicitation.

Before you know it, you've turned over the envelope from [fill-in-the-blank], slit it open, and dumped the contents out onto your lap. Now there's no question what these people want from you: the self-addressed envelope with those telltale broad stripes and the reply card with a hefty checkmark and a big bold "YES!" above a string of dollar amounts leave no doubt whatsoever that this is a fundraising solicitation. But [fill-in-the-blank] is a fascinating group, and a photo and caption on the reply card give the impression this letter is definitely about whatchamacallit, so it's probably worth looking a little further.

Now let's take stock before we stumble deeper into the jungle of real-world fundraising. What's happening here, and how does it compare to the experience you've just had with that aggressive young canvasser?

1. You weren't expecting a fundraising letter from [fill-in-the-blank] any more than you were anticipating the young woman's visit to your home.

2. When you first glanced at [fill-in-the-blank]'s appeal, you weren't paying much attention at all—even less attention, no doubt, than you paid that canvasser. (After all, she was standing right there.) Vögele estimates we devote no more than 10 percent of our attention to reading unsolicited mail.

3. Despite your lack of attentiveness, you noticed one thing without fail: the group spelled your name correctly. That young woman didn't know your name, but she looked you in the eye, accomplishing much the same end.

4. Something else about the letter caught your attention, triggering curiosity or concern—enough to motivate you to open the envelope and pull out the contents. What did the trick? The [fill-in-the-blank] name? That photo of whatchamacallit? It's hard to know (but ultimately doesn't matter) exactly what made the difference, just as your decision to open your front door to that canvasser was impulsive and difficult to analyze.

5. As you opened the envelope and dribbled the contents onto your lap, a stream of questions started flitting nearly unnoticed through the depths of your consciousness, much like those that came to mind as the fundraiser delivered her pitch in your living room. These questions included the obvious ones ("What's this about? What do they want from me? What's it going to cost me?"), and many of them were answered at a glance as you observed the contents of [fill-in-the-blank]'s appeal. These casual little traces of wonderment or confusion are what Siegfried Vögele calls *unspoken readers' questions.* As many as twenty such questions pop into the average reader's mind on picking up a direct mail solicitation.

But all this slips by with amazing speed. So far the whole incident—from your first glimpse of the [fill-in-the-blank] solicitation to your dumping the contents onto your lap—has taken a maximum of five to eight seconds.

To get a better sense of just how quickly five seconds flit by, follow the second hand on your watch, or count backward slowly by thousands. Those five long seconds spell the difference between the success or failure of a fundraising appeal. Tonight, for [fill-in-the-blank], they've been enough for a very good start.

Now, let's pick up the trail of our story again.

## How a Fundraising Letter Is Like a Face-to-Face Dialogue

Taking a sip of your drink, then turning up the volume on the television set, you now fish out [fill-in-the-blank]'s letter from the jumble on your lap. Dangling it before you between thumb and forefinger, you glance at the front page. Briefly you take in a dramatic little photo in the upper-right-hand corner and note that the letter contains short paragraphs, subheads, and underlining. Then you quickly flip the letter over to the back page to see who's writing to you.

Your eyes temporarily fix on the signature and the typed name below it, then drop down to the postscript; it's only three lines long, so you read it through. Sure enough, [fill-in-the-blank] is hoping you'll send money to do something new about whatchamacallit. A whole new round of questions rushes to the surface—questions such as, "How are they going to pull that off again? Will my twenty-five bucks make a difference? Are they going to send me something if I mail them a gift?" So now you scan the subheads and underlined words in the letter at a rapid rate: first on the last page, then, very briefly, on the two interior pages, and finally on the first page again.

Now you begin reading the letter's opening sentence. It's the beginning of a story, and before you know it you're hooked. You read first one longish paragraph, then another—but that's enough. You're satisfied. [Fill-in-the-blank] is doing exactly what you'd hoped, and you're just as eager to be part of the act this year as you were before. Out of long-ingrained habit, you grab the reply card and scan it to be sure you didn't misunderstand what [fill-in-the-blank] expected of you. Satisfied there was no miscommunication, you add the reply card to [fill-in-the-blank]'s postage-paid return envelope and drop the little bundle on top of the gas and electric bill: both will go into the "bills to pay" file. You'll write both checks next Saturday—or at any rate, that's what you say to yourself.

Let's pause here to take stock again, reviewing what's taken place from the perspective of Siegfried Vögele.

1. You were still largely inattentive—after all, you had a drink in one hand and a TV set blaring—but something about the letter from [fill-in-the-blank] persuaded you to turn it over for a second look rather than toss it into the wastebasket along with the day's direct mail losers. Was it that photo on the first page? The way those short paragraphs, subheads, and underlining suggested the letter would be quick and easy to read? No doubt both factors helped.

2. Pay close attention now: your eyes may have skipped through quite a number of words in scanning the first page of the letter, but you didn't actually read anything. The first words you read were the signature; the first element of text, the postscript. In other words, *the P.S. was the lead of this letter.* Siegfried Vögele says his eye-motion research reveals that the postscript is the first text read by more than 90 percent of all direct mail recipients.

3. But what was it you saw on the final page of the letter that motivated you, first to read the P.S. and then to scan the subheads and underlining? Was it the easy-to-read format and accessible language—or was there something genuinely involving in what you read? Was [fill-in-the-blank] making it worth your while to read on—by answering your unspoken questions with carefully crafted subheads, addressing your concerns through judicious underlining, spelling out the advantages you would receive by supporting their work? Vögele says yes: that only by answering your silent questions through such devices as these will a solicitation be involving enough to induce you to read on. If the letter doesn't answer those questions in the most obvious and accessible way, it's unlikely to be read at all.

4. Notice that the first time you read a complete block of copy was when you took in the P.S. The second time was after you read the opening sentence of the letter and learned it was interesting enough to engage you; then you read one or two complete paragraphs—and that was the point where you were finally hooked. In Vögele's way of looking at these things, there are two stages in a reader's involvement in a direct mail letter. As soon as you read one full block of text from beginning to end, you passed from the first stage to the second and final stage. At that precise moment, you began to participate in the *comprehensive second dialogue.* Here's how Vögele describes the process: "We answer unspoken readers' questions in a simple, easily understood way, first

through a short 'dialogue' which makes the reader aware of the benefit to himself, then through a [second and] more detailed 'dialogue' built along the same lines as a real personal sales conversation."

5. But what was it that caused you to glide so smoothly from the *short dialogue* to the *comprehensive second dialogue*? Vögele would say many factors contributed—everything in the content, language, and format that made the letter easy to read, accessible, informative, and directly responsive to your concerns. All are examples of the response boosters he calls *amplifiers:* little signs and gestures of positive reinforcement that help the reader spot encouraging answers to his unspoken questions.

In Vögele's lexicon, *filters* are the polar opposite of amplifiers. They're the negative forces that come into play in a direct mail package: the elements of formatting or the contents that make the package hard to read, uninteresting, off-putting.

Amplifiers provide you with little yeses to answer those unspoken questions. Filters produce no's.

The canvasser used her own arsenal of amplifiers by speaking intelligently (but not over your head), answering your questions (whether vocalized or not), watching and responding to your body language, and shutting up quickly when your patience flagged.

She skillfully moved you to answer yes to your own unvocalized questions—again and again and again. She avoided all the little traps (or filters)—the distractions, the boring lists of facts, the self-centered emphasis on [fill-in-the-blank]'s needs. Instinctively, she knew those missteps were a surefire way to lead you to answer your own unspoken questions with no—over and over again. Whoever wrote that letter for [fill-in-the-blank] did much the same thing, guiding you to answer yes far more often than you answered no.

As Vögele sees it, getting to that big YES!—a checkmark on the reply form, along with a check—is merely a matter of helping the reader answer yes a lot more frequently than he answers no.

But something else was going on here, too, something much more basic: both fundraisers—the letter writer no less than the canvasser—took pains to *engage you in a dialogue*. They answered *your* questions (spoken or not). They both went out of their way to involve you in a conversation—silent and one-sided in the case of the letter but nonetheless involving.

Neither the young woman nor the writer of the letter was engaged in a monologue, preoccupied with [fill-in-the-blank]'s needs and problems. Both made the effort to *relate the organization's needs to you*—the listener or the reader—in a style, language, and presentation format that subtly moved you to adopt [fill-in-the-blank]'s needs as your own.

## Answering Your Reader's Questions Before They're Even Asked

The trick to this craft, Siegfried Vögele tells us, is to anticipate the questions that will be on the reader's mind and answer those questions clearly and forcefully. He admonishes us to pay extra special attention to those questions that highlight the advantages the reader will enjoy (what we call *benefits*). Your answers must find their way into photos or drawings (and accompanying captions) or into subheads or underlined phrases or words—because those are the items in your letter that the reader will notice before actually reading what you've written.

Much of the skill that a letter writer brings to the task, then, is to catalogue the questions readers are sure to ask and artfully weave the answers into the letter. Vögele says there are two types: *basic questions*—those that involuntarily leap to mind when someone picks up any fundraising letter—and *product questions*—those that relate specifically to your appeal and might not come to mind if your reader were instead examining an appeal from some other charity. Although Vögele's terminology is derived from the experience of commercial direct marketing, both categories of readers' unspoken questions have their equivalents in the realm of fundraising.

Here are some of the basic questions that donors or prospective donors might ask themselves when they pick up one of your fundraising letters:

- Where did this letter come from?
- What's inside the envelope?
- Who wrote this letter?
- Who signed this letter?
- Where did they get my address?
- What do they know about me?
- Why are they writing to me specifically?
- How much money do they want from me?
- Should I even bother to read this letter?
- Can they prove what they say?

- What happens after I respond?
- Do I have to sign anything?
- Do I have to put a stamp on it?
- What would my spouse think about this?
- What would my friends think?
- Can this wait?
- What would happen if I don't do anything?
- Can I throw this thing away?
- Have I received this before?
- Will they put my name on another mailing list?
- What's the catch?

Now consider some of the many product questions that might leap into your reader's mind at the first sight of your fundraising letter:

- Have I heard of this organization before?
- Have I given to these people before?
- Do they get any government funds?
- Do they really need my help?
- What difference will it make if I respond?
- Are they going to send me a newsletter?
- Will I get lots of other solicitations from these people?
- Will they expect me to give them money every year?
- How much of this gift will actually be used the way they say?
- How is this different from what other groups do?
- Are they going to send me a thank-you?
- Have they been doing this kind of work for very long?
- Is there a local branch of this organization?
- How do I know they're honest?
- Who runs this organization?
- Is there anybody famous who supports them?
- Is there a deadline?
- What do I have to do to fill out the reply card?
- Is there a better solution for this problem?

These questions are actually quite straightforward. Questions of both types are a natural human response to any unsolicited appeal, whether it comes by mail or in person. In a face-to-face visit, the fundraiser intentionally confronts the most promising of these questions and tries to provoke yet more questions, knowing that engaging a prospect in dialogue is the straightest path to a gift. In a written fundraising appeal, too, the skillful writer seeks to anticipate these readers' unspoken questions, knowing that the more directly readers' true private concerns are met, the more involved readers will become in silent dialogue.

# The Four Waves of Rejection

If the writer doesn't properly anticipate and answer the reader's unspoken questions, instead of a preponderance of little yeses that add up to one big beautiful YES! the no's have it, Vögele says—and plunk! goes that letter. Rejection can come at any moment, he warns us. There are four possible stages in which the reader might give up on you.

## Wave One

You've got up to twenty seconds to engage the reader—just long enough for her to open the envelope, examine the contents, and decide whether to spend any more time with your letter. Vögele refers to this as the *first run-through*. In this stage, you face your first and biggest hurdle; if your letter survives this test, the greatest danger is past. If, instead, the reader concludes, "I've never heard of these people before," or "I already sent them money this year," or simply "I'm not interested"—or any one of a thousand other possible excuses not to proceed—your appeal may well end up in the wastebasket. Most do. Even letters to your most loyal and generous donors may suffer this ignoble fate: few people have the time or the inclination to read everything they receive in the mail.

## Wave Two

If your appeal survives the first wave of possible rejection, your chances of securing a gift are greatly improved, but you don't have a lock on a gift. All that's happened, from Vögele's perspective, is that your reader has found satisfactory answers to the first round of silent questions. Now, reading more thoroughly, the reader looks for answers to a whole new round of questions. Previously, the reader has looked only at the pictures, read the subheads, and cruised through the underlined text. Now comes the true test: what you've written (or failed to include) in the blocks of text. What the reader encounters here must respond to questions and spell out the benefits she will receive as a result of giving a gift. If the blocks of text in your letter don't speak to the reader and if your text fails to provoke a preponderance of little yeses, chances are your appeal will make its way into the trash in this second throwaway wave.

## Wave Three

Even if your letter survives the second wave of rejection, there's yet more potential trouble in store for you—for starters, the *filing-away*, or *archiving*, wave. If your letter succumbs to the near-universal human fondness for putting off until later what could just as easily be done right now, it won't find its way into the trash—at least not immediately. But, Vögele points out, time acts as a filter: the reader who was impressed enough with your appeal to put it away for later reference may no longer remember why she was so moved after a week or a month has gone by. The effect achieved is little better than a big fat NO! Rarely will archived appeals result in donations.

## Wave Four

Vögele distinguishes between the phenomenon of archiving (or filing away) and what he terms *putting to one side.* The difference lies in the reader's intentions: in putting aside your appeal, the reader has resolved to do something but can't quite decide what that will be. This may happen because you've presented her with a decision to make, a question to answer, a form to fill out, a comment or greeting to write—or because she simply doesn't have enough money in her checking account at the moment. Vögele estimates that 50 percent of the solicitations that are put to one side will ultimately get lost. He explains: "One day, they may well end up in the wastebasket too, even if the advantage offered in them was once recognized. In the meantime, a long period of time has elapsed. New pictures and information have taken precedence."

## The Solution

Here's the key: the faster you get your reader to respond, the more likely she will. That puts an enormous burden on the first twenty seconds of your letter's exposure to the reader's indifference. So let's conclude by going back to the beginning of this process: the first twenty seconds.

## A Closer Look at the First Twenty Seconds in Your Letter's Public Life

Vögele divides the crucial first twenty seconds into three phases:

*Phase one, before the envelope is opened—eight seconds on average.* During this time, recipients turn over the envelope, note how it's addressed, read the return address and any text, look for a way to open the envelope, and finally tear it open.

*Phase two—approximately four seconds.* The reader picks up and examines the contents. Even before she has read a single word, the materials have an immediate impact on her. She unfolds them, forming a general impression of what they contain.

*Phase three—another eight seconds.* In what Vögele refers to as the first run-through, the reader examines the pictures and headlines, finding short answers to her silent questions. If the writer has done a good job, the reader is now fully engaged in the short dialogue.

Remember that the writer's objective is to involve the reader by persuading her to read some of the blocks of text in the letter—to become involved in the comprehensive second dialogue. "This means you need to get your reader's interest long before the twenty seconds are up," Vögele warns. The recipient will continue reading only if the benefits to her are obvious within the first few seconds. And that's why he insists a letter needs to "express the advantages to the reader by using pictures and headlines" and underlined words and phrases.

• • •

Now let's take a break from the quantifiable certainties of German research and venture into the realm of qualitative research—by taking a close look at what donors really think about fundraising letters.

# Chapter 3

# What Donors Really Think About Fundraising Letters

**SOME YEARS AGO,** as I was writing the first edition of this book, I took time out to observe a focus group in Los Angeles. For two hours I cringed behind a two-way mirror while ten people sat around a table, picking apart a direct mail fundraising letter for Camp Fire USA, then known as Camp Fire Boys and Girls. I was present because the leadership of Camp Fire had retained my firm to help launch a nationwide, direct mail fundraising program.

The letter those people were savaging was one I'd edited less than a week before. I'd thought the letter was pretty good to begin with, but I was convinced my brilliant editing had lifted it into the ranks of the fundraising hall of fame. Indeed, one of my senior associates went out of his way to congratulate me on my fine work, and for the first time ever, Camp Fire staff approved the text without changing a single word. They loved the letter. Nevertheless, Camp Fire had agreed that before mailing the letter, we would test our draft copy in focus groups and not rely exclusively on our own instincts. The Los Angeles group was the second of two organized exclusively for that purpose.

The group consisted of seven women and three men, diverse in age, ethnicity, religion, and income level as well as occupation: among them were a couple of retired people, a housewife, a teacher, a banker, and two business owners. Half had completed at least four years of college. Most had done volunteer work in the past three years.

Despite their differences, these ten people had one crucial element in common: in interviews over the telephone, they said they had previously contributed money by mail to human service organizations such as the Girl Scouts, Boys Town, Special Olympics, City of Hope, or Red Cross. In other words, they seemed to us like good prospects to support Camp Fire.

Now here's what happened.

## How Ten People Reacted to My Pride and Joy

Under the skillful guidance of a professional moderator, the participants quickly warmed up to the subject at hand by discussing their views of direct mail fundraising and youth programs. They revealed what they knew—mostly what they didn't know—about Camp Fire. Prodded by the discussion leader, they cited examples of "good letters" from charities (ones that were "interesting" and contained "local examples so you can see the money at work"). Their biggest concern about fundraising letters was "authenticity." They were worried about getting sucked into scams "like you hear about on TV."

The group analyzed what was then Camp Fire's tagline—"The first fire we light is the fire within"—which most of them seemed to like. (A typical comment: "I'm not sure what it means, but I like it.") Then they critiqued one of our two candidates for the outer envelope design. That envelope featured the Camp Fire logo, name, address, and tagline along with smaller type reading "recycled paper," plus a much bolder and larger teaser: "Inside: Our free gift to you." Here's what the members of the focus group had to say about the envelope:

"'Recycled paper.' I like that."

"Pretty good as an envelope."

"Camp Fire caught my attention. The logo."

"I focused on 'Inside: Our free gift.'"

"There might be too much on it."

"It's very feminine. Like Camp Fire Girls."

"You get the feeling there's something they're going to tell you about the spark" (a word nowhere to be found on the envelope).

"'Free gift'? I like that."

"They want something."

"I'd throw this away."

"Why are they offering a free gift?"

"I'd open it."

"So would I."

"I'd toss it."

"You think you have to send a gift and then they'll send something."

The reviews were mixed, but not too bad for starters. Then the moderator passed out copies of the one-and-a-half-page fundraising letter intended to be mailed in that envelope and asked the group to read it. This was the letter I'd edited, actually a version of a much longer letter my firm had drafted. My hunch was that a shorter letter would be better received in the market we expected to mail for Camp Fire, because appeals from many national charities already competing in that market were typically short.

Here's what the group had to say about the letter:

"I would throw it away."

"There's nothing in there that says anything about the free gift."

"There's not enough information in there."

"How are they going to teach kids to 'be somebody'?" (a promise made in the text of the letter)

"I don't know Camp Fire."

"I think it's very wordy."

"How do I know it's an authentic program?"

"It didn't sell me."

"There are a lot of programs out there that are trying to do the same thing."

"I'd rather contribute to an L.A.-based organization. I'd contribute if it said kids in L.A. would be helped."

"The letter just doesn't flow very well."

"I don't like this 'Dear Caring American' [the salutation]. Leave that out."

"Are these kids from poorer areas, or is this like the Boy Scouts?"

"Is 'kids' acceptable? Shouldn't you say children? Teens? Youth?"

"This doesn't sound like Camp Fire. There's nothing camp-y here."

"They've been in business for over fifty years. Why don't they say that?"

"They need an 800-number. A hotline or somewhere you can call."

At various points along the way, the moderator turned the group's attention to specific elements in the letter copy:

- The letter's headline: "I'm gonna be dead by the time I'm 18."

    "It's not big enough."

    "It wouldn't mean anything unless I read the rest."

- The name we'd chosen for contributors of $12 or more: "Leadership Circle."

    "Too long a name."

    "Do I become a member?"

- The title we promised to early respondents: "Charter Member."

  "It sounds like the group [Camp Fire] is new."

  "I'm not important enough to be a Charter Member."

  "This letter's going to ten million people."

  "Just ask me for the money."

  "Does it mean they'll expect more money next year?"

To clinch matters, the moderator asked the group, "If you received this letter in the mail, would you consider making a contribution?" The unanimous response: "No."

Oh, ignominy! Oh, pain and suffering!

But am I glad that answer came from a focus group and not from an equally uncaring public—after Camp Fire spent a small fortune mailing 50,000 copies of the letter all over the country!

## Why Did We Set Up That Exasperating Focus Group, Anyway?

Now listen to a few of the comments about the four-page version of the Camp Fire appeal our firm had drafted. That version led with a gripping story about an inner-city child whose life was turned around by Camp Fire:

"I personally like this. I would give."

"It gives you an actual person."

"It's lovely."

"The lead grabs you—real hard."

A similar sentiment had prevailed the evening before in a focus group assembled in Tulsa, Oklahoma. I'm told the Tulsa group had a somewhat different take on the first letter: they were much more familiar with Camp Fire, were much less critical of the copy, and showed none of the Los Angeles group's cynicism about charity. But emphasis and nuances aside, there's no question that both groups favored the longer letter instead of the shorter one, and by a huge margin.

Camp Fire didn't go to all the trouble and expense of organizing focus groups merely to choose between two versions of one appeal. Hearing unguarded comments from representative prospects helped us fine-tune our copy. We were able to answer major questions we hadn't anticipated and clear up ambiguities in the copy and artwork, any one of which might have had a profound impact on the results. In other words, we learned in advance what our readers' unspoken questions were likely to be and made changes in the copy to answer those questions. For example, each of the following comments was helpful in making final copy revisions:

"How come there are boys as well as girls?"

"What makes this organization different? What are they going to do?"

"Are there Camp Fire programs here in Los Angeles?" (There are.)

"What is AIDS counseling? As a parent, I would be very interested in knowing what approach they take."

"If it were Girl Scouts, we wouldn't be as critical. We see them here."

"Teaching kids how to survive. This is a key point."

"It doesn't tell exactly where the money goes—like, '30 percent to this.'"

"What's it going to do for my city?"

## What Those Ten People Taught Me (All Over Again)

So lest you too stumble into the wilderness of indifference—armed only with a pitiful little one-and-a-half-page fundraising letter—please keep the following lessons in mind:

*Donors need lots of information to be persuaded to send gifts by mail.* They may say they want to read only short letters, but what they really crave are answers to their questions. And questions produce doubt or disinterest, the parents of inaction. If it takes an extra page or two to answer every question you can anticipate, increase the budget and stifle your natural tendency to keep your message short and sweet. The results will vindicate you.

*Donors are skeptical.* It's best to head them off at the pass by volunteering information about the unique character, the impact, and the cost-effectiveness of your work. And they want proof you're really doing the things you say you're doing. Abundant details—facts—will get that point across.

*An appeal is too long only if it doesn't convey the information that donors want.* My one-and-a-half-page version was "wordy" because it lacked the particulars of the four-page letter. The longer version was not wordy.

*Human interest sells—and probably doubly so in human service appeals.* A story, especially about children, is a great way to humanize a fundraising letter. That is what we did in the longer letter.

*If there's a way to misunderstand your message, donors will find it.* They'll miss important points if you don't emphasize them. They'll be thrown off by awkward transitions, unfamiliar words, poor word choices, and attempts to gloss over details. Words matter.

*Format and design affect understanding.* In a fundraising letter, the only tools you've got are words, numbers, typography, pictures, paper, and ink. Use them all wisely; you have no other way to establish your credibility by mail.

Most of the time, I remember all these lessons when I sit down to work on a fundraising letter. Yet I still sometimes write letters that don't work well.

Raising money by mail is an endlessly tricky business, and no amount of knowledge will equip a fundraiser to avoid occasional unpleasant surprises. But experience, insight, and market research like the focus group reported in this chapter can all help narrow the uncertainties and enlarge the odds of success.

Focus groups may not be cost-effective for your organization, and they're certainly not needed for every fundraising letter. But friends, family, and coworkers can informally evaluate your writing and the design of your package. That way, you too might find you're not achieving the effect you thought you were.

• • •

Now that we've examined what really happens to fundraising letters when donors receive them in the mail, let's examine the characteristics of an effective fundraising letter—one that takes account of the insights we've gained through focus groups and other techniques that cast light on the whims and foibles of the human beings who read our appeals.

# Chapter 4

# Characteristics of an Effective Fundraising Letter

**MOST FUNDRAISERS** apparently think fundraising letters are all pretty much the same. Here's how their definition of a fundraising letter seems to run: "A fundraising letter is an appeal from a nonprofit organization, describing needs and requesting charitable gifts to fill them."

Right?

Wrong! Wrong on every count.

So banish that ill-conceived and misleading definition from your consciousness. Better yet, copy it down onto a sheet of scratch paper, cross it out with bold strokes of your pen, slice it up with scissors, and deposit the whole mess in the nearest wastebasket.

Now you're ready to get started on the right foot! Read this next part carefully:

An effective fundraising letter possesses three attributes.

---

### Three Attributes of an Effective Fundraising Letter

1. An effective fundraising letter is an appeal from one person to another.

2. An effective fundraising letter describes an opportunity for the recipient to meet personal needs or achieve personal desires by supporting a worthy charitable aim.

3. An effective fundraising letter invites the recipient to take specific and immediate action.

---

I'm sure you noticed that one all-important word is missing here: money. Money—a request for a charitable gift—is an indispensable element in the overwhelming majority of fundraising letters. Omit that request for funds, and your letter will fail the most basic test of effectiveness. What's worse, you'll almost certainly fail to raise much money.

But the action requested in a fundraising letter doesn't always consist of sending money, at least not right away. The specific action requested might be to complete and return a survey; to use a set of stamps, name stickers, or greeting cards; or to authorize regular bank transfers. There are hundreds of possibilities. The letter writer's first responsibility when writing for results is to determine what that action is. And understanding that duty leads to what I call a fundamental law:

---

### The Fundamental Law of Fundraising Letter Writing

When you set out to write a fundraising letter, make sure you know precisely to whom you're writing and why—and be certain your letter makes that point just as clear to them as it is to you.

---

That "point"—the equation that expresses the who, what, why, when, and how of your appeal—is what I've fallen into the bad habit of calling the *marketing concept*. I'll discuss this all-important notion in more detail in Chapter Six, where I sum up the central message of this book. For starters, though, let's take a stab at a working definition:

### Working Definition of the Marketing Concept

- The marketing concept embodies your purpose in writing: to secure a gift of $500 or more, for example.

- The marketing concept identifies the person to whom you're writing: to extend the previous example, a donor who has previously given your organization at least one gift of $100 or more.

- The marketing concept incorporates the benefits the person you're writing to will receive as a result of responding—in this example, great satisfaction from knowing how much your organization can accomplish with $500 or more, plus special recognition for giving such a generous gift.

The Fundamental Law, then, is to work out the marketing concept before you write a single word—and then to be sure every word you write speaks to that concept.

## Fundraising Letters: One Size Won't Fit All

Fundraising letters are of many different types, serving a broad variety of ends and thus involving a great many different marketing concepts. To write an effective appeal, you must first determine the target audience and specific purpose you want to serve:

### Determining the Target Audience

- Are you writing to people who have never before supported your organization, asking them to join? That's an *acquisition* (or *prospect*) letter. I cover that topic in Chapter Ten.

- Is your letter to be mailed to new members or donors, welcoming them to your organization? I call that a *welcome package;* others may describe it as a welcome packet or kit or even a new-donor acknowledgment. Chapter Eleven takes up this subject.

- Are you writing to previous donors, appealing for additional gifts for some special purpose? That's a *special appeal.* You'll find examples in Chapter Twelve.

- Are you writing to proven donors at the end of the year? That's a *year-end appeal.* The topic is covered in Chapter Thirteen.

- Are you writing to persuade your donors to enroll in a monthly giving program? That's a *sustainer, pledge, or regular giving program,* the subject of Chapter Fourteen.

- Are you writing to some of your most generous donors, seeking large gifts? I refer to an appeal of that sort as a *high-dollar letter,* the subject of Chapter Fifteen.

- Is the specific purpose of your letter to induce previous donors to increase their support? If so, you're writing an *upgrade appeal.* You'll learn about that topic in Chapter Sixteen.

- Are you writing to your new and regular supporters to ask them to renew this year's annual gift or membership dues? Then you're writing a *renewal.* That's the theme of Chapter Seventeen.

- Is your letter intended to acknowledge a donor's recent gift? That's a *thank-you letter,* the subject of Chapter Eighteen.

- Are you writing to encourage your donors to consider legacy (or planned) giving? That's a *legacy promotion.* It's the subject covered in Chapter Nineteen.

The case studies in Chapters Ten through Nineteen, which contain examples of all ten of these types of fundraising appeals, will prepare you for many letter-writing challenges—but hardly all of them. There are important types of fundraising letters that don't appear in this book—for example, lapsed-donor reactivation letters, cultivation letters, and dozens more. No author can anticipate every need you may face. No book can supply you with models to follow in every contingency.

But in spite of such great variety in fundraising letters, the most productive fundraising appeals I've read share six qualities, as listed on page 42.

From a mechanical perspective, however, the only things common to all appeals are an *offer* (or *proposition*)—which incorporates the ask, if any, as

# Six Qualities of Successful Fundraising Appeals

1. *Clarity.* There's no doubt or ambiguity about the writer's intent or what the reader is asked to do. The message is delivered in unmistakably clear and simple terms that rule out guesswork. Early on, the reader gets the point of the appeal, and that point never wavers throughout the package.

2. *Cohesiveness.* Every component of the package works with every other to reinforce the message. If the message is complex—as, for example, in an appeal that combines a petition with a request for money—the close connection between the components is absolutely clear. The message isn't mixed. This means, for example, that an appeal for funds shouldn't be muddied by including a catalogue or a flyer that offers merchandise for sale, an invitation to a special event, or an update on a project discussed in an earlier appeal.

3. *Authenticity.* From beginning to end, the appeal is credible. The style and approach of the letter fit smoothly with what readers are likely to know about the signer, and the text includes enough revealing personal information to drive home that fit. Similarly, the nature of the appeal is consistent with what readers know about the organization and its work. In short, it's natural for this signer and this nonprofit to be sending this particular appeal. Conversely, a Hollywood starlet, no matter how popular, might not be the most credible signer of an appeal from a research institute.

4. *Ease of response.* The appeal contains everything the reader might need to respond without a moment's delay after reviewing the appeal. At a minimum, the package includes a clearly marked response device and a preaddressed response envelope, and there's no doubt that these two items are included exclusively for the purpose of responding to the appeal. In direct mail, the fundraiser's job is to make it easy for the reader to respond. Experience shows that if it's not easy, the recipient is likely to set the appeal aside and never respond at all.

5. *Appropriateness.* The message is calculated to be of interest to the intended reader, and the appeal requests assistance of a sort that the reader might naturally be assumed to be able to provide. For example, I might write an extraordinarily interesting letter about the cuisine of Kyrgyzstan, but I would be unlikely to generate much response to my appeal unless I were writing to people with either a demonstrated interest in exotic cuisine or a fascination with Kyrgyzstan, or even less likely, both. In other words, it's always important to write to the audience.

6. *Engaging copy.* There's something inherently intriguing about this appeal in the story it tells, the character of the request (or offer) it makes, or the language in which it's written. It's interesting and holds the reader's attention. Sometimes this can be accomplished with a clever outer envelope teaser (which is appropriately followed through inside the package). Sometimes a fascinating personal story about a recipient of the agency's help connects with the reader on a deeply emotional level. Sometimes a writer's style is so fresh and compelling that the reader is inexorably drawn through the copy. Whatever it is, something catches the reader's attention—and holds it.

well as the benefits to the donor—and the *case*—which is the argument that justifies the offer and spells out the benefits. If the appeal is framed as a letter, as are almost all successful fundraising efforts, it's likely to include a salutation and signature that clarify the relationship between the letter signer and the person to whom the letter is addressed, a lead that starts off the letter, a close that ends it, a P.S., and a response device (or reply device) that the donor may use to return a gift. That's about it.

Many fundraisers relate these elements to a formula, insisting there's a standard structure or sequence a writer may follow in constructing an appeal. I disagree. To understand how to write successful fundraising letters, you must study appeals that have worked well, determine what made them successful—and then put them aside and focus on your own donors and your own organization. Your fundraising letters will be successful only if they reflect what's unique about your organization and uniquely attractive to your donors.

• • •

To bear down hard on this important point, let's take a stroll through the pages of a single well-written fundraising letter. By accompanying me on this paragraph-by-paragraph tour in the next chapter, you'll gain an overview of the approach I'll spell out later in more detail. In the process, you'll gain insight about how to frame the unique attractions of your own organization in ways that will be compelling to your donors.

# Chapter 5

# A Leisurely Tour Through One Successful Appeal

**WE'LL MEANDER SLOWLY,** paragraph by paragraph, through a four-page fundraising letter and its companion package components in an excellent example of the fundraiser's craft. Before we embark on our journey, however, I urge you to read the whole package in its entirety (Exhibits 5.1 through 5.5). As you do, weigh it against the six characteristics of successful appeals that I discussed in the previous chapter: clarity, cohesiveness, authenticity, ease of response, appropriateness, and engaging copy.

My colleague and friend Bill Rehm wrote this fundraising appeal for the San Francisco Conservatory of Music a decade and a half ago. The conservatory had retained our firm to assist it in building its membership base, part of a broader development strategy to lay the foundation for a significant capital campaign several years hence. Like other outstanding appeals, this letter is just as fresh and compelling today as it was when it was first printed.

## The San Francisco Conservatory of Music Appeal

### The Outer Envelope

1. My eyes leap first to the signature in the upper-left-hand corner (called the *corner card*). Colin Murdoch, the president of the conservatory, signed the appeal inside, and printing his signature on the envelope (in blue ink, to contrast with the red of the logo and return address) lends a personal touch that previous testing suggests may improve results—regardless of how well known he is.

2. With the same glance, I take in the extraordinary woodblock print in the corner card: the conservatory's logo.

3. The typefaces used in the conservatory's name and address are consistently repeated throughout the contents of the package, as they should be. A typeface can be an organization's signature as surely as the most distinctive logo design.

**EXHIBIT 5.1**

## Outer Envelope, San Francisco Conservatory of Music

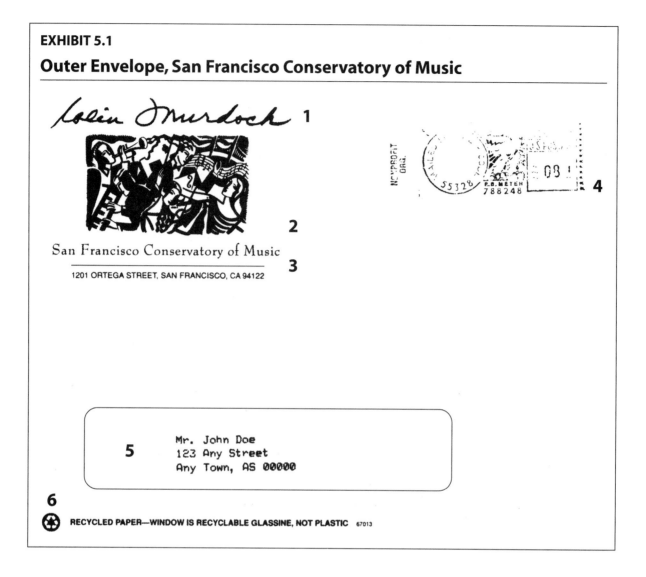

4. A postage meter has been used instead of a postal indicia (that is, a permit imprint). Testing sometimes shows that metered postage outpulls an indicia (but both are usually far less successful, though not necessarily less cost-effective, than first-class stamps).

5. Now, you and I may have noticed all four of the features of this envelope I've already enumerated, but a recipient of this appeal is much more likely to have found her eyes leaping first to the mailing label. Why? Because, research shows, she'll notice her own name before anything else. So she sees a so-called Cheshire label, a strip of plain paper machine-affixed to a card inside that shows through a glassine (recyclable) window, revealing a computer-imprinted name and address plus a five-digit key code (upper right in the window) and a postal bar code. (Cheshire labels are virtually extinct today, when inkjet printers can address the reply device more

cost-effectively than a label, but window envelopes live on.) The bar code enabled the conservatory to mail this particular envelope at a savings of three cents off what was then the standard nonprofit bulk rate (8.1 cents versus 11.1 cents).

6. The envelope advertises "recycled paper," though testing may show that using recycled paper doesn't improve results, even among donors who describe themselves as environmentalists. So what? As my grandmother would have said, "What can it hurt? And it might help!" Besides, it's the right thing to do.

## The Letter
### Page One

7. The size of the original page, 7 by 10 inches, is important. This so-called Monarch letter has a personal touch to it, because it's notably smaller than standard business size (8½ by 11 inches), much more like personal stationery. And there's that lovely logo again. It appears above the address—a street address, not a post office box—and a telephone number. Nowadays we might add a Web site address as well. Using the conservatory's actual address, telephone number, and Web site address may help inspire confidence in me as a prospective donor. It may also lead me to pay an unexpected visit or place a telephone call out of curiosity or suspiciousness—but that's very unlikely.

8. The use of "Thursday afternoon" is a copywriter's conceit. Still, it may subliminally convey an illusion that the letter bears a specific date. There's no real date here because this appeal was mailed via bulk rate, making it likely that at least some of the letters will be delivered two weeks or longer after the mail date.

9. "Dear Friend and Neighbor" is a neat variation on the standard "Dear Friend"; it's a signal that this appeal was mailed only locally. This is, in its way, a form of personalization, shortening the distance between the conservatory and me. However, since this letter is not addressed to me personally, it's obviously not personalized within the generally accepted meaning of that term. This is a bulk appeal, mailed in quantity, and there's no way around that.

10. In its five opening words, "I'm writing to invite you," this appeal simply and directly establishes the basis of a relationship between the signer and me. (Most people who receive this letter probably will flip to the bottom of page four to view the signature, to see who is sending the letter, and to read the P.S. But let's be orderly about this, and stick to our

**EXHIBIT 5.2**

## Solicitation Letter, San Francisco Conservatory of Music

**7**

San Francisco Conservatory of Music

1201 ORTEGA ST., SAN FRANCISCO, CA 94122
415/759-3463

**8**
Thursday afternoon

**9**
Dear Friend and Neighbor,

**10**    I'm writing to invite you -- and a select group of other music lovers in the Bay Area -- to take your seat, please.

**11**    Sit down, as our guest, at the Faculty Trio Concert this November 15th, and listen to some of the most beautiful chamber music that San Francisco has to offer.

**12**    It's our way of saying thank you -- for becoming a Friend of the San Francisco Conservatory of Music.

**13**    As the Conservatory begins its 76th season, we've set a goal of enlisting <u>333</u> <u>new</u> <u>Friends</u> <u>of</u> <u>the</u> <u>Conservatory</u>.  We've chosen that number because there are exactly 333 seats in Hellman Hall -- the concert hall where we hold our New Member Concert each year.

**14**    I'd like to see all 333 seats filled with new members this year.  And I'd like to see you in one of those seats.

**15**    In just a minute, I'll tell you about several other benefits you'll receive as a new member of the Conservatory.  But first, let me tell you what your membership support means to the Bay Area.

**16**    Like the Bay Area itself, the San Francisco Conservatory of Music represents many things to many people.  But above all else, the Conservatory is a community of musicians who experience the joy, the promise, and the pursuit of musical excellence. Every day, we celebrate the teaching, learning, composing, and performance of music.

**17**    That's been our proud mission for over 75 years

RECYCLED PAPER    67011  **18**

**EXHIBIT 5.2 (*Continued*)**

Page two  **19**

**20** -- ever since the Conservatory was first founded by pianists Ada Clement and Lillian Hodghead in 1917.

**21** Today, the San Francisco Conservatory of Music is one of the most respected institutions of music education in the country, offering instruction to more than 1,500 students ranging from pre-school to post graduate levels.

**22** Conservatory students, faculty and guest artists perform more than 300 concerts on campus each year.

**23** And over the past seventy-five years, the Conservatory has trained some of our country's most brilliant musicians -- violinists Isaac Stern and Yehudi Menuhin, pianist Jeffrey Kahane, and guitarist David Tanenbaum, to name just a few.

**24** The Conservatory's faculty of 78 professional musicians are drawn from some of the finest musical organizations in the country, including 32 musicians who are currently playing with either the San Francisco Symphony, the San Francisco Opera, or the San Francisco Ballet.

**25** It goes without saying that all of us at the Conservatory share a love for music. But more than that, we possess the desire to help talented and motivated students realize their dreams.

**26**

With a student-faculty ratio of just six to one, teachers give special attention to every student.

**EXHIBIT 5.2 (Continued)**

Page three **27**

**28**     I see our role at the Conservatory as one of
helping to nurture and develop the creativity,
skill, and genius residing within each musician.

**29**     I also see it as the responsibility of the
Conservatory to share the music we help create with
the community.

**30**     Through the Conservatory's Community Service
Program, our students give more than 400 performances
each year.  We bring music to hospitals, convalescent
homes, day care centers, retirement homes -- reaching
people who otherwise would never have the pleasure of
hearing live classical music.

**31**

*Conservatory students contribute to our community by performing more than 400 free concerts each year.*

**32**     The San Francisco Conservatory of Music has a
long, proud tradition of teaching and providing
musical excellence to the Bay Area.  And, I assure
you, this will continue to be our overriding mission
in the years ahead.

**33**     But the Conservatory is only as great as its
supporters.  Tuition and fees cover just 59% of our
annual budget.  The remainder must come from
generous individuals in our community.

**34**     Currently, we have a very special group of
Friends -- people like you -- who help support the
Conservatory with a tax-deductible membership
contribution each year.

**35**     That's why I hope you'll accept my invitation
to become a Friend of the San Francisco Conservatory

**EXHIBIT 5.2 (*Continued*)**

Page four

**36** of Music today -- and support one of San Francisco's oldest and most respected institutions.

**37**    When you become a Friend of the Conservatory, you'll receive <u>all</u> <u>these</u> <u>membership</u> <u>benefits</u>:

      **38**  o  A subscription to <u>At</u> <u>the</u> <u>Conservatory</u>, the monthly newsletter and calendar of events.

      **39**  o  Free tickets to the special Faculty Trio Concert for new members on November 15.

      **40**  o  Free attendance at the "Friends Only" Tour and Concert in January, 1994.

      **41**  o  Membership discounts for Conservatory concerts throughout the year and special discounts for Conservatory extension classes.

      **42**  o  Advance ticket purchase for the <u>Sing-It-Yourself</u> <u>Messiah</u> concerts at Davies Symphony Hall this December.

**43**    Perhaps the greatest benefit you'll receive, though, is knowing you're helping to ensure that students will continue to get the best musical instruction available.

**44**    So please, right now while everything is in front of you, take a minute to write your tax-deductible check and send it to the San Francisco Conservatory of Music.

**45**    With many thanks.

      **46** Sincerely,

      Colin Murdoch
      President

**47** P.S.  To reserve your free ticket to the Faculty Trio Concert at the Conservatory's Hellman Hall on November 15, we must receive your membership contribution by November 8.  Please send your gift <u>today</u>.  Thank you very much.

paragraph-by-paragraph story.) The opening sentence (the *lead*) identifies me in two important ways—as a music lover and a resident of the San Francisco Bay Area—and seizes my attention with an unfamiliar request: to take a seat.

11. The second paragraph quickly explains that unfamiliar request with specifics: *what* (a concert), *when* (on a particular day), and *where* (in San Francisco), in time-honored journalistic fashion. You'll note too that the conservatory is appealing to my love for chamber music. (How do they know that? They don't, of course. But they know how popular chamber music is among classical music fans.)

12. Now Colin Murdoch makes clear exactly why he's writing this letter to me. He wants me to become a "Friend" (and since I receive lots of letters like these, I've got a pretty good idea what he means).

13. Now come more facts—details that tell me this is a letter about something specific. Numbers and capitalized words capture my interest because they supply information that answers questions I may have about a topic that (as we've already established) is of general interest to me. The unusual number "333" is itself engaging, because it's unexpected. You'll also note that "333 new Friends of the Conservatory" is underlined—the only underlining on this page, so it really stands out. A different writer might have chosen different words to emphasize, but what's most important here is that underlining is used sparingly, to lessen the impression this is simply one more direct mail appeal.

14. That intriguing number is repeated. And so are the words "you" and "I," each for the third time so far. This is not an impersonal institutional appeal. It's a letter from Colin Murdoch to me.

15. There's "you" again: three more times. And "me" counts as a form of "I." Just as important, the concept of membership, broached in each of the two preceding paragraphs, is introduced in terms of its benefits, both to me and to the area where I live (not San Francisco, you'll notice, but the entire, and much larger, Bay Area).

16. In this seven-line paragraph—the longest on all four pages of the appeal—the conservatory is described in emotional and conceptual terms, not as brick and mortar. Murdoch is connecting with me where I really live—on the plane of values: "joy," "promise," "excellence," "teaching," "learning," "music."

17. Note that only one line of this paragraph appears on this page: that's a device to draw my eye onto the second page.

18. There's that "recycled paper" again.

## Page Two

19. This letter consists of two sheets of paper that form four pages. The notation "Page two" at the top helps orient me, minimizing the possibility I'll be confused (and thus less likely to send a gift).

20. Take note of specifics again. Facts and figures (used with reasonable restraint) heighten reader interest.

21. This reference to the conservatory's nationwide reputation helps establish credibility. The additional facts lend authority to the reference, making it more than a boast.

22. Here's a significant and surprising fact. Most concertgoers are aware that 300 performances per year is a very large number for any arts group.

23. More facts here, and interesting ones at that. These names, familiar to classical music lovers, help reinforce my interest while enhancing the credibility of the appeal.

24. Facts again (numbers). By now, I'm really getting acquainted with the conservatory.

25. We're back to values and abstracts again: "love," "desire," "talented," "motivated," "dreams." This fellow Murdoch isn't sending me a press release. He's connecting with me about things that matter.

26. This intense and charming photograph and its handwritten caption convey important facts about the conservatory and its work. They also lend added human interest to the appeal.

## Page Three

27. The words "Page three" reassure me that I'm on the right page. But I haven't been hit over the head with a "Next page, please" or the equivalent on the bottom of page two. (No doubt some direct marketer has tested that obnoxiously condescending device and found it improves response. I tend to avoid using it. I doubt it makes much difference other than to serve as one more subtle but unwanted reminder that an appeal is really, after all, just an impersonal direct mail letter sent to large numbers of people.)

28. Again, Colin Murdoch reveals his personal feelings. He uses the lofty language that gets to the heart of the subject: the teaching of music.

29. Continuing in the first person, Murdoch now reveals the outward-looking dimension of the conservatory's mission: relating to the community—my community.

30. I see that by supporting the conservatory, I won't just be helping to bring out the genius in future world-class performers. I'll also help support my community's social safety net.

31. This photograph depicts an obviously diverse group of schoolchildren, and the caption repeats the number "400." The effect is to drive home the point that the conservatory serves far more than its own students and faculty or affluent concertgoers like me. Those 400 concerts are free.

32. Now we're back to values again: tradition and musical excellence. Even the word "mission" connotes passion and an orientation to values.

33. Citing the central financial fact about the conservatory brings me back into the picture once again. There's little doubt in my mind that I'm (supposedly) one of those "generous individuals."

34. Any doubt I may have is now quickly dispelled: Murdoch is talking about "people like" me. But the contribution he wants is more than simply that. It's "tax deductible," it buys me a "membership," and it's to be annual.

35. That, obviously, is what Murdoch means when he asks me to become a "Friend." But I'm going to have to go on to the next page to learn whether there's some qualification or exception to his request.

**Page Four**

36. There is no exception here—just another argument for supporting the conservatory: its long and respected institutional history.

37. Here, in the first underlined words since the phrase on page one, Murdoch introduces the subject of membership benefits. (Note that the words are individually underlined. Some people prefer continuous lines, but I think the underlining of spaces distracts the eye from the message and focuses it on what's less important: the fact of the underlining itself. It also eliminates the spaces between words, which readers use to "swallow" words and phrases one bite at a time.)

38. As a "Friend," I'll receive a monthly newsletter and calendar. Murdoch cites the newsletter's name, emphasizing the unstated promise of events I may want to attend at the conservatory.

39. In fact, I'll receive free tickets to a specific concert—one that's coming up very soon.

40. More free tickets, and another event that's not too far off.

41. I'll get discounts—not only on admission to other concerts but for extension classes too. Here's a potentially important benefit that piques my curiosity. (I gave up trying the clarinet in fifth grade, but maybe I could learn it after all.)

42. Now—underlined again and deliberately placed last in the series, where it's most likely to be remembered—is a membership benefit that

could well be the most attractive of all: the conservatory's wildly popular sing-along *Messiah* concerts at San Francisco's elegant Symphony Hall.

43. Despite all these tangible benefits of membership, Murdoch rushes to remind me I'll get something even more valuable: the satisfaction of knowing I've helped achieve something I value highly: the teaching of good music.

44. If I'm tempted to set this appeal aside and make my mind up later about whether to respond, Murdoch's suggestion that I do it now may have no effect on me, but at worst it's a throwaway line. And I'm reminded once again that my gift will be tax deductible, a fact that may be of special interest to me since the end of the year is fast approaching.

45. Ever hopeful, Murdoch thanks me.

46. He signs off "Sincerely," rather than with a more formal "Yours truly" or a flamboyant "See you at the Conservatory!" He is, after all, the president of a respected institution. His flowery signature has an artful flair; it's printed in dark blue ink, to set it off from the typed text and reinforce the illusion of personal (or, rather, business) correspondence.

47. As you'll remember, most readers read the P.S. first. This P.S. makes good use of that opportunity. It restates the date of the fast-approaching faculty concert and, for the first time, lays out a specific deadline for membership contributions. To be sure I'll beat that deadline, I may really have to mail in my gift today, as I'm asked to do. (Although I rarely recommend including specific dates in letters written to recruit new members—or for that matter, in any other letters mailed at bulk rate—this case is an exception. The appeal was mailed within a narrow region and likely to be delivered well in advance of the concert date. And conservatory faculty and students perform so frequently that similar offers can be made almost any time of the year.)

## Lift Letter

48. Yes, that intense-looking fellow in the upper-right-hand corner photo is the renowned cellist Yo-Yo Ma. Classical music lovers probably know that. It's likely to be the photograph that first catches attention. That's what the eye-motion studies reveal. Then your eyes swept leftward to take in the musician's name, and finally down to the salutation and lead. This musical celebrity has signed what is called a *lift letter*—a brief, supplementary letter or note that strengthens the main appeal by emphasizing an important endorsement (as in this case) or providing significant information not found in the main letter.

49. While Colin Murdoch addressed me as a "Neighbor," Yo-Yo Ma finds common cause with me as a "Music Lover." It's a flattering reference. (He obviously never heard me play clarinet!)

50. From this first paragraph until the fifth and last, this testimonial lift letter from Yo-Yo Ma is a credibility-building exercise. It means a lot for one of the world's most illustrious concert performers to write about the conservatory's "high standards."

51. Similarly, it's useful—and impressive—for a celebrity in the world of music to name several of the conservatory's faculty members, who are far less likely to be known to the readers of this appeal. (I, for one, knew none of the three names cited.)

52. In a longer letter, Yo-Yo Ma might have revealed how frequently he visits the conservatory and how much time he spends there, thus establishing his authority as a judge of the conservatory's participation in the Bay Area community. In this context, I'm not impressed with the claim he makes in this paragraph.

53. He's back on more solid ground in this paragraph, speaking about musical tradition and the "next generation of musicians."

54. Most celebrities try to get off easy in lift letters like this one, omitting explicit endorsements such as the last paragraph. But without such a direct statement, a lift letter's value is limited. Now I know that Yo-Yo Ma really wants me to lend a hand. (His appeal would have been even stronger if he had written, "I urge you to join me as a Friend of the San Francisco Conservatory," thus leaving not a shadow of a doubt about his own deep commitment.)

55. He signs off "Sincerely," his name alone sufficing to identify himself. His signature, like Colin Murdoch's, is printed in dark blue ink to set it apart from the typewritten text.

## The Reply Device

56. "BRAVO!" What an appropriate variation on the more commonly used "Yes!" (The applause line is printed in dark red, as are the checkmark boxes and suggested gift amounts; the logo, name, address, and telephone number; and the headline below the line of dashes near the bottom. That bottom portion is tinted a gentle shade of red. All the text and every other element on this reply device is printed in black.)

57. In three terse sentences, the response device sums up the essence of the *offer* spelled out in Colin Murdoch's letter.

58. I'm offered three choices here. (Unfortunately, I have to read the text at the bottom of this reply device closely to be certain "Regular

**EXHIBIT 5.3**

# Lift Letter, San Francisco Conservatory of Music

**48**

**Y O · Y O   M A**

**49** Dear Friend and Music Lover,

**50**     Some of the finest cello teaching in the country today takes place at the San Francisco Conservatory of Music, where high standards are combined with an openness to new trends.

**51**     The San Francisco Conservatory of Music has a sense of tradition in the best sense of the word.  Generations of great cello teachers from Margaret Rowell to Bonnie Hampton and Irene Sharp have nurtured some of the finest young cellists today.

**52**     The Conservatory is a working community -- it not only functions as an institution, but it participates as a vital member of the Bay Area community.

**53**     The high standards, tradition and a sense of community are the reasons why the San Francisco Conservatory of Music continues to be such a strong, creative force in producing the next generation of musicians.

**54**     I urge you to support this fine institution.

**55**     Sincerely,

Yo-Yo Ma

Membership" really entitles me to all the benefits I'll get as a "Friend" of the conservatory. It might have been better to label the $40 option "Friend of the Conservatory" and devise a new name for the $100 option, while spelling out special benefits for the higher level of support. But no appeal's perfect.)

59. Here I'm reminded of the deadline, November 8. It's also clear to me that the offer of free tickets to the Faculty Trio Concert is a serious

---

**EXHIBIT 5.4**

**Reply Device, San Francisco Conservatory of Music**

**56** *BRAVO!*

**57**  I accept your invitation to become a Friend of the San Francisco Conservatory of Music. I want to help continue the long, proud tradition of musical excellence in San Francisco. Enclosed is my membership gift of:

**58**  ☐ **$40**      Regular Membership
☐ **$100**     Special Friend of the Conservatory
☐ **$**_____

**59**  ☐ Send me my FREE ticket(s) to the Faculty Trio Concert on November 15. Request must be received by November 8.      ☐ one ticket      ☐ two tickets

**61**

**60**  Mr. John Doe
123 Any Street
Any Town, AS 00000

San Francisco Conservatory of Music

**62**
**Your contribution to the San Francisco Conservatory of Music is fully tax-deductible. Thank you very much.**

1201 ORTEGA ST., SAN FRANCISCO, CA 94122
415/759-3463

- - - - - - - - - - - - - - - - - - - - - - - - - - - - - - - - - - - - - - - - - - -

**63** ▲ **DETACH HERE**

**64 Your Membership Entitles You to Receive:**

**65**  1. A subscription to *At the Conservatory*, the Conservatory's monthly newsletter and calendar of events.

2. A special New Member Fall Concert.

3. Membership discounts for Conservatory concerts throughout the year—and for Conservatory extension classes.

4. Advance ticket purchase for Sing-It-Yourself Messiah Concerts at Davies Symphony Hall.

5. Free attendance at the "Friends Only" Tour and Concert (January 1994).

**66** *Please detach top portion, fold and return with your check in the enclosed postage-paid envelope. Keep bottom portion for your records.*

**RECYCLED PAPER**   67012B

one: this is an excellent and appropriate use of a premium in membership acquisition.

60. Here's the Cheshire label (noted in paragraph number five, describing the outer envelope).

61. That wonderful logo again!

62. I'm reminded, for the third time, that my gift will be tax deductible.

63. It's almost always wise to include instructions such as "Detach Here." Certainly I could figure out that the reply device is perforated along the line of dashes, but it's courteous to relieve me of the (admittedly very slight) burden of determining that for myself. Instructions of this sort also reinforce the action-oriented nature of direct mail appeals.

64. Now any lingering doubt that I might not actually receive the wonderful benefits that Colin Murdoch's letter described is totally dispelled.

65. Those benefits are listed, described in the same words as in the letter.

66. The last thing I want to do when signing up for a membership in the conservatory is to fumble around with unfamiliar slips of paper of odd shapes and sizes, so I'm pleased to be told exactly what to do.

## Reply Envelope

67. Once again I'm reminded that my gift to the conservatory entitles me to membership, with its attendant benefits. This handwritten tagline is printed in dark blue, like that of the signatures on both letters.

68. "Recycled paper" again!

69. This five-digit code helps production staff and envelope printers keep this envelope apart from those used with hundreds of other projects.

70. These vertical ruled lines are for the electronic scanning equipment used by the U.S. Postal Service to route the mail.

71. The indicia and the horizontal ruled lines are for the naked eye: unmistakable signs that this envelope is, as the words to the left explain, "Business Reply Mail." At the time, it cost the conservatory approximately 40 cents per envelope returned. Currently, the charge for business reply mail ranges from 28 cents to $1.11 per piece but would likely be 49 cents for a small but steady mailer such as the Conservatory's.

72. The envelope is addressed to the conservatory. In a more personal appeal—a membership renewal letter, for example—it might be appropriate to type Colin Murdoch's name above the institutional name. Its omission here is not a significant oversight: I would find it a little difficult to believe that the president of the San Francisco Conservatory of Music would be

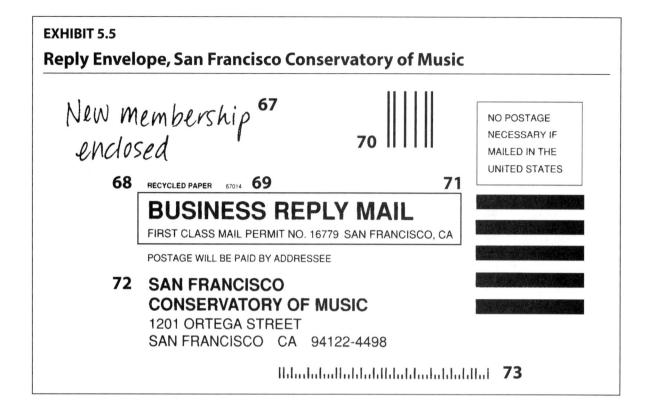

**EXHIBIT 5.5**

**Reply Envelope, San Francisco Conservatory of Music**

opening envelopes containing new memberships. Still, typing Murdoch's name on the reply envelope would reinforce the personality of this appeal; on balance, I would favor doing that.

73. This bar code enables the U.S. Postal Service to sort returning envelopes with minimal human intervention: the vertical lines are computer language for the letters and numbers contained in the address.

## What You Can—and Can't—Learn from This Example

This fundraising letter for the San Francisco Conservatory of Music is a singular appeal; it was written for a particular purpose on behalf of a particular organization at a particular time. As a result, there are several ways this letter may not work well as a model for your own fundraising efforts. The package was written to acquire members, whereas most fundraising letters are written to proven donors. The letter is benefit-driven, even to the point of offering prospective members admission to a specific performance, and most nonprofits have to reach far to come up with tangible donor benefits. There's a celebrity lift letter, a device that's appropriate for most nonprofits only in unusual circumstances.

Nevertheless, it's worthwhile for you to study this package closely because it does its job so well. I chose this fundraising letter because its varied contents illustrate how to meet so many different letter-writing challenges and, more to the point, because it dramatizes how different a particular fundraising letter can be from every other fundraising letter. There's no question what the conservatory is offering. The marketing concept couldn't be clearer.

## A Shorter Journey Through a Letter That Doesn't Work Well

For a contrasting example, let's take a look at an appeal (Exhibit 5.6) that's much closer to the dysfunctional definition of a fundraising letter that I referred to at the beginning of Chapter Four.

A. Glance at the outer envelope. You can't miss the return address rubber-stamped in the upper-left-hand corner or the incomplete (and, in many parts of the country, undeliverable) address on the mailing label. The only thing this envelope has going for it is a first-class stamp. But you've probably guessed, just as I did, that the reason this was mailed first class was one of the following: (1) the quantity wasn't large enough to qualify the appeal for bulk mail, (2) the organization didn't have or couldn't get a nonprofit bulk mailing permit, or (3) the list was in such bad shape the organization couldn't bundle the mail properly to suit postal personnel.

B. Now take a look through the text on the first page. It has its positive points: short paragraphs, white space, underlined subheadings, language that's clear and relatively readable. But there are precious few personal pronouns anywhere in sight—except for "we" a few times—and the rest is argumentative and rhetorical. It's not really even clear this is an appeal for funds because I'm asked if I can "assist in other ways." But there's no way I can tell how my "financial contribution"—or any other sort of help I might give—is connected to anything else in this letter.

C. The second page continues in the same vein, compounding the problems of the first page: more statistics, more rhetoric, a laundry list of organizations (some of them little known), a dual signature—and no ask. It's hard to imagine a letter better calculated not to raise money.

D. Apparently the Federal Jobs Program outlined in the top two-thirds of this reply device is the principal program of the organization that sent this appeal, although I'm forced to guess that's really the case. Only at the bottom of the page do I find a way to respond to the letter (assuming I'd be so inclined). You'll note it's called an "Endorsement Form." However, there's no way for me to indicate my endorsement (for the Federal Jobs

Program? the Campaign to Abolish Poverty?). There's also no suggested gift amount and no return address (in case the form becomes separated from the letter or the return envelope).

E.  This rubber-stamped little reply envelope doesn't inspire confidence. Major gift fundraisers speak of an organization's readiness to receive big gifts. This organization doesn't appear ready to receive little gifts.

---

**EXHIBIT 5.6**

## Outer Envelope (A), Campaign to Abolish Poverty

CAMPAIGN TO ABOLISH POVERTY
942 MARKET STREET #708
SAN FRANCISCO, CA 94102

Mal Warwick
2550 Ninth
Berkeley CA 94710

**EXHIBIT 5.6 (*Continued*)**

## First Page (B), Campaign to Abolish Poverty

# Campaign to Abolish Poverty

**942 Market Street, #708, San Francisco, CA 94102 ● Ph: 415-397-4911  Fx: 415-434-3110**

November 6, 1992

Dear Friend:

Electing Bill Clinton President certainly creates new opportunities in Washington, D.C.  The pendulum is beginning to swing in the opposite direction.

But it remains to be seen how much difference Clinton will make, particularly for the poor and near-poor.  If history is any guide, strong grassroots pressure will be necessary to push Clinton beyond his election-year program.

The Campaign to Abolish Poverty (CAP) aims to push the pendulum as hard as possible.  Our current focus is to build support for the Federal Jobs Program -- a proposal to create two million new, permanent, public service jobs -- as a first step toward ending poverty in this country.

**We urge you to help this effort by sending a financial contribution now, and letting us know if you can assist in other ways.**

Clinton has committed himself to a number of good positions.  But there is a downside to most of them.

Jobs

On the one hand, for example, it is encouraging that Clinton proposes federal funding for public works jobs.  But he's only talking about one-shot infrastructure repair -- temporary jobs which largely would exclude women, minorities and low-income people who need them the most.

**We need to persuade Clinton and Congress to support <u>sustained</u> federal funding for** local human service jobs  - jobs for which the poor and near-poor would qualify, with relevant on-the-job training.

Tax Reform

It is also positive that Clinton advocates increasing taxes on the wealthy.  But his proposal would roll back only one-fifth of the tax breaks received by the top 2% of all households during the last fifteen years.  If these families with annual incomes over $200,000 paid 34% of their income in federal taxes, as they did in 1977, $80 billion in addition to the $20 billion targeted by Clinton could be generated.

**We need to persuade Clinton and Congress to restore 1977 tax rates for the wealthy.**  All other income groups are now paying higher federal taxes (including payroll taxes).  The wealthy could pay what they paid in 1977 without undue hardship.

**EXHIBIT 5.6 (*Continued*)**

## Second Page (C), Campaign to Abolish Poverty

Military Spending

Clinton's proposals for reductions in the military budget are inadequate. **We need to persuade Clinton and Congress to move in the direction of a 50% cut in military spending,** which could free almost $150 billion per year to help put Americans to work.

Federal Jobs Program

In consultation with a wide range of recognized experts and community organizations, CAP has developed a specific program -- the **Federal Jobs Program** -- that would appropriate $50 billion to create two million permanent public service jobs, paid for by higher taxes on the wealthy and reductions in the military budget (see enclosed).

A broad range of community-based organizations, community leaders, and elected officials have already endorsed this program, including American Friends Service Committee, Catholic Charities of San Francisco, California Legislative Council for Older Americans, Coleman Advocates for Children and Youth, San Francisco Lawyer's Committee for Urban Affairs, and Maryland United for Peace and Justice. Considering that we have been gathering endorsements only since early October, this support is very encouraging.

But in order to influence the next session of Congress, the Campaign to Abolish Poverty and its membership must broaden its base and press its case effectively in Washington. We have recently begun encouraging discussions with a number of national organizations with lobbyists in Washington to build support for our jobs program.

The desperation and misery experienced by growing millions of Americans compel us to make this effort and to continue until economic security for all is established as a human right.

So please give what you can financially, and if possible contribute time and energy as well. Please complete the form enclosed and return it with your tax-deductible donation as soon as possible.

With your help, we have a chance.

Sincerely,

Wade Hudson
Chair

Barbara Arms
Director

**EXHIBIT 5.6 (*Continued*)**

# Reply Device (D), Campaign to Abolish Poverty

## FEDERAL JOBS PROGRAM

**Purpose:**  To appropriate $50 billion to create 2 million new public service jobs in both urban and rural areas, as the first step toward guaranteeing every adult the opportunity to work at a living wage.  Each year, funding should increase by 20% until these jobs go begging due to lack of applicants.

**Types of Work:**  These funds shall be used to hire workers in repair/maintenance/ rehabilitation of publicly-owned facilities, conservation/rehabilitation/ improvement of public lands, child care, health care, in-home caregiving, education (including tutorial services), peer counseling, housing and neighborhood improvement, recreation, arts programs, community centers, and other vital public services.

**Wages:**  Wages shall range from $7-$12 per hour, plus benefits, and shall be indexed to inflation. The compensation for these positions shall not be less than the prevailing compensation for individuals employed in similar occupations.

**Allocation of Funds:**  Two and one-half percent of all funds shall be allocated for Native American tribes and Alaska Native villages.  Remaining funds shall be allocated by the Secretary of Labor to the states based upon the number of people living in poverty in each state.

**Administration:**   The Secretary of Labor shall distribute the funds to the states for distribution to local governments.  The cost of administration shall be no more than the standard for similar programs.  Each recipient of funds shall be responsible for ensuring equal employment opportunities, equal pay for equal work, and the full participation of traditionally underrepresented groups, including women and racial and ethnic minorities.

**Displacement:**  The following shall be prohibited: a) any displacing of current employees, including partial displacement such as a reduction in the hours of nonovertime work, wages, or employment benefits; b) impairing of existing contracts or collective bargaining; c) filling of openings created by related layoffs or terminations; or d) infringing on promotional opportunities of current employees.

**Oversight:**  Prior to submitting its plan to the State, each eligible entity shall conduct an open public review and comment process, and during the year, shall conduct at least one public hearing to receive input into its evaluation process.  Workers hired by these funds shall be encouraged to participate in this review process.

**Source of Funds:**  The funds needed for this program shall come from increasing personal income taxes on the richest 2% of households and from reducing the military budget.

------------------------------------------------------------------------------------------------

## ENDORSEMENT FORM

\_\_\_Please find enclosed a check for _____ (made payable to: Campaign to Abolish Poverty) to help with building support for the Federal Jobs Program.  (Contributions are tax-deductible.)

\_\_\_I would like to volunteer some time to help.

\_\_\_Please send me more information about CAP and the Federal Jobs Program.

Name (print) _____

Organization (if any)_____

Address _____

City_____State_____Zip_____

Day Phone_____Eve Phone_____Fax_____

---

**EXHIBIT 5.6 (*Continued*)**

## Reply Envelope (E), Campaign to Abolish Poverty

CAMPAIGN TO ABOLISH POVERTY
942 MARKET STREET #708
SAN FRANCISCO, CA 94102

---

# Building Relationships

Throughout the first journey we made, you must have recognized the emphasis I placed on the relationship between the conservatory and the donor. Relationship building is the essence of good fundraising; the biggest rewards come with time.

To gain perspective on the techniques that will allow you to use fundraising letters to maximum advantage in building strong, long-term relationships with your donors, please join me now in Part Two, "The Letter Writer's Plan of Action."

# Part Two

# The Letter Writer's Plan of Action

**IT'S NUTS-AND-BOLTS** time. In this part, we'll approach the task of writing a fundraising letter from a strictly practical, down-to-earth perspective. In successive chapters, we'll cover these topics:

- What to do before you sit down to write a fundraising appeal

- The nine steps I recommend you follow in crafting a fundraising package

- The eight concrete Cardinal Rules that determine whether your appeal will be a success (or a dud), along with a self-assessment form that will help you evaluate the likely effectiveness of a fundraising letter in light of these rules

- The practical guidelines of style and syntax I urge you to follow when you're writing a fundraising appeal—or, for that matter, any other prose that's meant to persuade a reader to act

# Chapter 6

# What to Do Before You Write Any Fundraising Letter

**HOW DO YOU** get started writing that fundraising letter that's due at the printer's next month?

You *think.*

Effective writing begins with clear, uncluttered thinking. Before you set down on paper a single word of your next fundraising appeal, you must understand precisely to whom you're writing, why you're writing, and what you're writing. That's what the following twenty questions are about. Asking yourself these questions won't guarantee you'll write a better letter (much less a more successful letter), but they will help you think clearly about the task at hand and focus your writing on the specific points you most need to make.

Answering these questions will enable you to construct a powerful marketing concept, the idea that's at the core of any piece of writing conceived to produce results. The marketing concept is a tapestry woven of need, opportunity, and circumstance. It's the pure essence of the message you're conveying. Or think of it as an executive summary of your letter.

The marketing concept is at the heart of the dialogue that Siegfried Vögele describes (see Chapter Two). Incorporated into it are the answers to many of your readers' unspoken questions.

Never forget this: the words you write will obtain the objectives you desire only to the extent that those words convey a marketing concept powerful enough to motivate your donors. You must appeal to them clearly and unambiguously, which requires that you begin with an absolutely clear understanding of why you're writing a letter in the first place. That's where the twenty questions start.

# The Twenty Important Questions You Need to Ask Before You Begin Writing

## First, Think About Why You're Writing This Particular Letter

1. What is the purpose of your appeal? To acquire new donors or members? Solicit larger gifts or major gifts? Urge your donors to consider planned giving? Reactivate lapsed members or donors? Or meet any of a multitude of other specific fundraising needs?

## Now, Think About the People You're Writing To

2. What do the people you're writing to have in common with one another? For example, do they share a powerful experience: an earthquake, religious conversion, new citizenship, a rare disease, a crushing personal loss? Are they patriotic or dedicated to a particular cause? Are they all likely to be concerned about global climate change?

3. What fact, or facts, may be true about almost all of these people—facts to distinguish them from the rest of the world's population? Are they all over the age of sixty? Do they all live in a single community? Were they all once patients in your hospital? Are they all women? Baby boomers? Donors? Nondonors? Members?

4. What do you know about the feelings of the people you're writing to? Are they likely to be angry (or elated) about a recent turn of events in the world or in your local community? Have recent economic setbacks made life more difficult for them, or changes in tax laws made them more comfortable? Are they likely to be skeptical about charity? Concerned about declining moral values? Fearful of old age?

5. What's the relationship of these people to your organization? What do they know about you, your organization, or the issue or problem you're addressing? What don't they know? What do they want to know? Have they been contributing regular gifts for several years and demonstrated interest, even commitment, to your agency? Is the typical reader of the letter you're about to write a longtime subscriber to your newsletter or a new donor who lacks basic information about your work? Is there likely to be a personal relationship between the readers and your executive director or a member of your board?

6. Consider the typical recipient of your letter. What experiences, feelings, and thoughts is that person likely to have that would help her understand the issue or problem you're addressing? Is it likely that this typical reader will feel very deeply, based on her own personal experience, about some issue

or problem that underpins your agency's work? For example, if you serve the homeless, is she likely to come into contact with homeless people on a daily basis—or almost never? Put yourself in her position, and think how she might think and feel about the challenges your organization faces every day.

7. What leads you to believe that the typical person you're writing to will respond favorably? Does she have a long history of supporting your agency or, at least, other organizations like yours? Has she expressed interest in knowing how she might help? Is there some personal connection, such as a child who was a patient, a parent who benefited from your services, or an old school tie? Is this a time of crisis, and have earlier appeals to the same or similar groups amply demonstrated that people like those you're writing to now are likely to respond?

## Now, Think About What You'll Ask People to Do

8. What is it exactly that you want recipients to do? Renew their memberships? Send larger annual gifts than they did last year? Join an exclusive giving club? Commit to making monthly gifts via electronic funds transfer? Support a special new project? Respond to an emergency with an additional $10 or $15?

9. What is the minimum amount of money (if any) that you hope to receive from each recipient? Few other questions are more important in appeals sent by mail. The amount of your ask, particularly the minimum amount, will often predetermine the amount you receive. A prospective donor may be incredulous at a request for $1,000, while a long-loyal supporter thinks the same sum too small. (That's one reason why the same appeal usually can't be sent to both prospective and proven donors.) To be successful, your appeal must ask for a specific amount, and that must be the right amount.

10. Is there anything else you want recipients to do right now? Will your appeal ask for a cash contribution and nothing more? Or will you request a three-year pledge, a monthly commitment, a signature on a credit card authorization form—or something entirely different? For example, will your appeal include an *involvement device,* such as a postcard to the governor, a membership survey, or an offer to supply information about wills and bequests?

## Now, Think About the Circumstances in Which You're Writing This Appeal

11. What problem, need, issue, or opportunity prompts your agency to send this appeal? Be specific; don't state the need as simply that "funds are

tight" or "we need money." Think about the particular set of circumstances that makes it necessary for your agency to raise funds right now. Is there a profoundly exciting new opportunity that your organization wants to meet by launching a new program? Has there been an unanticipated demand for your services—or a shortfall in funding from corporate and foundation donors? Is a trustee or a friendly foundation offering a challenge grant (or willing to do so)?

## Think About the Person Who Will Sign the Appeal

12. What is the signer's name? It's dangerous to draft an appeal not knowing who will sign it. A fundraising appeal—a letter from one person to another—is most powerful when it reflects the personal views and feelings of both people—the sender and the receiver. The appeal will be most effective if you can bring it to life with a relevant anecdote or two, or a typical statement that will ring true—something that might cause a knowledgeable reader to nod and say, "Yes, that's ol' Fred in a nutshell, all right!"

13. What is the connection between the signer and the problem, need, issue, or opportunity that prompts the appeal? If the signer is your president or executive director, the connection may be obvious—and rife with possibilities to bring that opportunity to life. If the signer is instead someone who has no day-to-day connection with the events or circumstances that prompt your appeal, think about what might move the signer to write an emotional appeal at this particular time. Is there something in his past: his education, his childhood, his experience as a soldier at war, his business achievements?

14. What is the connection between the signer and those who will receive the appeal? Do they share the experiences of a generation? For example, are most of them over the age of fifty-five—or under forty? As loyal members of a single organization, have they shared a particular event or intense experience: the death of a president, a Super Bowl victory, the landing on the moon, the fall of the Berlin Wall? Or are they all well-to-do, or members of a particular community? Have they received similar honors, attended the same school, watched the same shows on television?

15. What are the signer's feelings and thoughts about the problem, need, issue, or opportunity that underlies the appeal? If you don't know the answer to this question, ask it. Sometimes the signer—even an in-house, staff, or board signer—can suggest a powerful line of argument or

an evocative story that will bring your appeal to life. Emotional copy is usually more effective than intellectual copy, but a powerful fundraising letter is built on ideas and facts as well as feelings. Look for both to flesh out your appeal.

### Consider What Benefits People Will Get If They Respond to Your Appeal

16. List all the tangible benefits, if any. Are you offering a newsletter, for example, or discounts on products or services, or the promise of invitations to events with celebrity supporters? Or have you enclosed a premium such as a bookmark, name stickers, photographs, or a calendar?

17. List the intangible benefits of sending a gift in response to your appeal. Will donors help you change the course of human history, or save the life of a tiny child? Will they be ensuring that their values and beliefs will be passed along to generations of descendants or raising the quality of life in their community? Will donors gain salvation, learn about a headline-grabbing issue, prevent the abuse of pets?

### Why Do the Readers of Your Appeal Need to Respond Right Now?

18. Is there an especially urgent need or opportunity that justifies this appeal? Is Thanksgiving approaching, and with it increased demand for the hot meals your agency serves to the poor? Is a regional war about to break out, shutting down communications with your field office? Is the congressional debate drawing to a close? Will the board of directors be forced to shut down the program soon if funding goals aren't met?

19. Is there a deadline by which you must receive responses? For instance, have you arranged—or can you arrange—a challenge grant with an imminent deadline? Is the end of the calendar year approaching, and with it the opportunity for donors to save on this year's taxes? Is Easter special to your organization, representing a traditional time for your supporters to demonstrate their compassion for the less fortunate?

20. What will happen if you don't receive responses before that deadline? Will you lose the challenge grant? Will poor people go hungry? Will children be turned away from the door to your agency? Will small animals die, or the supply of autographed books run out, or people with AIDS suffer needless pain?

If you crave a shorthand way to remember these twenty questions, think of the journalist's old saw about including the who, what, when, where, and why into a story's lead (and add a how for good measure). You can even diagram these thoughts as follows:

| | |
|---|---|
| **Who?** | Who will sign the letter? |
| | Who will receive the letter? |
| **What?** | What is it you want the reader to do? |
| | What will the reader receive in return? |
| **When?** | When do you want the reader to respond? |
| **Where?** | Where will the proposed action take place? |
| **Why?** | Why should the reader take this step? |
| **How?** | How will the proposed action make a difference? |

## How to Write a Marketing Concept

Once you've answered those twenty questions (or cheated by using the table I just gave you), sum up all this information in one paragraph. Be as specific and precise as possible, and write the paragraph in the first-person singular (just as you'll have to do when you write the letter itself). Address it to that one typical individual who will be receiving your letter. This paragraph will be the marketing concept for your appeal. Once you've written it, the rest of your job will be easy.

Keep in mind that the marketing concept is not the letter itself or even its opening paragraph; it's simply a way to get started. Others might call it the *copy platform.* It's the foundation on which you'll construct your appeal. It's what you'll write about: facts, information, feelings, circumstances—that is, specifics. The marketing concept is the skeleton on which you hang them all together. In writing your letter, you'll put flesh on these bones.

To help you get the hang of it, here are examples of two typical marketing concepts:

*Because you've been so generous to the Center in the past, you've heard from me from time to time about exciting new developments here. I've told you before how far we stretch your contributions to serve the underserved in the Community. Now, a renewal gift from you of as little as $25 will go twice as far as before! Your $25 will help house the homeless children of the Community by enabling the Center to buy $50 or more worth of lumber and tools—because your gift will be matched, dollar for dollar, by an anonymous donor through the Center's new Matching Gift Program. That way, you'll get double the satisfaction from your act of* *generosity—and bring new hope to twice as many of your neighbors in the Community.*

• • •

*You may not know me, but I'm sure you're familiar with the Museum, which has been the centerpiece of my life during the past twenty years of my tenure as its Director. I'm writing to you, a fellow resident of the City, because I want you to be among the first to know about the Museum's unique new Charter Membership program. As a person who appreciates the finer things in life, you'll cherish for many years to come each magnificent issue of our new bimonthly magazine on the visual arts. You'll receive the magazine absolutely free of charge as a Charter Member of the Museum. And you'll have the satisfaction of knowing that your Charter Membership contribution of $45, $75, $150, or more will help us to showcase the exciting work of emerging new artists in our region.*

If cramming so much information into one paragraph strikes you as daunting, it may be useful to consider the construction of a marketing concept as a multistage process. Begin by thinking, answering the twenty questions I posed earlier. Then read all the available material that might help you flesh out the concept with those telltale facts that often work like magic in a fundraising letter: reports from program officers, foundation proposals, postings on the organization's Web site, and so forth. If necessary, ask questions of senior staff members, program officers, clients or beneficiaries, gift processing staff members, or donors. Then think some more before you (finally) draft the marketing concept. Once you're pleased with the result, shop it around the office. Ask your colleagues to poke holes in your argument and identify shaky claims or missing facts. Revise accordingly.

Often, but not always, the reply device in a successful direct mail fundraising package restates the marketing concept. That's why many experienced direct mail copywriters (including me) tackle the reply device first when they set out to write a package. Keep in mind that the reply device has four functions: to affirm the donor's decision to take the action you're requesting, to restate the marketing concept, to detail the donor's benefits, and to guide gift processing.

To get a stronger grip on the central role of the marketing concept in the reply device, study the examples in Exhibits 6.1 through 6.4. You'll soon get the gist of the marketing concept behind each of the fundraising appeals from which these response forms were selected. It stares you right in the face. That's what your marketing concept needs to do every time you write an appeal!

Remember always that your reader has only twenty seconds to get the message. (Think back to Siegfried Vögele's eye-motion research.) If your message—the central reason that your readers should respond—isn't clear at a glance, there's little chance your letter will be read at all, much less generate contributions.

---

**EXHIBIT 6.1**

## New Donor Enrollment Form, Doctors Without Borders

# YOU CAN HELP SAVE A LIFE

**Yes, I want to help Doctors Without Borders USA bring medical humanitarian relief around the world. I am making a tax-deductible gift of:**

❑ $35     ❑ $75     ❑ $100     ❑ $200     ❑ $500     or ❑ $ _____

**We desperately need your financial support.  Please help us.**

F306256291 ADQ070301A1V

Mr. Mal Warwick
~~2763 Ashby Pl Apt E~~
~~Berkeley, CA 94705-2323~~

DOCTORS WITHOUT BORDERS
MEDECINS SANS FRONTIERES
PO BOX 5023
HAGERSTOWN MD  21741-5023

A1

**Please make your check payable to Doctors Without Borders USA.  TO CHARGE YOUR GIFT, PLEASE SEE OTHER SIDE.**
**Please tear at perforation and return this reply slip with your gift.  Thank you for your support.**

Printed on Recycled Paper
Q73A-1

✂ *Detach here*

- - - - - - - - - - - - - - - - - - - - - - - - - - - - - - - - - - - - - - - - - - - - - - - - - - - - -

© Kris Torgeson

*"Many people tell us that this is the first time that they have seen a qualified doctor and received treatment.  People have told me that they don't know what might happen to them if we weren't here and there were no international witnesses to what they are going through."*

– Matthias Hrubey, MD for Doctors Without Borders,
Kass, South Darfur, Sudan

**Your contribution to Doctors Without Borders allows our volunteers to save lives around the world.**

**$35 –** Supplies a basic suture kit to repair minor wounds.

**$75 –** Provides 1,500 patients with clean water for a week.

**$100 –** Provides infection-fighting antibiotics to treat nearly 40 wounded people.

**$200 –** Supplies 40 malnourished children with special high-protein food for a day.

### *Thank you for your generosity.*

**www.doctorswithoutborders.org**

**EXHIBIT 6.1** (*Continued*)

**Fill in the following to charge to your credit card:**

**American Express, MasterCard, Visa, and Discover accepted.**

Authorized signature                                    Date

Account number                                      Expiration date

Name as it appears on your credit card

### Doctors Without Borders Meets. or Surpasses All Standards

Doctors Without Borders has consistently met all standards of watchdog agencies and has recently been awarded an "A" rating from the American Institute of Philanthropy. The watchdog agencies' reports are available to the general public.

Please read our *Commitment to Our Supporters* at http://www.doctorswithoutborders.org/donate/donorcommitment.cfm.

*For more information, please call Donor Services at 212-763-5779.*

**Doctors Without Borders, PO Box 5023, Hagerstown, MD 21741-5023**

## In 2005, donations to Doctors Without Borders USA, Inc. were spent as follows:

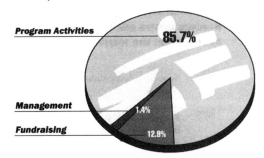

Program Activities — 85.7%
Management — 1.4%
Fundraising — 12.9%

Doctors Without Borders strives to direct at least 85% of our spending to program activities, which include emergency and medical programs, program support, and public education.

We have surpassed this standard every year from 1995 to 2005. We are committed to this goal.

### NOTICE TO CONTRIBUTORS

Many states require charities that solicit funds from the public to register with the state agency regulating charities. Although our financial report is always sent free to anyone requesting a copy, certain states require us to advise you that a copy of our financial report is also available from them.

If you desire a copy of our financial report, you may write to: **Doctors Without Borders USA, Inc.,** 333 Seventh Avenue, 2nd Floor, New York, NY 10001 or State of New York. Our annual report is also available on our website: www.doctorswithoutborders.org.

**State of Florida:** A copy of the official registration and financial information may be obtained from the Division of Consumer Services by calling toll-free, within the state 1-800-HELP-FLA. Registration does not imply endorsement, approval or recommendation by the state. Florida registration #SC-03413. **State of Georgia:** The following information will be made available from the organization by request: 1) a full and fair description of the charitable program for which the solicitation campaign is being carried out and, if different, a full and fair description of the programs and activities of the charitable organization on whose behalf the solicitation is being carried out; and 2) a financial statement or summary which shall be consistent with the financial statement required to be filed with the Secretary of State pursuant to Code Section 43-17-5. **State of Kansas:** The annual report is filed with the secretary of state, Kansas registration number 219-017-1. **State of Maryland:** For the cost of postage and copying, documents and information filed under the Maryland charitable organizations laws can be obtained from the Secretary of State, Charities Division, State House, Annapolis, MD 21401. **State of Mississippi:** The official registration and financial information of Médecins Sans Frontières/Doctors Without Borders may be obtained from the Mississippi Secretary of State's office by calling 1-888-236-6167.

Registration by the Secretary of State does not imply endorsement. **State of New Jersey:** Inform filed with the attorney general concerning this charitable solicitation may be obtained from the atto general of the state of New Jersey by calling 1-973-504-6215. Registration with the attorney ge does not imply endorsement. **State of New York:** A copy of the latest annual report may be obta from the organization or from the Office of the Attorney General by writing the Charities Bureau, Broadway, New York, NY 10271. **State of North Carolina:** Financial information about this organization a copy of its license are available from the State Solicitation Licensing Branch at 1-888-830-4989. The licer not an endorsement by the state. **State of Pennsylvania:** The official registration and financial inform of Médecins Sans Frontières/Doctors Without Borders USA, Inc. (registration #0011941) may be obtained the Pennsylvania Department of State by calling toll-free, within Pennsylvania, 1-800-732-0999. Regist does not imply endorsement. **Commonwealth of Virginia:** Financial statements are available from the Division of Consumer Affairs, P.O. Box 526, Richmond, VA 23218. **State of Washington:** Inform relating to the financial affairs of Médecins Sans Frontières/Doctors Without Borders USA, Inc. is avai from the Secretary of State, and the toll-free number for Washington residents: 1-800-332-4483. **Sta West Virginia:** West Virginia residents may obtain a summary of the registration and financial docum from the Secretary of State, State Capitol, Charleston, WV 25305. Registration does not imply endorsen

Unless otherwise noted, Doctors Without Borders will use your gift for the project(s) that Do Without Borders determines is in need of funds.

Doctors Without Borders USA, Inc. is recognized as tax exempt under section 501(c)(3) of the Int Revenue Code.

**EXHIBIT 6.2**

# New Donor Enrollment Form, Ocean Conservancy

## New Member Reply Form

☐ **YES!** I want to help protect dolphins, whales, sea turtles and other endangered marine wildlife. My tax-deductible gift (made payable to The Ocean Conservancy) is for:

*Your gift of this level or higher will really help!*

☐ $50    ☐ $25    ⬭ $15*    ☐ $10    ☐ Other $_____

* For your gift of $15 or more, you'll receive full membership benefits *plus* our exclusive Ocean Conservancy sea turtle plush!

☐ Please put my gift to work entirely for the oceans—don't send me the sea turtle.

07DPBCKAAX 27102297101

Mr William P Rehm
XXXXXXXXXXXXXXXX
XXXXXXXXXXXXXXXX
Illdnluldlluullllunulllunulddddddlunull

The Ocean Conservancy
**Advocates for Wild, Healthy Oceans**

**Please return this form with your check, or complete the reverse to give by credit card. *Thank you!***

62305

The Ocean Conservancy • 2029 K Street, NW • Washington, DC 20006 • www.oceanconservancy.org

7-PB2A

---

Charge my credit card:    ☐ MasterCard    ☐ VISA    ☐ American Express    ☐ Discover

Card Number: [_____]    Exp. Date: _____

Print name (as shown on card): _____

Signature: _____

---

**EXHIBIT 6.3**

## New Donor Enrollment Form, Interfaith Alliance

07 0418457

### I Want to Help Preserve Our Constitution!

☐ **Yes, I am disturbed by the manipulation of religion for political gain. The Religious Right must be stopped from using the alleged "war on Christianity" as a tactic to advance their divisive agenda.** To help protect religious freedom, promote inclusive policies, and advocate for civility in politics, I am joining THE INTERFAITH ALLIANCE with my gift of:

☐ $25    ☐ $50    ☐ $100    ☐ $250    ☐ Other $_____

Please make your check payable to **The Interfaith Alliance.** To make your contribution by credit card, please complete information on reverse side.

By signing up for timely e-mail updates, you can stay informed about the activities of The Interfaith Alliance and issues that impact you. **My e-mail address is:**

_____@_____._____
(We will never sell or share your e-mail address.)

Mr. Stephen Hitchcock
~~1100 Stannage Ave~~
~~Albany, CA 94706-2022~~

‖l··l··l·ll··ll···ll··ll·l·l·l·l·l·lll····l·l·l·ll

P107031T

**THE INTERFAITH ALLIANCE**

1331 H Street, NW
11th Floor
Washington, DC 20005
Toll-Free: (800) 510-0969
Fax: (202) 639-6375
www.interfaithalliance.org

Mr. Hitchcock, it's so important that you and I tell President Bush and Members of the 110th Congress to stop funding religion with government dollars. We must remind our leaders that we, as people of faith, good will and conscience, believe the separation of church and state is good for both religion and government. Please include the petition below along with your gift and return this entire form to The Interfaith Alliance. We will deliver your message to the President, *thank you!*

---

## PETITION TO THE PRESIDENT

FROM:  Mr. Stephen Hitchcock
          Albany, CA

As a person of faith, good will and conscience, I am offended by the Religious Right's attempts to curtail religious freedom under the guise of a "war on Christianity."

I am opposed to all attempts to funnel my tax dollars into houses of worship and religious organizations, and to any other efforts that undermine the appropriate relationship between government and houses of worship as dictated by the First Amendment.

President Bush, I believe with all my heart that my values call for understanding, healing, and inclusion — not intolerance, divisiveness, and bigotry.

I respectfully urge you to preserve freedom of — and from — religion for ALL Americans, as mandated in the Constitution.

Sincerely,


_____          _____
SIGNATURE                                    CITY, STATE

---

## EXHIBIT 6.3 (*Continued*)

☐ I prefer to charge my contribution of $ _____ to my:

☐ **VISA**      ☐ **MasterCard**      ☐ ▮▮▮      ☐ **DISCOVER NOVUS**

Card Number _____   Expiration Date _____/_____

Authorized Signature _____

E-mail _____ @ _____ . _____

Religious or Spiritual Affiliation (optional) _____

Your gift could go twice as far if your company has a matching gift program. Please ask your personnel office for the appropriate forms and guidelines.

The Interfaith Alliance is making a difference in America by promoting the positive role of religion in public life and challenging religious political extremism. TIA is located at 1331 H St.,NW, 11th Floor,Washington, DC 20005 and can be reached at (202) 639-6370. Contributions to TIA are not tax-deductible for federal income tax purposes. TIA is a 501(c)(4) non-profit organization. You may obtain a copy of the charity's financial report by writing to the charity's name and address. NY – New York residents may obtain a copy of TIA's annual report by writing to the Office of the Attorney General, Department of Law, Charities Bureau, 120 Broadway, New York, NY 10271; PA – The official registration and financial information of The Interfaith Alliance may be obtained from the Pennsylvania Department of State by calling toll-free, within Pennsylvania, 1-800-732-0999. Registration does not imply endorsement.WV – Residents may obtain a summary of the registration and financial documents from the Secretary of State, State Capitol, Charleston,WV 25305; WA – A notice of solicitation required by law is on file with the Washington Secretary of State.You may obtain financial disclosure information by contacting the Secretary of State at 1-800-332-GIVE; MD – Copies of documents and information submitted by TIA under the Maryland Charitable Solicitations Act are available for the cost of copies and postage from the Secretary of State, State House, Annapolis, MD 21401, 410-974-5534; VA – A financial statement for the most recent fiscal year is available upon request from the Division of Consumer Affairs, Department of Agricultural and Consumer Services, P.O. Box 1163, Richmond,VA 23209, 804-786-1343; Registration by the Secretary of State does not imply endorsement; NC – Financial information about TIA and a copy of its license are available from the State Solicitation Licensing Section at 888-830-4989. The license is not an endorsement by the state; FL – Registration # CH9499.A COPY OF THE OFFICIAL REGISTRATION AND FINANCIAL INFORMATION MAY BE OBTAINED FROM THE DIVISION OF CONSUMER SERVICES BY CALLING TOLL-FREE, WITHIN THE STATE, 1-800-435-7352 or 1-800-FLA-Yuda POR ASTENCIA EN ESPANOL; NJ – INFORMATION FILED WITH THE ATTORNEY GENERAL CONCERNING THIS CHARITABLE SOLICITATION MAY BE OBTAINED FROM THE ATTORNEY GENERAL OF THE STATE OF NEW JERSEY BY CALLING 973-504-6215. KS: TIA's registration number is: 339-588-6 and Epsilon's registration number is ID# 0000027. The annual financial report for the preceding fiscal year is on file with the Secretary of States, 1st Floor, Memorial Hall, 120 SW10th Ave., Topeka, KS 66612. Registration with any of these government agencies does not imply endorsement.

Made in the USA

**EXHIBIT 6.4**

## New Donor Enrollment Form, AmeriCares

# Please Help AmeriCares Save More Lives Around the World

Mr. Hitchcock, here are some examples of how your gift can save lives:

- ❏ $25 can provide 125 patients with tests for tuberculosis and malaria
- ❏ $50 can provide 1,000 children with treatments for cholera
- ❏ $100 can provide 1,500 infants and children with oral-rehydration treatments
- ❏ $250 can provide 5,000 children with anti-parasitic treatments
- ❏ $500 can provide 400 patients with rapid malaria tests
- ❏ Other $_____

802228278   Q071101196
Mr. Stephen Hitchcock
XXXXXXXXXXXX
XXXXXXXXXXXX

**AmeriCares**
HUMANITARIAN LIFELINE TO THE WORLD
88 Hamilton Avenue
Stamford, CT 06902
www.americares.org

*Photo Courtesy of: Debra Phillips*

To receive updates and information via e-mail, please provide your e-mail address:
_____ @ _____

*Contributions to AmeriCares are tax-deductible to the extent permitted by law. Please make check payable to AmeriCares.*

## Contribute to AmeriCares with Confidence

For nearly 25 years, the success of AmeriCares has been characterized by timely response, meaningful impact and intense passion. For every $100 donated to AmeriCares, more than $3,000 in aid is delivered due to partnerships and in-kind contributions.

*For the past five years, AmeriCares has been awarded the highest four-star rating from Charity Navigator, the nation's premier independent charity evaluator.*

*Photo courtesy of Kate Moxham*

*"The fact that we cannot solve all the world's problems does not absolve us of the responsibility of solving the ones we can."*
— Bob Macauley
AmeriCares Founder & Chairman

AMC-Q0711-PBRply

• • •

Join me now in Chapter Seven on a step-by-step journey through the route I usually take when setting out to write a fundraising letter.

# Chapter 7

# Eight Steps Toward Successful Fundraising Letters

**NOT LONG AGO,** a man who has been raising money by mail for more than thirty years bragged to me that he rarely spends more than an hour or two writing a fundraising letter—and he has been responsible for some big winners. Some of the most successful appeals he has ever written, he claimed, took no more than forty-five or sixty minutes of work.

You may choose to believe his claim or not. (I, for one, am skeptical.) But you won't hear me making similar assertions. I've been known to spend hours—even, occasionally, days—wrestling with a marketing concept before I set a single word down on paper.

In other words, I sometimes spend just as long thinking about what I'm going to write as another writer might require to do the job from start to finish. It's usually time well spent, as far as I'm concerned. Once I know what I'm going to write, the rest goes much more smoothly (at least most of the time).

Developing the marketing concept is just the first of eight steps I take when writing a fundraising letter, but it may occupy half or three-quarters of all the time I spend on a project.

The eight-step sequence I follow may not work for you. In fact, you may believe you're better off working like my colleague Stephen Hitchcock, who swears he writes in order to think (rather than the other way around). I suspect the truth is that Steve simply thinks a lot faster than most of the rest of us. You may too. Nevertheless, I hope you'll try it my way at least once. You might even like it!

So let's run through the eight steps, one by one. Assume that you've been assigned the task of writing a simple, straightforward special appeal to the active donors of a charity called Hope Is Alive! Here is the way I recommend you go about the project.

## Step 1: Develop the Marketing Concept

Write a complete marketing concept, so you'll understand the offer you'll be making in the letter. Writing this concept down will force you to decide how much money to ask for, who will sign your letter, and whether you'll include a donor involvement device (such as a survey), a premium, or a deadline—all the things you're writing the letter about. In this case, let's say you've determined that the marketing concept runs as follows:

> *As Executive Director of Hope Is Alive! I've written you many times in the past about the terrible challenges faced by the homeless in our city. Now I'm writing to you, as one of our most loyal and generous supporters, to tell you about a challenge that's a wonderful opportunity: two members of our Board of Trustees have volunteered to match your gift on a dollar-for-dollar basis if we receive it before January 15—up to a total of $10,000. The money raised in this Challenge of Hope will be used to outfit our new shelter, so that thirty more homeless families can find a warm and secure place to sleep in the difficult weeks still to go before winter ends.*

Now you're *almost* ready to start writing the appeal itself.

## Step 2: Determine the Contents of Package

Exactly what are you going to write? A long letter or a short one? A window envelope with text (a *teaser*) on the outside or a businesslike, *closed-face* (no window) envelope with no printing except the name Hope Is Alive! and the return address? In other words, it's time to determine how your marketing concept will be implemented as a fundraising package. What will the appeal consist of? In preparing this particular appeal, you might decide the following components are adequate to the task:

### Contents of Package

- A Number 10 closed-face outer envelope printed in black on the front only, with the addressee's name and address laser-printed on the front, and mailed first class with a postage stamp

- A two- or three-page letter, 8½ by 11 inches, printed in two colors, on one side only on two (or if necessary, three) sheets, with page one laser-personalized and subsequent pages printed to match but not personalized

- A reply device, approximately 3¼ by 8½ inches (to fit unfolded in a Number 10 envelope), printed on one side only, in two colors, on card stock, with name, address, and the ask amounts laser-personalized

- A Number 9 business reply envelope printed in one color on one side only

I suggest you write all this information down on a sheet of paper. Label it something like "Contents of Package." And take the time necessary to describe in some detail the paper stock and other specifications for each of the items you've decided to include in the package.

These should never be casual choices. Here, you've settled on a closed-face outer envelope with no teaser because you reason that committed donors will be inclined to open an appeal from Hope Is Alive! without an extravagant promise on the envelope. You've picked a two- or three-page letter with no brochure or other graphic enclosures because the story of the matching gift challenge is easily told and the January 15 deadline fosters a sense of urgency that might be undermined by a photo brochure that takes time, trouble, and expense to design and print.

Note how much closer you're getting now to knowing exactly what you're going to write. If you were writing a package to acquire new members rather than solicit support from proven donors, you might feel the need for a longer letter, a bigger reply device (perhaps to accommodate a full listing of membership benefits), plus a brochure or other insert, and maybe a premium such as name stickers as well. You might also find laser personalization is impractical in such a member acquisition package (because it's unlikely to be cost-effective). Before you actually write a letter, you need to know such things for two reasons: (1) the person in charge of getting the letter printed and mailed will need to secure printing and letter-shop bids, and (2) you need to know the space limitations you'll be facing when you write.

Even what might seem like inconsequential details can make a big difference in the way you go about writing a letter. Take, for example, the way the choice of printing technology affects the choice of minimum suggested gift levels in the letter. The choice of laser personalization on the reply device and the first page of the letter allows you to ask for gifts commensurate with each individual's giving history, because those amounts appear in the same computer file as the names and addresses. However, if you don't laser-personalize the letter's subsequent pages, you can't repeat the specific ask amounts printed on page one. If the final page of the letter is to be reproduced on an offset printing press rather than a laser printer, any ask amounts printed there will be identical in all the letters—something of a disadvantage, since it's customary and advisable to repeat the ask close to the end of an appeal.

But now your choices have been made. You know what you're writing, and you're ready to start.

## Step 3: Draft the Reply Device

Drafting the reply device may take no more than a minute or two, since you've already written a complete marketing concept. And as you write the device, you may find yourself fleshing out the marketing concept. For instance, if there are to be several different ask levels or segments in your appeal for Hope Is Alive! now's the time to think through the implications. A gift of $500 might require a dramatically different justification from one of $25. Waiting until later to figure that out might oblige you to do a lot of rewriting.

But this appeal, I've said, is simple and straightforward. So let's assume different versions of the letter aren't needed for different donor segments. The language on the reply device, then, will read somewhat as follows:

*Yes, I'll help meet the Challenge of Hope! so that thirty more homeless families can find a safe, warm place to sleep in the difficult weeks remaining before winter ends. To beat the January 15 deadline—so my gift is matched dollar-for-dollar by the Trustees—I'm sending my special tax-deductible contribution in the amount of:*

☐ *$[Last + 50%]*     ☐ *$[Last + 25%]*     ☐ *$_____*

## Step 4: Write the Outer Envelope

Here's the point where I'm likely to get hung up all over again, even after developing a gem of a marketing concept. If a letter I'm writing requires an outer-envelope teaser—one of those brassy, cute, provocative little half-statements and promises—I might find myself dithering for hours before I can get past this crucial fourth step in the process. I can write two thousand words in the time it takes me to devise a really good teaser. Sometimes, I'm forced to settle for one that's less than ideal. More often, I choose to omit the teaser, since my agency's tests repeatedly confirm that teasers rarely make much of a difference.

Yet a teaser can entice the reader to open the envelope, which nothing else may be able to bring off. A teaser that's doing its job will challenge, question, or intrigue the reader, drawing her more deeply into the silent dialogue that may later lead right to a gift.

Like everything else in a fundraising package, the outer-envelope teaser must be appropriate to the appeal type. For example, it's hard to imagine how any of the following teasers could be used on an outer envelope for a donor acquisition package: "It's time to renew!" "Special Bulletin for Members Only," or "Your newsletter is enclosed." All of these are teasers as surely as the most outrageous come-on for a "free gift" or a petition to the president of the United States. So are such seemingly offhanded statements as "First Class Mail" or "Official Documents."

Often the best teaser is no teaser at all. Fundraising letters are almost always crafted to mimic personal letters, so teasers may well cheapen or undermine the effect the writer hopes to achieve. In fact, extensive testing suggests that response isn't necessarily higher when you use a teaser, even when it seems eminently appropriate to do so. I believe that only *really good* teasers have the intended effect. Teasers that fall short of the mark probably have no effect whatsoever—or worse, they may persuade the reader *not* to open the envelope. After all, for most people, teasers are a dead giveaway for what all too many reflexively look on as junk mail.

The outer envelope in Exhibit 7.1, an oversized (9 by 12 inches), closed-face carrier, was part of a high-dollar fundraising package. The envelope bears first-class stamps, and the only words in sight are those in the address and the corner card, where the return address appears. There is no teaser in the generally accepted sense of that term. But for that appeal, at that time,

**EXHIBIT 7.1**

## Exemplary Outer Envelope, Mills-Peninsula Hospital Foundation

Arthur H. Bredenbeck

**Mills-Peninsula Hospital Foundation**

100 South San Mateo Drive, San Mateo, CA 94401

Mr. John Doe
123 Any Street
Any Town, AS 00000

the absence of a teaser was the best possible come-on. Words calculated to call greater attention to the contents or otherwise hype the appeal would likely have depressed response rather than boosted it. That's why I regard the teaser in Exhibit 7.1 as the best ever, bar none.

Let's assume that you've decided the appeal you're crafting for Hope Is Alive! will be mailed in a closed-face, personalized outer envelope with no teaser. You're ready to move along to the fifth step.

## Step 5: Write the Lead

If the opening paragraph of a letter doesn't engage the reader's attention, he's unlikely to read further. Research shows the lead of the letter has higher readership than any other element but the outer-envelope copy and the P.S. The lead paragraph—a simple sentence, more often than not—is one of the most important elements in a fundraising letter, which may help explain why the lead is another one of those points where I've been known to clutch.

You won't clutch, however. You know exactly how you're going to lead off your letter for Hope Is Alive! You'll begin with a brief, inspiring story about a six-year-old client of the agency who personifies everything that's best about its work—something like this:

> *Jennifer just <u>knew</u> things were going to get better. Molly told her so.*
>
> *Jennifer was only six years old, and she'd spent most of those years on the streets. Drifting from town to town with a dad who could never find work that lasted. No school. No friends, really. No pretty clothes like the other girls she saw sometimes.*
>
> *But one day Jennifer and her dad showed up at our Front Street shelter. Molly D'Alessandro was on duty and greeted the new arrivals. You might say it was love at first sight.*

Telling a story is just one of several common approaches to writing a lead. You might also respond to or elaborate on the outer-envelope teaser, ask a provocative question, challenge the reader, make the offer, or simply establish the reader's relationship with the signer. Some of the most powerful letter leads combine several of these elements.

While you're engaged in writing this lead, you might find it convenient to write the close of the letter as well. Just as the lead ought to be directly connected to the outer-envelope teaser, if any, the close should relate to the lead. If you began by asking a question, answer it now. If you started by challenging the reader, refer to the challenge again, and note how the offer you've made will enable the reader to respond in a meaningful way. Complete the circle; round out your letter with a satisfying close. In this case, you'll want to be sure that Jennifer and her dad and Molly D'Alessandro all figure in the way you wind up the letter.

## Step 6: Write the P.S.

We've learned from Siegfried Vögele that the postscript is the real lead more than 90 percent of the time because that's where readers usually turn first. This step deserves your full attention.

After a lot of thought, you've decided to use the P.S. to emphasize the deadline for receipt of matching gifts in the trustees' challenge grant campaign. The postscript would go something like this:

> P.S. Your gift will be matched dollar-for-dollar—but only if we receive your check by January 15. In this difficult winter, please help us outfit the new shelter and take thirty more homeless families off the streets!

This P.S. conveys three of the strongest elements of the appeal—the deadline, the dollar-for-dollar match, and the thirty families who will benefit—at just the place in the letter that's bound to have the highest readership of all.

Don't conclude on the basis of this example that you should use the postscript to restate and reinforce the ask. The overwhelming majority of fundraising letters make that mistake. Simply pleading with the reader to "act now" or "send your gift today" is a waste of this valuable real estate. That's boring. Use the P.S. instead to disclose some benefit or intriguing fact or to comment on an enclosure in the package that's not discussed in the body copy. Make the P.S. irresistibly interesting. After all, its function is to involve the reader and motivate him to turn to the lead of the letter.

Now you're ready to move along to the body of the letter itself.

## Step 7: Consider Subheads and Underlining

Do you remember Vögele's observations about the behavior of real-world direct mail recipients—how they skip about the text, glancing at a phrase here and a highlighted word or two there? If so, you'll want to decide at the outset what points to highlight visually within the body of the letter.

The items to underline or to feature in subheads aren't necessarily the ones you think will break up the text at the most convenient intervals or help convey your tone of voice. Rather, subheads and underlining must *appeal directly to the reader.* Ideally, such emphasis is used to spotlight donor benefits, tangible or intangible—the payoff to those who respond to the appeal with contributions.

Let's assume you've decided that subheads are inappropriate for the appeal you're writing for Hope Is Alive! Perhaps they're out of character for the signer, the executive director, who tends to be a bit stuffy, or perhaps you think subheads detract from the upscale image the agency wants to convey. There's still an easy way for you to accent the benefits offered in your appeal, answer readers' unspoken questions, and make your letter easier to read: by underlining. Do it sparingly, on only a few key words and phrases. Limit yourself to no more than three or four per page, and emphasize donor benefits. If possible, choose them before you write the body of the letter. One way you can determine which points warrant underlining (or subheads) is to outline the letter before you write it. If you construct your outline paying particular attention to the benefits you're offering, the appropriate words and phrases may jump off the page.

As you may be aware, this advice of mine on underlining flies in the face of common practice in the direct mail fundraising field. Pick up almost any fundraising letter at random, and what are you likely to find? Sentence after sentence, paragraph after paragraph, line after line—underlined. Overuse of underlining defeats its purpose, which after all is emphasis. Emphasize everything, and you emphasize nothing.

In this case, you'd be likely to decide that among the points requiring underlining are these two important ones:

> *If you respond by January 15, <u>your gift will be matched dollar-for-dollar.</u>*
> *With your generous support, Hope Is Alive! will be able to open the new shelter on time—and <u>thirty homeless families will be off the streets</u> for the rest of the winter.*

Instead of emphasizing Hope Is Alive!'s $10,000 budget to outfit the new shelter, you've wisely chosen to stress the thirty homeless families who will have a warm and secure place to sleep. Obviously, your readers will care much more about Jennifer and her dad and the other families than about an agency's budget!

## Step 8: Write the Text (At Last!)

This is the easy part. You've already written the reply device; you've developed the lead, the close, and the P.S.; you've drafted the principal underlined points. What else is there to do? A game of fill-in-the-blank.

Take care, though; it's all too easy to stumble off course in the stretch. Tell the story you started about Jennifer and Molly, but don't turn it into a novelette. Make sure the story shows the benefits the reader will receive if she accepts your offer: that Jennifer now has hope for a better life, and so will dozens of other good people trapped in terrible circumstances. Stick to the points you selected for emphasis by underlining. You picked those points because they answer the unspoken questions you know your reader will have—and because they emphasize the benefits that you hope will motivate the reader to send a gift without delay. If you stay on this course, Hope Is Alive! will raise its $10,000, and those thirty families will be off the streets. You, the author, will be a hero. And so will everyone who responded to your appeal.

$$\bullet \quad \bullet \quad \bullet$$

In the next chapter let's recap the essentials by reviewing what I call the Cardinal Rules of Fundraising Letters.

# Chapter 8

# The Cardinal Rules of Fundraising Letters

**IN MANY WAYS,** the techniques required to write an appeal for funds share a lot with any other sort of writing that's intended to persuade or otherwise produce results. But there are guidelines that apply specifically to writing fundraising letters. I call these axioms the Cardinal Rules of Fundraising Letters.

## The Cardinal Rules

To illustrate the eight rules spelled out below, I'll refer to the direct mail package in Exhibits 8.1 through 8.6. It's an appeal mailed by St. Joseph's Indian School, in Chamberlain, South Dakota; this package was one of several efforts to secure an additional gift from one of my newsletter's correspondents in the year after I sent the school an unsolicited $15 check as part of an annual exercise to learn how nonprofits respond to small gifts. The appeal isn't without flaws, but it does illustrate the eight rules.

### Rule 1: Use "I" and "You" (But Mostly "You")

"You" should be the word you use most frequently in your fundraising letters. Your appeal is a letter from one individual to another individual, not a press release, a position paper, or a brochure.

Studies on readability supply the fundamental reason the words "you" and "I" are important: they provide human interest. Stories, anecdotes, and common names (and capitalized words in general) have some of the same effect, but the most powerful way to engage the reader is by appealing directly to her: use the word "you."

In the St. Joseph's Indian School fundraising letter (Exhibit 8.1), notice how Brother David Nagel uses these powerful personal pronouns to establish intimacy:

**EXHIBIT 8.1**

**Appeal Letter, St. Joseph's School**

St. Joseph's Indian School
Chamberlain, South Dakota 57326

October 30, 1992

Dear Friend,

You are a dream catcher.

The Lakota (Sioux) believe that good dreams and nightmares float in the air, and that a special willow frame strung with sinew can screen out nightmares and let only good dreams pass through.

They call the ornament a dream catcher and put one in every tipi and on the cradle board of every baby.

The other evening I was walking through the William House, one of our childrens' homes.  I peeked in on some of the younger kids who were already asleep. I watched the children sleeping and dreaming peacefully.

Sweet dreams are something new for so many of the children.  They've come from such troubled homes — and nightmares are far more common on the reservations. I thought about the Lakota (Sioux) dream catcher and my thoughts turned to you.

You protect our children from nightmares.  You save them from poverty, illiteracy, and despair — a nightmare fate that befalls so many Native Americans on the reservations.

You bring them good dreams — of a bright future as well-educated, young adults with a purpose and strong values.  And you help make those dreams come true. You are a dream catcher!

Because you are a guardian of good dreams for the children of St. Joseph's, we want you to have a special gift.  I've enclosed a Thanksgiving Card that features the Lakota dream catcher.

**EXHIBIT 8.1** (*Continued*)

I hope you'll keep this card to bring good dreams to yourself and your family, or pass it on to bring good dreams to a faraway loved one at Thanksgiving.

Because so many of our friends are interested in Lakota traditions, we have ordered a small number of Lakota dream catchers in antique brass.

If you can send a special gift today of $25 or more, I'd love to send you one of these unique ornaments as a special gift from the children of St. Joseph's.

These highly detailed dream catchers make wonderful gifts for children and new parents, and make unique Christmas Tree decorations.

In any event, please send a gift today of whatever you can afford to bring dreams of hope to the children of St. Joseph's. Without people like you, their lives would be a nightmare.

Thanks!

Yours in Christ,

Bro. David Nagel
Director

P.S. Thanksgiving is a special, happy time around here. It's one of the few times when America remembers all the gifts Native Americans gave to this country — and how little they received in return. Please remember the children of St. Joseph's when you offer thanks over your Thanksgiving dinner. We'll be praying for you.

**EXHIBIT 8.2**

**Appeal Reply Device, St. Joseph's School**

# Dreams of Hope for the Children

2150050. 079

Mr. Karps:
Send a gift today of $25 or more, we'll send you a beautiful antique
brass Dream Catcher ornament as a special gift from the children of
St. Joseph's.

# YES!

**I want to be a dream catcher to help bring dreams of hope to the children of St. Joseph's.**

2150050. 079

Enclosed is my gift of:

( ) $25     ( ) $15     ( ) $48     ( ) $_____

( ) I have enclosed a gift of $25 or more, please send an antique
brass Lakota dream catcher ornament.

Please make your tax-deductible gift payable to St. Joseph's and mail it with this slip.
Use the other side for your prayer requests and intentions. Please be sure the return
address on the reverse side shows through the window of the enclosed envelope.

## St. Joseph's Indian School Chamberlain, South Dakota 57326

**EXHIBIT 8.2 (*Continued*)**

# PRAY FOR ME

Dear Brother David, I am in need. Please pray for the following intentions.

☐ For the health of my loved ones                    ☐ For my peace of mind

☐ For the strength of my marriage                     ☐ For my children

☐ Other _____          ☐ For my health

_____

_____

☐ Please send information about your Charitable Gift Annuity.

**Please be sure this address shows through the window of the enclosed envelope:**

ST. JOSEPH'S INDIAN SCHOOL
CHAMBERLAIN SD 57326

**EXHIBIT 8.3**

## Dreamcatcher Premium, St. Joseph's School

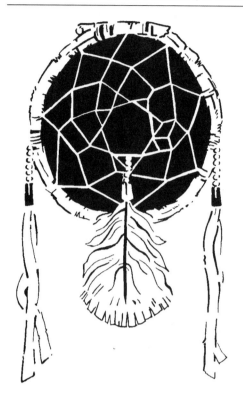

### THE LEGEND OF THE DREAMCATCHER

The native Americans of the great plains believe that the air is filled with both good and bad dreams.

Historically, the dream catchers were hung in the tipi or lodge, and also on a baby's cradle board.

Legend has it that the good dreams pass through the center hole to the sleeping person. The bad dreams are trapped in the web, where they perish in the light of dawn.

**EXHIBIT 8.4**

## Dreamcatcher Thanksgiving Card, St. Joseph's School

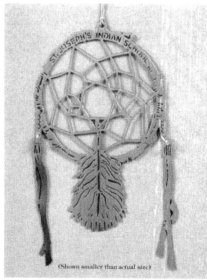

### Dreamcatcher

This Dreamcatcher is produced in solid brass. The beautiful details of the brass hanging are brought out by the antique finish. For a special gift I will send you this beautiful Dreamcatcher for you to display in your home.

*Bro. Dave*

(Shown smaller than actual size)

*You are a dream catcher.*

*I peeked in on some of the younger kids who were already asleep.*

*You protect our children from nightmares. You save them from poverty, illiteracy, and despair . . .*

*I hope you'll keep this card to bring good dreams to yourself and your family . . .*

Note that the singular "Dear Friend" is used here—and the same singular salutation appears even if the letter is addressed to a married couple. (Only one person at a time reads a letter.) Abolish the plural "you" from your vocabulary (as in "Dear Friends," for example). Try to avoid the royal "we" too; it smacks of condescension and will detract from the personal character of your appeal.

Use of the singular will require that you stick to a single letter signer. You'll cause yourself two problems by using more than one signer. First, you won't be able to enliven your letter with the personal details and emotional asides that might come naturally in a letter from one person to another. And second, with multiple signers you'll sacrifice suspension of disbelief: your reader's willingness to accept that your letter is actually a personal, one-to-one appeal.

Think about it: how am I, as the receiver of this letter, to believe that two or three busy people who don't live together or work in the same office have collaborated in writing a fundraising letter to me? Which one of them typed the letter? (Or was it really someone else?) Did they both actually sign it? These are not questions you want your readers to be asking!

**When to Break Rule 1**  You may write a letter in the first-person plural if—and only if—there's a special reason to do so—for example, if the letter is to be signed by a married couple or your organization's two venerable cofounders or a famous Republican and a famous Democrat. Even in such exceptional cases, however, I advise you to craft the letter *as though it were written by only one* of the two signers, in much the same manner as one of those annual family letters that arrive by the bushel every December. Something like this: "When Bob and I agreed to cochair this fundraising drive, it was absolutely clear to both of us that we'd have to turn first to the agency's most loyal and generous donors—people just like you."

## Rule 2: Appeal on the Basis of Benefits, Not Needs

Donors give money because they get something in return (if only good feelings). To tap their generosity, describe what they'll receive in return for

**EXHIBIT 8.5**

## Charitable Gift Annuity Brochure, St. Joseph's School

### make a note!

It's Time For
A Little
End Of The Year
Pre-Planning

You may discover that a timely charitable contribution this time of the year could increase your personal joy of helping the Lakota boys and girls at St. Joseph's and play an important role in reducing your income taxes.

With a little PRE-PLANNING NOW, you may pleasantly learn that you have more charitable gift possibilities than you realize!

One of the ways, as you know, to save on your taxes and do some good at the same time is with a gift to charity. Those who have adequate deductions to itemize, may include their gifts as charitable deductions.

Perhaps you have found in the past that you did not have enough deductions to benefit by itemizing. However, a Larger-Than-Usual gift this year, might enable you to hoist your deductions and allow you to itemize as you benefit from a tax savings.

As we advance toward the final months of 1992, it is wise to begin making plans for gifts that could help you before the year ends.

THIS IS AN IDEAL TIME OF THE YEAR TO CONSIDER A ST. JOSEPH'S CHARITABLE GIFT ANNUITY.

If you have been "thinking about" an annuity but kept putting it off — NOW, BEFORE THE YEAR'S END — is a good time to find out how our Gift Annuity works.

Keep in mind, it is a Gift as well as an Investment! With a St. Joseph's Gift Annuity you are giving to some of the neediest children in our country as well as guaranteeing yourself a lifetime income. PLUS, you are allowed definite tax advantages the year the gift is made. About 45 to 50 percent of your initial gift is considered a charitable deduction by the IRS, and as we pay you, part of your annuity is not taxed.

Our Gift Annuity program is very simple: you give a specified amount ($1,000 or more) to the school and we in turn pay you a FIXED rate of return for as long as you live. The older you are the higher the return. You may be interested in the Single Life contract only — or perhaps the Joint Life plan may be best (even if rates are a bit lower) if you are married.

If you are between the ages of 50 to 65, you might like to investigate our Deferred Gift Annuity plan. With this type of annuity, you contribute your gift right away and claim the Charitable Deduction portion the year it is given. However, your income payments do not begin until a later-specified time, perhaps the year you retire. In the meantime, your gift

is safe and accruing interest. This is a very useful plan for individuals or married couples who could use the Charitable Deduction during their working years but will not need the income until they retire.

You may wish to consider exchanging appreciated stocks or bonds for a St. Joseph's Charitable Gift Annuity. This can be a wise way to make a gift, which may eliminate some of your capital gains tax, and earn a charitable deduction the year the gift is made.

Now as the year is rapidly ending it is an excellent time to find out more about a St. Joseph's

Charitable Gift Annuity. Fill out the attached coupon and return it to us. We would be delighted to send you a personalized proposal before the year ends.

**EXHIBIT 8.5 (*Continued*)**

# REMEMBER

1) Donations made to St. Joseph's on or before December 31 are deductible this year if you itemize.

2) A gift that is larger-than-usual might enable you to itemize for your 1992 taxes.

3) Consider a gift of appreciated stocks and avoid capital gains tax or receive a considerable savings if exchanged for a Charitable Gift Annuity.

4) This is a beautiful time of the year to give a memorial gift in honor of a loved one while making a charitable gift to us.

5) The IRS allows a charitable deduction for gifts of property such as antiques, artwork, jewelry, and any type of collection if we can actually use it for the school. The deduction would be for the fair market value of the object given.

6) The joy and satisfaction of making a major type gift to the Lakota boys and girls at St. Joseph's Indian School.

It is always wise to consult your tax advisor before any final contribution is made that may affect your tax outcome.

**Special Gifts**
**St. Joseph's Indian School**
P.O. Box 100
Chamberlain, SD 57325-0100

---

Dear Brother David,

Please use the following information to calculate my Gift Annuity benefits. I understand that I am under no obligation and this personalized proposal is FREE.

☐ Immediate Gift Annuity      ☐ Deferred Gift Annuity (payments to begin year _____)

Amount of Gift Being Considered: $ _____ (Minimum Annuity Amount $1,000.)

Frequency of Payment Desired: ☐ Annual      ☐ 2 Times/Year      ☐ 4 Times/Year      ☐ Monthly
                                                   ($5,000 Min.)      ($10,000 Min.)

Name (Mr., Mrs., Miss) _____

Address _____

City _____ State _____ Zip _____

Telephone _____

☐ We are interested in a Two (Joint) Annuity plan.

Name of Second Annuitant: _____ Birth Date: Month ____ Day ____ Year ____

Birth Date: Month ____ Day ____ Year ____

Relationship of Second Annuitant: _____

**Please Note:** For proposed annuitant(s) less than 50 years of age, we write only Deferred Payment Annuities—payments typically to start at age 65. *(All information is confidential.)*

**EXHIBIT 8.6**

## Appeal Outer Envelope and Reply Envelope, St. Joseph's School

their money—such benefits as lives saved, or human dignity gained, or larger causes served. And don't be shy about emphasizing tangible benefits. Donors may tell you they give money for nobler reasons, but premiums often make a difference. (Most donors read your letters in the privacy of their own homes. They don't have to admit their own mixed motives to anyone—not even themselves.)

Look at how Brother David bases his request for funds to the St. Joseph's Indian School on the benefits to the donor, both tangible and intangible:

> *If you can send a special gift today of $25 or more, I'd love to send you one of these unique ornaments as a special gift from the children of St. Joseph's.*
>
> *These highly detailed dream catchers make wonderful gifts for children and new parents, and make unique Christmas Tree decorations.*
>
> *In any event, please send a gift today of whatever you can afford to bring dreams of hope to the children of St. Joseph's. Without people like you, their lives would be a nightmare.*

**When to Break Rule 2**  If you're sending a genuine emergency appeal, you'd be foolish not to write about your organization's needs—and graphically so. But if it isn't a real emergency (and you'll really be in trouble if you habitually cry wolf), then write about benefits, not needs. In the long run, you'll raise a lot more money that way. An annual "emergency" could put you out of business!

## Rule 3: Ask for Money, Not for "Support"

Almost always the purpose of a fundraising letter is to ask for financial help. Be sure you do so clearly, explicitly, and repeatedly. The ask shouldn't be an afterthought, tacked onto the end of a letter; it's your reason for writing. Repeat the ask several times in the body of the letter as well as on the reply device. A successful fundraising letter might include as many as half a dozen asks. It may even be appropriate to lead your letter with the ask.

Note in the St. Joseph's appeal that the ask appears twice in the letter and twice again on the reply device (Exhibit 8.2). Notice, too, how clear and explicit the requests for funds are: ". . . send a special gift today of $25 or more," ". . . please send a gift today of whatever you can afford," "Send a gift today of $25 or more," and "Enclosed is my gift of . . ."

**When to Break Rule 3**  Many direct mail packages are structured not as appeals for funds but as invitations to join a membership organization.

Others feature surveys or other donor involvement devices. In these cases, deemphasize the financial commitment, and highlight membership benefits—or stress the impact of completing the survey or mailing the postcard you've enclosed.

## Rule 4: Write a Package, Not a Letter

Your fundraising letter is the single most important element in the mailing package, but it's only one of several items that must fit smoothly together and work as a whole. At a minimum, your package will probably include an outer (or carrier) envelope, a reply envelope, and a reply device in addition to the letter. When you sit down to write, think about how each of these components will help persuade donors to send money now. Make sure the same themes, symbols, colors, and typefaces are used on all elements, so the package is as memorable and accessible as possible. And be certain every element in the package relates directly to the big idea or marketing concept that gives the appeal its unity. (I spoke about marketing concepts in Chapter Six.)

Notice that the St. Joseph's Indian School package contains seven components:

- Outer (carrier) envelope (Exhibit 8.6)
- Two-page letter (Exhibit 8.1)
- Reply device (Exhibit 8.2)
- Photograph in full color of the dreamcatcher premium (Exhibit 8.3)
- Dreamcatcher Thanksgiving card (Exhibit 8.4)
- Charitable gift annuity brochure (Exhibit 8.5)
- Reply envelope (Exhibit 8.6)

Examine these components carefully, and you'll see several earmarks of a successful effort to package the contents of this appeal in a unified way:

- *Theme.* The dream catcher theme, the big idea in this appeal, is emphasized on every component of the package except for the brochure on gift annuities and the nearly text-free reply envelope.
- *Subtext (or underlying theme).* The subtext of gift giving is explicit almost everywhere and implicit everywhere else. There's no mistaking that this is an appeal for funds, but it's couched as an exchange of gifts.
- *Color.* Although you can't see them in this book's black-and-white reproduction, the colors used on the outer envelope, the letter, and the

reply device are identical: black text with bright orange accenting and imagery. The brochure is printed in red and black.

**When to Break Rule 4**  Sometimes it pays to spend a little extra money on a package insert that doesn't directly relate to the marketing concept. For example, a premium offer might be presented on a *buckslip*—an insert designed to highlight the premium—but the offer might not appear anywhere else in the package (with the possible exception of the reply device). Often, in fact, a buckslip works best if it doesn't use the same color and design as other package elements, so that it stands out more clearly.

## Rule 5: Write in Simple, Straightforward English

Use compact, powerful words and short, punchy sentences. Favor words that convey emotions over those that communicate thoughts. Avoid foreign phrases and big words. Minimize the use of adjectives and adverbs. Don't use abbreviations or acronyms; spell out names, even if their repetition looks a little silly to you. Repeat (and underline) key words and phrases.

Brother David's simple, unadorned language, free of pretense, in his letter (Exhibit 8.1) helps convey the strength of his appeal: "good dreams and nightmares," "the younger kids," "You bring them good dreams," and "to bring dreams of hope to the children."

**When to Break Rule 5**  A letter that could have been written by a twelve-year-old might not look right bearing the signature of a college president or a U.S. senator, so follow this rule judiciously. But don't make the mistake of confusing big words, complex sentences, and complicated thoughts with intelligent communication: the most literate fundraising letter needs to be clear and straightforward. The very best writing is easy to understand.

## Rule 6: Format Your Letter for Easy Reading

The eye needs rest, so be conscious of the white space you're leaving around your copy:

- Indent every paragraph.
- Avoid paragraphs more than seven lines long, but vary the length of your paragraphs.
- Use bullets and indented paragraphs.

- In long letters, try subheads that are centered and underlined. Underline sparingly but consistently throughout your letter—enough to call attention to key words and phrases, especially those that highlight the benefits to the reader, but not so much as to distract the eye from your message.

Take another look at the St. Joseph's appeal in Exhibit 8.1. Notice that not a single paragraph in the body of the letter is longer than five lines (and there's only one that long). Only the P.S. exceeds that limit, with seven lines. Every paragraph is indented the standard five spaces, although the letter is printed on Monarch-sized paper. There are neither underlining nor bulleted points in Brother David's appeal, but they aren't needed here; the letter is short enough and sufficiently appealing. It's easy to read.

**When to Break Rule 6**  Don't mechanically follow this rule. Some special formats, such as telegrams or handwritten notes, have formatting rules of their own. Don't ignore them. Remember that you want the reader to believe—or at least to *act* as though she believes—that you've sent her a telegram, a handwritten note, or a personal letter (or whatever else the communication might be).

## Rule 7: Give Your Readers a Reason to Send Money NOW

Creating a sense of urgency is one of your biggest copywriting challenges. Try to find a genuine reason that gifts are needed right away: for example, a deadline for a matching grant or an approaching election date. Or tie your fund request to a budgetary deadline so you can argue why "gifts are needed within the next 15 days." There is always a reason to send a gift now. And the argument for the urgency of your appeal may bear repeating.

Keep in mind, though, that urgency isn't a simple matter of time alone. Circumstances such as children dying of hunger, troops massing for an invasion, or the imminence of an environmental catastrophe may require urgency despite the absence of deadlines.

There are several ways Brother David builds a sense of urgency in his appeal for the children of St. Joseph's Indian School:

- The emphasis on Thanksgiving in an appeal dated October 30 provides a natural and easily understood deadline.

- The brochure headlining "It's Time for a Little End of the Year Pre-Planning" (Exhibit 8.5) sets a fallback date, December 31, thus laying down a second line of urgency.

- Brother David's comment that "we have ordered a small number of Lakota dream catchers" implies that the supply could run out quickly, leaving the donor *without* "wonderful gifts for children and new parents."

- The topic of "poverty, illiteracy, and despair," set out in the letter, is freighted with urgency all its own.

**When to Break Rule 7**  Be very careful about fixed deadlines if you're mailing by bulk rate, which might delay delivery by two weeks or more. (Instead of giving a date, use a phrase like "within the next two weeks.") Don't overuse the same arguments for urgency, lest your credibility suffer. And try not to depend on deadlines based on actual dates in large-scale mailings to acquire new donors: the value of those letters will almost always be greater if you can continue to use the same letter over and over again.

## Rule 8: Write as Long a Letter as You Need to Make the Case for Your Offer

Not everyone will read every word you write, but some recipients will do so, no matter how long your letter. Others will scan your copy for the information that interests them the most. To be certain you push their hot buttons, use every strong argument you can devise for your readers to send you money now. And to spell out every argument may mean writing a very long letter; it may also mean repeating what you've written to the same donors many times in the past. But don't worry about boring your readers by restating your case: research repeatedly reveals that even many of the most active donors remember very little about the organizations they support.

Brother David's appeal for St. Joseph's is only two pages long. If all the information contained in the two inserts devoted specifically to the dream catcher offer were to be included in the letter rather than printed as separate items, the appeal would run to three pages. (It's much better the way it is.) Still, this letter doesn't convey enough information about St. Joseph's to answer the questions that might occur to a prospective donor who has never before heard of the school. (For starters: "How many kids attend the school? Where is Chamberlain? Does all the money come from donors like me, or does the government pay too?") This appeal was mailed to a previous donor who presumably has had those questions answered.

**When to Break Rule 8**  Not every organization and not every appeal calls for a long letter. A well-known organization with a readily identifiable purpose—the American Red Cross, for example, or a prominent children's hospital—might be able to make its case with only a sentence or two. Similarly, in writing to your proven donors, you can sometimes state the argument for a straightforward membership renewal or special appeal in just a few words. "It's time to renew your membership" is a good example.

## Three More Things to Keep in Mind

If you follow the eight rules I've just described, you won't go far wrong when you write your next fundraising appeal. But I suggest you also keep in mind the psychology of the position you've placed yourself in as the signer of your letter. You might want to consider the following as three additional rules of writing fundraising letters:

1. You (the signer) are an individual human being, with hopes, fears, convictions, and experiences. Look at how Brother David takes up that challenge, writing about "sweet dreams," "nightmares," "despair," "loved ones," and "wonderful gifts." This is no masterpiece of self-revelation, but it gives a sense of a man who is engaged in his work and feels strongly about the children at the school.

2. You are writing to one person, the addressee, who has hopes, fears, convictions, and experiences too. Notice how Brother David appeals directly to the donor's feelings: "You bring them good feelings"; "to bring good dreams to yourself and your family"; "Without people like you, their lives would be a nightmare."

3. Regardless of its mission, your organization addresses human needs on many levels, intangible as well as concrete, emotional as well as practical. Those are the things people care about. Remember that Brother David doesn't write about budgets, fiscal years, and funding shortfalls. He writes about *the kids*—their dreams, their nightmares.

## Rating Your Writing

Some people think that writing fundraising letters is pure art. Others insist the work is simply a matter of building on well-known formulas. Judging from the hundreds (sometimes thousands) of fundraising appeals I see every year, they're both wrong. There's precious little art in evidence. And if formulas really work in writing fundraising letters, they're not well known because their influence doesn't show either.

Without a formula for success, most level-headed folks would be likely to think that there is no systematic way to assess the effectiveness of a fundraising letter. But as a lifelong contrarian, I maintain that there are two ways to do so:

*The standard way.* Just mail the letter, and you'll see how well it works. However, if you've been doing a little too much of that and with too little to show for it, you might try using the following method to review your work before the market renders its own, possibly costly, opinion.

*My way.* With my Cardinal Rules as a point of departure, I've developed a simple self-assessment form for a fundraising appeal, reproduced as Exhibit 8.7. (Note that in the course of converting the Cardinal Rules into a method of evaluation, I've lent more weight to some factors and less to others.) If this is a formulaic approach, so be it. It works for me.

• • •

Let's move on to Chapter Nine, where we'll examine some of the more general considerations that come into play when you're writing for results.

**EXHIBIT 8.7**

# How to Assess a Direct Mail Fundraising Package

*Rate package on each criterion, circling the rating, with 5 = best, 0 = worst.*

| # | Criterion | Rating | Weight | Total |
|---|-----------|--------|--------|-------|
| 1 | Speaks to the reader, *from* the signer. Uses the singular personal pronouns "you" and "I." | 0 1 2 3 4 5 | × 2 = | |
| 2 | Talks about benefits, not needs. | 0 1 2 3 4 5 | × 3 = | |
| 3 | Has an unmistakably clear *offer*. Benefits to donor are compelling. Asks for a specific amount of money or other explicit act. | 0 1 2 3 4 5 | × 5 = | |
| 4 | Establishes urgency—that is, makes the case to take action now. | 0 1 2 3 4 5 | × 2 = | |
| 5 | Is unified into a whole package, with components reinforcing each other. | 0 1 2 3 4 5 | × 2 = | |
| 6 | Has a powerful writing style: short words; emotion; short sentences; short paragraphs; no ten-dollar words, foreign expressions, abbreviations, acronyms. | 0 1 2 3 4 5 | × 2 = | |
| 7 | Is formatted and designed for easy reading. Uses white space, indents, bullets, underlining, a P.S. Looks like a typewritten letter. | 0 1 2 3 4 5 | ×1 = | |
| 8 | Letter is as long (or as short) as necessary to make the case. Must address all the unspoken questions a reader's likely to have. | 0 1 2 3 4 5 | × 1 = | |
| 9 | Outer envelope commands attention, provokes curiosity. | 0 1 2 3 4 5 | × 3 = | |
| 10 | Response device makes it easy to take action. | 0 1 2 3 4 5 | × 2 = | |
| 11 | Effectively uses color, graphics, white space to emphasize essentials: benefits, deadline, call to action. | 0 1 2 3 4 5 | × 1 = | |
| | TOTAL (Total the 11 ratings. Remember: $0 \times 5 = 0$!) | | | |

Now turn to the next page to evaluate your score.

**EXHIBIT 8.7 (*Continued*)**

**How to evaluate your score.**

*With as many as 5 points available for each of the eleven criteria, and weighting factors that total 24, a perfect score is 120 points. You may translate a numerical score into a letter grade as follows:*

| Rating | Letter Grade | Meaning |
|---|---|---|
| 110–120 | A+ | No more need be said. |
| 100–109 | A | Give that writer a pat on the back! |
| 80–99 | B | Shows lots of promise. |
| 60–79 | C | Needs some improvement. |
| 30–59 | D | Requires a lot of work. Maybe better to start from scratch! |
| 0–29 | F | Uh oh! |

# Chapter 9

# You're Writing for Results—Not for a Pulitzer Prize

**MY BROTHER HAS** never forgiven me. Art was eighteen and about to enter his first year of college. He has since become a respected psychiatrist and has taught at universities that rival any I've ever attended. But back then—to my mind, at least—he was just my snot-nosed younger brother. And Art was absolutely, positively guaranteed to stumble over freshman English—or so everyone else in our family was convinced.

Since I was three years older than my brother and a veteran of hundreds of essays, letters, stories, reviews, and critiques, not to mention a few political speeches, our mother pressed me into service during that summer of 1962. As a former English teacher, she was suffering from acute embarrassment in addition to her maternal fear for Art's future.

"Make yourself useful for a change," she told me. "Help your brother. Teach him how to write."

This assignment pleased neither Art nor me, but orders were orders. (Our parents were still paying the bills, after all.) With mutual ill will, we took up our new roles: I as a teacher, he approximating the role of the obedient younger brother.

Things went from bad to worse after I gave Art his first assignment: a 500-word essay entitled "How to Tie Your Shoelaces."

Art wrote and then rewrote that essay at least a dozen times, each successive draft a mosaic of my notations in red, blue, and black pencil. The essay was finished only after painful daily sessions stretching over several weeks. Along the way, there were countless changes in word order and sentence structure. We discarded adjectives and adverbs, shifted prepositions, changed verbs, and thumbed through Roget's Thesaurus for sparkling new nouns. But when the job was complete and we were ready to proceed with the second assignment, it was obvious that what Art had learned about writing had little to do with any of the changes we'd made in his labored drafts. The essence of what he learned (and I "taught") was this:

## Art's Lessons Learned

1. To write clearly and effectively, the writer must *think* before setting pen to paper (or, more likely now, fingers to the keyboard). Clearly written communication is nothing more—and nothing less—than a reflection of disciplined, logical thinking.

2. When writing to achieve results, the writer must *make things easy for the reader.* Unless held at gunpoint or facing the loss of a job, the reader has no obligation to the writer and nothing to fear. The reader is free to abandon what she or he is reading and turn to something more personally rewarding—like badminton or Beethoven, for example.

3. The right word is not necessarily the most colorful or even the most precise. The right word is the strongest, the most expressive word—the word that communicates the writer's meaning most effectively.

4. A skillful writer can make any subject interesting, amusing, or at least palatable.

Perhaps I'm kidding myself. Art may never have learned those four things at all. Or his freshman English teachers might have forced some discipline into his writing where I'd utterly failed. But I cherish the thought that my brother's subsequent academic success had at least a little to do with my drillmaster's brand of summertime writing instruction.

As in so many of the other times in my life when I thought I was helping someone else, I was really helping myself a lot more. That summer, acting in the belief that a good teacher needs to be thoroughly familiar with his text, I reread Strunk and White.

If you're not familiar with this legendary little volume, I suggest you pick up a copy and devour it. If you already know the book, reread it before you start your next writing job. Its title is *The Elements of Style,* its coauthors William Strunk Jr. and E. B. White. It's readily available in inexpensive paperback editions throughout North America, and—perhaps best of all—*The Elements of Style* is truly a little book. My 1950s-vintage paperback version is all of seventy-one pages long.

Some writers claim they can get along quite well without Strunk and White or any other grounding in the basics of writing. I'm told there are hugely successful advertising and public relations copywriters who learned everything they know on the job. I'm skeptical of this assertion, which I ascribe largely to the self-promotion that's so common among people who traffic in myths. But for the sake of argument, let's accept the claim that copywriters can learn their craft even if they're ignorant of the fundamentals of English style. That doesn't mean it's a good idea to violate all the rules. In fact, I believe the copywriter's life will be easier—and probably more successful—if it starts with training in the basics. That brings us to Rudolf Flesch.

# Rudolf Flesch's Rules of Effective Writing

Generations of Americans have turned to Rudolf Flesch for advice on effective writing and speaking, and no wonder. Flesch's books, written decades ago, contain insights as fresh today as when they were newly written. I especially recommend *How to Write, Speak and Think More Effectively* (an inexpensive and widely available paperback available from NAL/Signet and described in Resource H). Flesch's "Rules of Effective Writing" are well worth reading in full, but here's the gist of them:

- Write about people, things, and facts.

- Write as you speak.

- Use contractions.

- Use the first person.

- Quote what was said or written.

- Put yourself in the reader's place.

- Don't be too brief.

- Plan a beginning, middle, and end.

- Go from the rule to the exception and from the familiar to the new.

- Use short forms of names.

- Use pronouns rather than repeating nouns.

- Use verbs rather than nouns.

- Use the active voice.

- Use small, round figures.

- Be specific. Use illustrations, cases, and examples.

- Start a new sentence for each new idea.

- Keep sentences and paragraphs short.

- Use direct questions.

- Underline for emphasis.

- Make your writing interesting to look at.

These aren't arbitrary rules of taste or style. They're the result of Flesch's studies of readers' reactions to written material.

Rudolf Flesch is the all-time master of the study of readability, which means the likelihood that what you've written will actually be understood (and possibly remembered) by your readers. Flesch held sway in an era when numerical measurements inspired more faith than they do in today's skeptical society, but his charts, graphs, and scores are still useful. In fact, they're incorporated into the readability statistics in Microsoft Word.

Flesch found, for example, that two key indicators of the readability of writing were the number of syllables per 100 words and the average length of a sentence (expressed in number of words).

I won't go into the precise way Flesch defined these two measurements. You can read it yourself in his book (and I hope you will). But look at how Flesch interprets these measurements (Table 9.1).

In Flesch's lexicon, "very easy" writing is to be found in comic books. "Standard" writing is the earmark of such magazines as *Time,* and "very difficult" writing is found in scientific and professional journals.

This chapter averages eleven words per sentence, according to my word processor—pretty easy reading, Flesch would say. Judge for yourself whether you find my writing readable.

But short words and short sentences alone won't make your writing easy to read. Flesch insists (and I agree) that a factor of equal importance is the human interest in what you write. Human interest is a function of the proportion of personal words (such as personal pronouns and proper names), the frequency with which quotations are used, and the extent to which you engage the reader by challenging, questioning, or directly addressing her.

Flesch's suggestions about how to increase readability are equally useful. Here are some of them:

- Focus on your reader.

- Focus on your purpose.

**TABLE 9.1**
## Rudolf Flesch's Measurement of Readability

| Description of Style | Syllables per 100 Words | Average Sentence Length (number of words) |
|---|---|---|
| Very easy | 123 | 8 |
| Easy | 131 | 11 |
| Fairly easy | 139 | 14 |
| Standard | 147 | 17 |
| Fairly difficult | 155 | 21 |
| Difficult | 167 | 25 |
| Very difficult | 192 | 29 |

- Break up sentences and paragraphs.

- Find simpler words.

- Help your reader read (emphasize, anticipate, repeat, summarize).

- Learn to cut unnecessary words.

- Rearrange for emphasis.

- Write to be read aloud.

- Don't write down to your reader.

To write for results, you'll need to do more than polish your writing style. Writing for results is different from writing meant merely to describe or report to the reader. Let's take a look at the differences now.

## How Writing for Results Is Different from Writing to Describe or Report

There are at least nine differences between writing for results and writing merely to describe or report, all of which might prove to be crucial elements in your fundraising or sales letters.

1. *Colloquialisms.* Writing for results requires you to use everyday language and patterns of speech because you need to communicate readily, without delay or complication and without forcing the reader to work for understanding. There are exceptions to this rule, but like much else that can be said about writing for results, the exceptions revolve around the audience, not the writer.

In many fundraising letters (depending, of course, on the signer and the cause), I might use such phrases as "No way!" or "Guess again" to underline the informality of the appeal. Such examples of colloquial speech and even slang are more than just acceptable; they're sometimes essential. Like a chatty personal letter, a masterpiece of copywriting will read much more like a conversation at the supermarket than an article in the *Harvard Business Review.*

2. *Clichés.* Most people think, speak, and write in clichés. That, I believe, is not a good thing, but it's important for the copywriter to take it into account. Clichés, after all, are only one step removed from garden-variety colloquialisms; precisely because of their familiarity, they offer an easy way to communicate thoughts rapidly. For the same reason, many readers also find clichés boring, so a tired and overused turn of speech shouldn't be your first line of defense against the difficulty of explaining a complex set of circumstances or making a subtle argument. But sometimes when writing for results, an old chestnut can help you fill the understanding gap.

Consider, for example, that old cliché, the "pot of gold at the end of the rainbow." I wouldn't be caught dead using this phrase in everyday speech, even in a defenseless moment. But I can think of no other phrase that more readily communicates the concept of fabulous wealth and could better provide an appropriate image for a sweepstakes featuring large cash prizes. (Naturally it's been used—time and time again.)

3. *Figures of speech.* You'll probably remember from high school English that similes and metaphors are among the earmarks of fine literature. A simile is one of those hard-working figures of speech that crawls up the hillside "like a train trailing a hundred cars." In contrast, a metaphor forces the reader to do much of the work, taking it on faith that an abstraction in a figure of speech might be a train, a Bengal tiger, or a pot of gold.

I have a simple rule about the use of similes and metaphors in writing for results: *Don't use them.* Metaphors require thought; even similes can slow the reader down, or worse. These figures of speech help communicate complex thoughts and feelings, but only by indirection; any complexities in your message need to be spelled out more directly, or you may lose your readers.

4. *Humor and irony.* Creative advertising copywriters notwithstanding, humor is rarely advisable in writing for results. And entirely avoid irony, that wry, sophisticated form of humor. It's not just that some people have no discernible sense of humor or even that what's humorous to one person might seem tragic to another. The fundamental problem, I believe, is that the written word is an imperfect medium to convey good humor.

In speaking to an audience, you might get a laugh for even a poorly told joke by communicating the humor through tone of voice, gestures, facial expressions, and even the use of props, aided by the natural tendency for most people to feel sympathy for you when you're standing right there. You have none of those advantages when writing to that same audience. I suggest you keep the jokes to yourself, or tack them up on your refrigerator or the office bulletin board.

5. *Sentence structure.* I'll call her Miss Forsythe because, truth to tell, I can't remember her name. More than half a century ago, she taught me in ninth-grade English that every sentence must contain a subject and a predicate. Among a great many other rules, all of them delivered in commanding tones and in language that inhibited questions, Miss Forsythe also insisted that a sentence must never begin with "and" or "but" and must never end with a preposition.

In some forms of writing, those rules are as true today as they were in the 1950s. But not in writing for results. To convey meaning simply and clearly—to respect the informal practices of natural, spoken language and place emphasis where it's needed—Miss Forsythe's rules sometimes need to be ignored. The result may be writing that fails all the tests of conventional sentence structure, punctuation, and grammar—but yields the results you want.

Try these rules instead of Miss Forsythe's:

- A sentence expresses a single thought. Sometimes a thought can be expressed in just one word. One. And one's enough.

- Don't worry about ending sentences with prepositions. Sometimes a preposition is the very best word to end a sentence with.

- And it's okay to start a sentence with a conjunction. (But don't overdo it. Two sentences in a row that start with "but" are likely to confuse the reader.)

- If at first you're not convinced by these three rules, reread them carefully. You might change your mind.

6. *Punctuation.* We'll look at three specific forms of punctuation here.

*Semicolons.* I despise semicolons. My thoughts tend to break up into little pieces that don't quite justify sentences of their own, but I still refuse to follow the grammarian's rulebook and set one apart from another with a semicolon. Much better, I think, just to pretend I've written a sentence. Miss Forsythe would disapprove with her customary hauteur. But no matter: I get no complaints from my latter-day readers. And when I'm seeking results with my writing—when I want my readers to take action—I am especially zealous to root out all the semicolons.

Why? Because sentences are easier to read without semicolons. The eyes glaze over at the sight of long sentences. Periods provide rest and comfort. The capital letters that begin new sentences heighten interest. Besides, Miss Forsythe isn't here to kick me around anymore.

*Dashes.* In writing for results, it's often wise to use a dash—what typesetters call an *em dash* (about twice the width of a hyphen—technically, the width of a capital M). I use a lot of dashes when writing fundraising letters—and I don't feel guilty in the least, no matter what Miss Forsythe might say. Dashes lend emphasis to your thoughts by setting them apart and increasing the white space that surrounds them. (The German professor you met in Chapter Two insists that dashes arrest the reader's eye and make writing less readable, but I choose to ignore his advice on this highly personal matter of style.)

*Ellipses.* Miss Forsythe would cringe . . . but I don't care. Ellipsis points (. . .) have much the same effect as a dash, particularly when they are set off by blank spaces before and after the points. Both help convey meaning by splitting complex or urgent thoughts into their component pieces.

7. *Contractions.* Lawyers, top business executives, and even some journalists advocate the sparing use of contractions. Don't pay any attention to them if you want your readers to take action. Listen instead to Rudolph Flesch. And to me.

Purists would rather you spell out every word, erring on the side of precision, so there can be absolutely no confusion in the minds of your readers. I'd rather you use fewer words, favoring informality and natural speech patterns, so your readers won't feel that you're talking down to them.

Contractions such as "I'm," "you've," "don't," and "can't" are usually preferable in copywriting to the longer expressions they're derived from: "I am," "you have," "do not," and "cannot." The shorter form is more easily taken in by the ear, and the eye quickly comprehends the meaning of contractions. Also, negatives catch the reader's attention, sometimes conveying precisely the wrong impression. The word "not" may lodge in the reader's eye like a cinder, causing him to misread the following sentence—or the point of the whole letter.

8. *Repetition.* Grammarians are often repelled by writing intended to persuade because it's likely to be riddled with repetition. The repetition is not accidental. Just as a journalist leads an article with the most important piece of news, the copywriter is likely to emphasize the points of greatest potential interest to the reader by repeating them—the ask in a fundraising letter, for example.

The English language possesses almost unmatched variety, so a writer can describe any benefit or make any offer in a hundred or a thousand different ways. The demands of writing a letter intended to sell products or secure contributions may force the writer to use precisely the same words over and over again.

9. *Underlining and italics.* Miss Forsythe told us never to italicize words unless they're book titles or come from a foreign language. In the days when handwriting and using a typewriter were the writer's only options, she meant not to underline words. Today some editors follow the same rule: I sometimes find my articles or columns appearing shorn of all their carefully chosen italicized emphasis. I keep submitting articles peppered with italics anyway, in hopes my editors will wake up and see what's obvious to me: *italics enhance the reader's understanding*—when used sparingly.

Emphasizing important facts or thoughts makes it easier for the reader to grasp the writer's meaning and easier to review and remember key points. In writing typewriter-style—as, for example, in most fundraising letters— I generally prefer underlining instead of italics, even though I might have hundreds of alternative typefaces at hand (and most of them available in italic as well as roman fonts). Often it's important to preserve the illusion that I'm really writing on a typewriter.

## When Does the Fun Start?

Some writers can produce readable copy in a first, fluid draft. It seems as though the words just keep streaming out of their fingertips, all neatly arranged in precisely the right order. (God, I hate those people!) Within the ranks of the top freelance writers, stories abound about the geniuses who can sit down at the keyboard (a typewriter, often enough) at 9:00 in the morning and type without interruption for three hours. They knock off for an hour's lunch, return for four more hours of unruffled word processing in the afternoon—and end the day with five thousand salable words, or even ten thousand. But these are people who write hundreds of books or thousands of stories or articles (or both). They've had a lot more practice than you're likely to get. And I don't mind admitting they've got a lot more innate talent for writing than I have.

So most of us have to revise and rewrite and revise again. Don't make the mistake of believing you've got it right the first time. Chances are that you don't. Whatever it is you're writing, set it aside for a day or two or a week after you've completed your first rough draft. Then take a fresh look at it. And don't forget to read your letter aloud. If you can't find something on every page that cries out for revision, you're either a far better writer than I am or you're kidding yourself.

• • •

Join me now in Part Three, "Customizing Your Appeal," where we'll review the ten common types of fundraising letters and the unique requirements each poses.

# Part Three

# Customizing Your Appeal

**IN THE FOLLOWING** ten chapters, we'll take a walking tour through the thickets of fundraising, visiting, one at a time, each of the most common types of fundraising appeals to examine their unique characteristics and the distinctive demands they impose on a writer. In the course of Part Three, we'll study letters designed to

- Recruit new members or donors
- Welcome new donors
- Appeal for a special (additional) gift
- Request a year-end contribution
- Recruit monthly sustainers
- Solicit larger, high-dollar gifts
- Persuade donors to send bigger gifts
- Seek annual gifts
- Thank donors
- Seek legacy gifts

On the CD-ROM that accompanies this book, you'll find two full-color examples of each type of package discussed in Part Three.

# Chapter 10

# Recruiting New Donors
## Starting Intimate Conversations with Strangers

**THE TERM *DIRECT MAIL*** is most commonly associated with the letters that nonprofits mail, often in extremely large quantities, to enlist new members or donors from among a broad population of prospects. In reality, the other types of fundraising letters covered in the following chapters are in many ways (such as the substantial net revenue they generate) far more important to the financial health of nonprofit organizations than the *acquisition* (or *prospect*) packages that bring in new donors. Still, it's the acquisition letters that make the rest of the process possible by supplying a steady stream of new, first-time donors.

The reply device in Exhibit 10.1 is typical of those used to accompany acquisition letters mailed to prospective donors. How do you know this form comes from an acquisition (or prospect) package? Because the reference to "my membership gift" on the front and the phrase "I wish to join Bread for the World" in the credit card copy on the back make it unmistakably clear that the package is intended to recruit new members. This form is typical of acquisition packages in several other ways as well:

- The language on this response device makes it clear that Bread for the World is dedicated not just to the specific, top-priority campaign that is the subject of this appeal (a "Citizen Petition" to end hunger in Africa) but to a broader array of issues affecting "hungry and poor people," and the accompanying letter (not illustrated) makes that even clearer. Note, too, the organization's tagline next to the logo: "Seeking Justice. Ending Hunger." Although this appeal focuses on one campaign, as a whole it asks the recipient to buy into the organization's mission and goals. That's what "joining" means. This is not an appeal to support a specific project.

- You'll note that the suggested gift amounts are typeset, so the amounts are probably the same for all recipients of this letter. The amounts are comparatively small, affording an easy entry level for new members. But there are three gift choices, covering a fairly wide range, because

---

**EXHIBIT 10.1**

## New Donor Response Device, Bread for the World

---

## Help turn Africa's crisis of hunger into a harvest of hope

I've signed the Citizen Petition below. I'm urging my members of Congress to take action that will save the lives of those ravaged by famine and the AIDS epidemic — and that will enable Africans to feed themselves.

☐ **$10**    ☐ **$25**    ☐ **$50**    ☐ **$** _____

☐ I prefer to make my membership gift by credit card and have filled out the necessary information on the reverse side.

Mr. John Doe
123 Any Street
Any Town AS 00000-0000
BFW07PA/01-25-07/pkg.1 Control

**Bread for the World**
*Seeking Justice. Ending Hunger.*

50 F Street NW, Suite 500
Washington, DC 20001
1-800-822-7323     www.bread.org

07PADOE1  *See other side for important information.* ▶
00000

---

## CITIZEN PETITION

**WHEREAS,** drought, flooding, and civil strife have created a food crisis where one in three people in sub-Saharan Africa suffers from hunger;

**WHEREAS,** cost-effective programs have proven to reduce hunger—and lower the risk and impact of AIDS;

**WHEREAS,** the AIDS epidemic is killing 6,500 Africans every day—even though life-saving medicines are available for less than one dollar a day per person;

**THEREFORE, I URGE** the Senate Majority Leader and the House Speaker, along with other leaders in Congress to:

(1) Rush humanitarian assistance to Africa where drought and flooding have made food production impossible;

(2) Dramatically increase poverty-focused development assistance for Africa and other poor parts of the world; and

(3) Fulfill our nation's promise to fund global AIDS initiatives that support cost-effective drug-therapy and life-saving prevention.

Signed _____    Date _____    City, State _____

RECYCLED & RECYCLABLE / PRINTED WITH SOY INK     7-PA2A

---

little is known about those to whom the letter was mailed: they're strangers.

- Note also that the "Citizen Petition" at the bottom of the front of this reply device provides an opportunity for the prospect to become directly and immediately involved in Bread for the World's current lobbying campaign. Involvement devices of this sort aren't unique to acquisition letters, but they're more commonly found in that context. Involvement typically boosts response. It's a way to get strangers to pay attention.

**EXHIBIT 10.1 (*Continued*)**

I wish to join Bread for the World with a credit card gift of $_____

☐ VISA ☐ Mastercard ☐ Discover Expires _____ (Month/Year)

Card #_____

Card security code* _____

Name on card *(PLEASE PRINT)* _____

Your signature _____

\* *For your protection, we are now required to request the 3 or 4 digit security code on the back of your credit card.*

*Visit www.bread.org/give to make a secure gift online.*

**We use your contributions wisely and effectively**

You are welcome to request a copy of our latest financial report by visiting www.bread.org, or by contacting: Bread for the World, 50 F Street NW, Suite 500, Washington, DC 20001-1565, 202-639-9400 or 1-800-822-7323.

Gifts to Bread for the World are not tax-deductible since our members lobby Congress on behalf of hungry and poor people. If you prefer to make a *tax-deductible contribution* to support research and education efforts (such as the Hunger Report, the ONE Campaign, and research on trade), please make out your check to Bread for the World Institute.

If you are a resident of one of the states below, you may obtain financial information directly from the state agency: **FLORIDA —** A COPY OF THE OFFICIAL REGISTRATION AND FINANCIAL INFORMATION MAY BE OBTAINED FROM THE DIVISION OF CONSUMER SERVICES BY CALLING TOLL-FREE, (800) 435-7352 WITHIN THE STATE. REGISTRATION DOES NOT IMPLY ENDORSEMENT, APPROVAL OR RECOMMENDATION BY THE STATE. (SC-05787) **MARYLAND —** For the cost of copies and postage: Office of the Secretary of State, State House, Annapolis, MD 21401. **MISSISSIPPI —** The official registration and financial information of Bread for the World may be obtained from the Mississippi Secretary of State's office by calling 1-888-236-6167. Registration by the Secretary of State does not imply endorsement. **NEW JERSEY —** INFORMATION FILED WITH THE ATTORNEY GENERAL CONCERNING THIS CHARITABLE SOLICITATION MAY BE OBTAINED FROM THE ATTORNEY GENERAL OF THE STATE OF NEW JERSEY BY CALLING (973) 504-6215. REGISTRATION WITH THE ATTORNEY GENERAL DOES NOT IMPLY ENDORSEMENT. **NEW YORK —** Office of the Attorney General, Department of Law, Charities Bureau, 120 Broadway, New York, NY 10271. **NORTH CAROLINA —** Financial information about this organization and a copy of its license are available from the State Solicitation Licensing Branch at (919) 807-2214. The license is not an endorsement by the state. **PENNSYLVANIA —** The official registration and financial information of Bread for the World may be obtained from the Pennsylvania Department of State by calling toll-free, within Pennsylvania, (800) 732-0999. Registration does not imply endorsement. **VIRGINIA —** State Division of Consumer Affairs, Department of Agricultural and Consumer Services, P.O. Box 1163, Richmond, VA 23218. **WASHINGTON —** Charities Division, Office of the Secretary of State, State of Washington, Olympia, WA 98504-0422; 1-800-332-4483. **WEST VIRGINIA —** Residents may obtain a summary from: Secretary of State, State Capitol, Charleston, WV 25305. 12/06

*Registration with any of these states does not imply endorsement, approval or recommendation by the state.*

# How Donor Acquisition Letters Are Different from Other Fundraising Appeals

Successful appeals written to recruit new donors or new members come in all sizes, shapes, and flavors. They may be fat or thin, colorful or drab, up-to-the-minute or timeless. They're sometimes mailed using third-class bulk postage, sometimes (though less often) with first-class stamps. But there are five characteristics that the majority of donor acquisition letters share.

### Five Characteristics of Donor Acquisition Packages

1. Donor acquisition letters are often long and occasionally contain lots of additional material too: brochures or folders, flyers, lift letters,

buckslips, and premiums. Many charities fare better without using any of this stuff. Some well-known groups can get away with short letters too. Chances are, though, that a letter you write to prospective donors will need to be at least a little longer than the letters you usually write to previous donors. Otherwise prospects may not have enough information about your organization to decide whether they'll make a gift.

2. They typically appeal to prospects to support a charity's larger agenda: its goals, the full range of its programs (though one project or aspect of the work may get the lion's share of the attention in the letter). If prospective donors send gifts in response to such a letter, they're more likely to respond favorably when asked later for additional support.

3. References to "you" (the reader) are normally vague and general. Although your organization may know a great deal about the people on one of its prospect lists, it probably knows next to nothing about those on its other lists. With these other people, there isn't much to hang a relationship on. Chances are the demands of economy will require that you mail the same letter, unchanged, to all your prospect lists.

4. Typically, acquisition letters are undated and make few references to time or the calendar. That's because you'll probably want to use this appeal over and over. Not just because of the need to economize but also because it normally takes repeated trial and error to fashion a really successful acquisition letter, with modifications tested and retested over time.

5. The minimum suggested gift amount tends to be low. Most charities seek to maximize the number of new donors: asking for less at the outset may serve that purpose.

## Case Study: Western Pennsylvania Conservancy

The Western Pennsylvania Conservancy (Pittsburgh) asked me to edit a new-donor acquisition package (Exhibits 10.2 and 10.3).

As you can see, I made a number of changes:

- The most important change was to include an explicit ask for money, citing specific dollar amounts. (I had no way of knowing what those amounts might be in practice. They would depend on the *string*, or range, of gifts that had traditionally worked well for the Conservancy.) With only the rarest exceptions, a fundraising letter must cite at least one specific suggested gift amount.

- I also made significant changes in the *Johnson's Box*—the boldfaced copy that precedes the salutation. I dropped the language proposed in the draft. The parallelism of the wording worked fine, but "We need you" is a weak case for giving. Instead, I selected donor benefits to highlight there.

- Similarly, I overhauled the lead to emphasize benefits even more. Writing fundraising letters is, ultimately, all about spotlighting the benefits to the donor. Contrary to the conventional wisdom in nonprofit circles, few people care about an organization's needs: it's results delivered to its beneficiaries that matter more to people—and those results, if good, are viewed as benefits by donors. As a result, I moved the "good neighbor" theme down a couple of pegs. But that was a good theme, so I fleshed it out a little.

- A four-page letter requires page numbers. Sometimes I like to dress them up a bit, as I did here, by adding a header consistent with the letter's theme.

- The copy called out for boldface and italics to emphasize key points, styling that was lacking in the draft. I focused on the major donor benefits and the most intriguing thoughts. Please note that I limited emphasis to two or three instances on each page—and that all of them are short.

- Generally, the executive director (or the equivalent) is the best signer. But if the statements made in the letter were more true of the director of membership or of someone else associated with the conservancy, then that person could sign the appeal instead. With notable exceptions, the selection of a letter signer is not that big a deal.

- I rarely write a direct mail letter without a P.S. Studies show that this copy receives very high readership, as I've noted earlier. That's why I placed the ask here.

**EXHIBIT 10.2**

# Original Acquisition Letter, Western Pennsylvania Conservancy

*We need you . . .*

*And, once you consider what we are doing to keep Pennsylvania's wild places wild and to make Pennsylvania's communities vibrant—I hope you'll say that you need us, too!*

Dear Friend,

My message is simple. I need you to help us to save the places we all care about. We need you to join with us at Western Pennsylvania Conservancy.

Here's why. We're *your neighbors,* and just like any good neighbor, we want to work with you, to save the places we care about.

If you're like me, you probably don't know every one of your neighbors. So, in case you don't know us, let me tell you a few things about us. We've been your neighbor for more than 60 years, working to protect the most important wild places in Pennsylvania . . . from the shores of Lake Erie to the hills and valleys in our southernmost counties . . . from wildflowers along the Ohio border to Cherry Run, in the center of the state.

We're also the organization that maintains and operates Fallingwater, the world-famous house that Frank Lloyd Wright built in Mill Run. And we work with over five thousand volunteers' help to create some of the most beautiful community gardens in the eastern United States.

In the time since we opened the doors to Western Pennsylvania Conservancy, in 1932, we have purchased more than 204,500 acres of land in Pennsylvania. *These 204,500 acres remain open to the public—you and I—to visit and enjoy.*

You've probably been to some of the areas we've purchased and helped to preserve. Have you rafted the Youghiogheny River, through Ohiopyle State Park? Walked the Laurel Highlands Trail, in Laurel Ridge State Park? Did you ever take a boat on Lake Arthur in Moraine State Park? Have you hunted on the State Game Lands in Fulton County? Has your family fished at McConnell's Mills?

In the last six decades, we purchased the bulk of the lands at all these public spots, and then sold them to one of the state or federal public agencies (often far below costs, by the way) to create these great havens.

I've spent some time in many other parts of the country, and I have to tell you that our region is fortunate to have the amount of open space we have here. There aren't many areas where the public has our kind of access to such beautiful places.

**EXHIBIT 10.2 (*Continued*)**

We, at Western Pennsylvania Conservancy, keep adding to the tally. Right now, we're working to protect another corridor of continuous open space—along the Clarion River. Starting more than 20 years ago, we have purchased more than 12,600 acres along a 41-mile stretch of this recreation corridor. We've already conveyed more than 8,000 of those acres to state and federal agencies, which protects them and gives you public access.

As I said in the beginning of the letter, we do more than protect these undeveloped lands. You might know us at Western Pennsylvania Conservancy as the neighbor who helps your community with a garden project. We have more than 400 separate garden projects all over western Pennsylvania.

We're proud of the success of our "community conservation" efforts in this region. We have a philosophy here that "communities make gardens grow, and gardens can help communities grow."

We bring together volunteers, corporate and foundation sponsors, and our understanding of how to produce a garden project in some of the most unlikely places. Working side-by-side, these partnerships have transformed some concrete flatland spaces into breath-taking displays of color, cultivated by the pride of every partner.

Through the generosity of partnerships, we facilitated garden projects in schoolyards, neighborhoods, at senior citizen complexes, and along highways. *We believe in the power of these garden projects to promote healthy and attractive communities.*

I know sprawl's a big word in conservation these days. Actually, I do believe that helping make existing communities more attractive helps reduce development pressures on undeveloped countrysides. It's a practical matter. *And we believe in practicality at Western Pennsylvania Conservancy.* We don't just talk about how to "protect land," or "improve urban living spaces." We don't think it's practical to just talk about it. We do it.

That brings me to Fallingwater, the house that Edgar J. Kaufmann entrusted to Western Pennsylvania Conservancy in 1963. It was his home; but he always knew it was more than that. "The union of powerful art and powerful nature into something beyond the sum of their separate powers deserves to be kept living," he said. He knew the house was an international treasure. *He thoughtfully pondered his choice for the organization to best protect this reverent location, and Mr. Kaufmann chose us—Western Pennsylvania Conservancy.*

We know why he entrusted Fallingwater to Western Pennsylvania Conservancy. *He knew that we understand the connection between man and nature.* It's in *why* we protect as much land as we do. It's in *why* we facilitate the growing number of garden projects we choose every year.

**EXHIBIT 10.2 (*Continued*)**

It's in *how* we preserve Fallingwater. And frankly, it's in how this staff approaches every work day here.

To give you a sense of what I mean, here's just a sample of what's on our organizational plate now.

—We must protect Fallingwater structurally. The famous "house on the waterfall" is more than 60 years old, and its signature cantilevers, which seem to hang in mid-air, have sagged, or deflected, past an acceptable point. We shored them up as a temporary measure. But we intend to strengthen the house internally without permanently impacting the visual integrity of this historic home.

—We intend to expand our traditional land protection through purchase by adding a community-based approach to conservation. Our field scientists have an amazing wealth of knowledge about the wildest places and their living resources of western Pennsylvania, and we know there are many more ways to use that information to create real progress in land protection without jeopardizing or diminishing in any way the human values.

Someone recently shared with me, "I don't know much about biodiversity, but I know it includes people!"

—It's always been our commitment to "include people," and here's how we intend to "do," not just "talk." We haven't uncovered every opportunity yet, but we are finding ways to link ecological health to local livelihoods, such as in agriculture, forestry and tourism, the top three economic forces in Pennsylvania today. In French Creek, we've already begun, with our partnership to form the French Creek Project, which works with landowners to protect this important and biologically rich watershed.

—As part of our mission to help connect people with nature, we are continuing to expand our members activities. In 2000, members will have a full year's worth of events to choose from—starting with our popular Valentine Day Hike at Bear Run; highlighting Earth Day, in the spring; and concluding the year with guided canoe floats and interpretive hikes all over western Pennsylvania.

—We aren't militant, by any means, but we do believe we are considered a reasonable voice for conservation. We are selective about the advocacy issues that we'll take on in Harrisburg or Washington, D.C. For instance, we delivered testimony to encourage the Pa. Fish and Boat Commissioners to approve changes to their list of Endangered and Threatened Species. After all, our scientists helped collect the data that led to some of the decisions about the list. We choose our involvements carefully, to save our most critical resources and to have the widest impact for the greatest good.

**EXHIBIT 10.2 (*Continued*)**

And that brings me back to the Clarion River. As I canoed it recently, I reflected on the notion that this was the crossroads of Conservancy's past, our present and our future. You see, 90 years ago, the Clarion was the most polluted waterway in the Commonwealth. Through the great efforts of a lot of people in the region, and beyond, the river was cleaned up. The river-side tannery industry was in decline, the paper industry changed their discharge habits, and community groups worked on abandoned mine drainage and other protection efforts. Then, 20 years ago, Western Pennsylvania Conservancy bought its first acre along the river. As I mentioned earlier, we've bought more than 12,000 acres in that watershed. Our goal is to see the Clarion River corridor connect with Cook Forest and Clear Creek State Park to form the largest State Park. With your help, we can make it happen.

To me, the future for Western Pennsylvania Conservancy is in continuing to work alongside the residents of the community as they cultivate the growing tourism as part of a sustainable economy while they maintain the serenity that attracts visitors in the first place! That's what we mean when we say we're "saving the places we care about!"

The way I look at it, *it's all part of being a good neighbor.*

So, neighbor, I hope you'll join us. Because, I need you! Please, join today.

You'll receive . . . . . . . .

**EXHIBIT 10.3**

# Edited Acquisition Letter, Western Pennsylvania Conservancy

**Have you rafted the Youghiogheny River through Ohiopyle State Park? Walked the Laurel Highlands Trail in Laurel Ridge State Park? Has your family fished at McConnell's Mills?**

**If so, the Western Pennsylvania Conservancy has directly benefited you.**

Dear Neighbor,

If you've ever taken a boat on Lake Arthur in Moraine State Park, or hunted on the State Game Lands in Fulton County, you've been to some of the land we've purchased and helped to preserve.

In the last six decades, the Western Pennsylvania Conservancy has purchased the bulk of the lands at all the public spots I've named. Then we turned right around and sold them to a state or federal agency—often far below cost—to create these priceless havens.

So, you might not know me, but I'm your neighbor—and like any good neighbor, *I want to help you enjoy the highest possible quality of life.*

If you're like me, you probably don't know every one of your neighbors. So, just in case you don't know me or the organization I'm so proud to lead, let me tell you a few things about the Western Pennsylvania Conservancy.

For more than 60 years, the Conservancy has been working to protect the most important wild places in Pennsylvania—from the shores of Lake Erie to the hills and valleys in our southernmost counties . . . from wildflowers along the Ohio border to Cherry Run, in the center of the state.

We're also the people who maintain and operate Fallingwater, the world-famous house that Frank Lloyd Wright built in Mill Run. And we work with over five thousand volunteers, helping to create some of the most beautiful community gardens in the eastern United States.

Since we opened the doors to Western Pennsylvania Conservancy in 1932, we have purchased more than 204,500 acres of land in Pennsylvania . . . and opened those acres to the public—to you and me and our children's children—to visit and enjoy . . . forever.

I've spent some time in many other parts of the country, and I have to tell you that our region is fortunate to have the amount of open space we have here. *There aren't many places in America where the public has our kind of access to such beautiful spots.*

But we keep adding to the tally. Right now, the Western Pennsylvania Conservancy is working to protect another corridor of continuous open space—along the Clarion River. Starting more than 20 years ago, we have purchased more than 12,600 acres along a 41-mile stretch of

**EXHIBIT 10.3 (*Continued*)**

An Appeal from Neighbor to Neighbor, page 2

this recreation corridor. We've already conveyed more than 8,000 of those acres to state and federal agencies, which protects them and gives you public access.

Of course, you might also know us at Western Pennsylvania Conservancy as the neighbor who helps your community with a garden project. We have more than 400 separate garden projects all over western Pennsylvania.

We're proud of the success of our "community conservation" efforts in this region. We have a philosophy here that *"communities make gardens grow, and gardens can help communities grow."*

We bring our know-how about garden projects together with volunteers and with corporate and foundation sponsors in some of the most unlikely places. Working side by side, these partnerships have transformed some concrete flatland spaces into breathtaking displays of color, cultivated by the pride of every partner.

Through the generosity of partnerships, we facilitate garden projects in schoolyards, neighborhoods, at senior citizen complexes, and along highways. I firmly believe these garden projects don't just enhance the beauty of our communities. They also promote *healthier community life.*

Consider that for a moment. I think you'll agree with me.

I also believe strongly that helping make existing communities more attractive helps reduce development pressures on undeveloped countryside. It's a practical matter. And we believe in practicality at Western Pennsylvania Conservancy.

We don't just talk about how to "protect land" or to "improve urban living spaces." We don't think it's practical to just talk about it. We do it.

The same was true at Fallingwater, the house that Edgar J. Kaufmann entrusted to Western Pennsylvania Conservancy in 1963. It was his home—but he always knew it was more than that.

"The union of powerful art and powerful nature into something beyond the sum of their separate powers deserves to be kept living," Mr. Kaufmann said. He knew the house was an international treasure. He thoughtfully pondered his choice for the organization to best protect this reverent location, and Mr. Kaufmann chose us—Western Pennsylvania Conservancy.

I know why Edgar Kaufmann entrusted Fallingwater to Western Pennsylvania Conservancy.

*He knew that we understand the connection between man and nature.*

---

**EXHIBIT 10.3 (*Continued*)**

---

> An Appeal from Neighbor to Neighbor, page 3

That connection helps explain why we protect as much land as we do. It explains why we support a growing number of garden projects every year. It shapes how we preserve Fallingwater. And it profoundly affects how my staff and I approach our work every day of the year.

To give you a sense of what I mean, here are just a few examples of what's on our organizational plate right now:

- The Western Pennsylvania Conservancy is working to protect the structural integrity of Fallingwater. The famous "house on the waterfall" is more than 60 years old, and its signature cantilevers, which seem to hang in mid-air, have sagged over the years. We shored them up as a temporary measure. But we intend to strengthen the structure internally without permanently impacting the visual integrity of this historic home.

- Someone recently shared an intriguing thought with me: ***"I don't know much about biodiversity, but I know it includes people!"*** Here at the Western Pennsylvania Conservancy, it's always been our commitment to "include people." We haven't uncovered every opportunity yet, but we are finding ways to link ecological health to local livelihoods, such as in agriculture, forestry, and tourism (the top three economic forces in Pennsylvania today). In French Creek, for instance, we and our partners have already begun to form the French Creek Project, which will work with landowners to protect this important and biologically rich watershed.

- As part of ***our mission to help connect people with nature,*** we are continuing to expand our members' activities. In 2000, members will have a full year's worth of events to choose from, starting with our popular Valentine's Day Hike at Bear Run . . . highlighting Earth Day, in the spring . . . and concluding the year with guided canoe floats and interpretive hikes all over western Pennsylvania.

- The Western Pennsylvania Conservancy is widely considered a reasonable voice for conservation. We're selective about the advocacy issues that we'll take on in Harrisburg or Washington, D.C. For instance, we delivered testimony to encourage the Pennsylvania Fish and Boat Commissioners to approve changes to their list of Endangered and Threatened Species. After all, our scientists helped collect the data that led to some of the decisions about the list! We choose our involvements carefully, to save our most critical resources and to have the widest impact for the greatest good.

And that brings me back to the recreation corridor we've been protecting along the Clarion River. As I canoed there recently, I reflected on the notion that this was the crossroads of the Conservancy's past, our present, and our future.

**EXHIBIT 10.3 (*Continued*)**

An Appeal from Neighbor to Neighbor, page 4

You see, 90 years ago, the Clarion was the most polluted waterway in the Commonwealth. Through the combined efforts of a lot of people in the region (and beyond), the river was cleaned up. The riverside tannery industry was in decline, the paper companies changed their discharge habits, and community groups worked on abandoned mine drainage and other protection efforts.

Then, 20 years ago, Western Pennsylvania Conservancy bought its first acre along the river—the first of more than 12,000 acres in that watershed so far. Our goal is to see the Clarion River corridor connect with Cook Forest and Clear Creek State Park to form the [STATE'S?] largest State Park. With your help, we can make it happen.

To me, the future for Western Pennsylvania Conservancy lies in continuing to work alongside the residents of our communities. We play a vital role in helping cultivate the growing tourism that sustains our economy—by helping maintain the serenity that attracts visitors in the first place! That's what we mean when we say we're "saving the places we care about!"

The way I look at it, ***it's all part of being a good neighbor.***

So, neighbor, I hope you'll join me and our fellow neighbors here at the Western Pennsylvania Conservancy—today! You may enlist as a member for as little as $XX.

As a member of the Western Pennsylvania Conservancy, you'll receive a number of valuable benefits:

- [BENEFIT 1. Newsletter??]

- [BENEFIT 2. Discounts, free passes, maps???]

- Most important of all, however, you'll gain the satisfaction of knowing that you're a good neighbor. Your support of the Western Pennsylvania Conservancy will help your neighbors—and all our children and our children's children—to enjoy the bounties of nature throughout all time.

In hope and gratitude,

[signature]

[Name of Executive Director]

Executive Director

P.S.　　Please take a moment right now to complete the enclosed membership enrollment form and attach your check for $XX, $YY, $ZZ or more. Then return both the check and the form to me in the attached pre-addressed envelope. ***You'll be glad you did!***

# Chapter 11

# Welcoming New Donors
## Treating People Like Part of the Family

**FUNDRAISERS ARE FINALLY** coming to understand that direct mail cannot be treated simply as a way to haul in gifts. The letters we send our donors or members are just as important for the contributions they make to the relationship-building process that lays the groundwork for more and larger gifts over a long period of time. A welcome package for new donors or new members is the best example of this growing trend. These packages, mailed soon after the receipt of a donor's or member's first check (in response to an acquisition, or prospect, package), are intended to open a dialogue between the individual and the organization by laying out, simply and clearly, all the benefits of supporting the organization and all the ways that a supporter may become directly involved.

The response device in Exhibit 11.1 comes from such a welcome package for new members. Its distinguishing characteristics are typical in many ways of welcome packages:

- The "Welcome!" message is impossible to miss.

- It contains a *bounce-back* form, which offers the new member the opportunity to obtain information about important Bread for the World programs.

- There's space on the bounce-back form to supply information that will be useful to Bread for the World in targeting future requests for help, including the new member's e-mail address, which may be used in the organization's future online fundraising program.

- On the reverse of the bounce-back form is information the new member may use when participating in future Bread for the World grassroots lobbying campaigns.

- Donor options on the bounce-back form include opportunities to opt out of mailing list rentals and exchanges, enlist in the Baker's Dozen monthly giving program, and sign up for Bread for the World's free *Hunger Sunday* newsletter offering resources and suggestions for action.

**EXHIBIT 11.1**

## New Donor Welcome Package Response Device, Bread for the World

# Welcome!

Thank you for joining Bread for the World with your . . .
. . .gift of $100, received on January 22, 2007.

I'm pleased you've become Bread for the World's *newest member.* Your financial support and your citizen action make a big difference as all of us work together to end hunger in the U.S. and overseas.

BFW07YA/Pkg. 1/New Member Welcome
Ms. Jane Doe
123 Main Street
Anytown, AS 11111

*—David Beckmann, President*

Tear off and keep this top portion. Please *return the bottom portion* to Bread for the World in the envelope provided. Thank you.

## We'd like to hear from you ...

The following information will help us serve you as a member of Bread for the World:

**E-mail address** _____     **Home phone: (_____)** _____

**Your denomination or church** _____

BFW07YA/Pkg. 1/New Member Welcome
Ms. Jane Doe
123 Main Street
Anytown, AS 11111

◀ *Please correct your name and address at left if they aren't complete and accurate. Thank you!*

44237806
WELC

### Bread for the World
*Seeking Justice. Ending Hunger.*
50 F Street NW, Suite 500
Washington, DC 20001
1-800-822-7323   www.bread.org

## Want to be more involved?

☐ Please start my free subscription to *Hunger Sunday* newsletter—with resources and suggestions to help churches and faith communities take action on behalf of hungry people.

☐ I'm interested in joining the *Baker's Dozen* and helping end hunger every month—by pre-authorizing my bank to send monthly gifts. Please send me details.

☐ I'd prefer that my name and address *not* be shared with other organizations. (Bread for the World occasionally exchanges its mailing list with select organizations whose activities might be of interest to our members.)

**To sign up for special e-mail alerts ...**

**For news about legislation ...**

**To order publications and resources...**

**Visit www.bread.org**

● Give  ● Learn
● Get Involved  ● Take Action

RECYCLED & RECYCLABLE / PRINTED WITH SOY INK     7-YA2W

*Please see reverse side for important information*

**EXHIBIT 11.1** (*Continued*)

## *Your letters and phone calls help end hunger*

**Please contact your senators and representative in the U.S. Congress. Urge them to support measures that give hungry people the tools and resources they need to feed their families. Visit www.bread.org — for the latest news about pending legislation as well as the names and addresses of your members of Congress.**

Bread for the World

*Seeking Justice. Ending Hunger.*

50 F Street NW, Suite 500
Washington, DC 20001

*Contributions to Bread for the World are not tax-deductible since its members work for legislative change.*

**How to contact
your members
of Congress:**

U.S. House of
Representatives
Washington, D.C.
20515

U.S. Senate
Washington, D.C.
20510

Phone for both
House and Senate:

**202-224-3121**

### We use your contributions wisely

*You are welcome to review our latest annual report with audited financial statements, which can be found at www.bread.org. Or write us at Bread for the World, 50 F Street NW, Suite 500, Washington, D.C. 20001. We'll be glad to send you a copy.*

**Questions or concerns about your membership?**

Call 1-800-822-7323

Or send an email message to memberservices@bread.org

## How New Donor Welcome Packages Are Different from Other Fundraising Appeals

In nonprofits' continuing search for heightened donor loyalty and higher renewal rates, welcome packages for new donors are becoming increasingly common. These packets of information mailed to newly recruited members or donors may be fat or thin, elaborate or simple. Typically, however, they share five attributes.

### Five Characteristics of New Donor Welcome Packages

1. They strive to be warm, emphasizing the organization's appreciation rather than its needs and offering additional information. Short copy

is common. The welcome letter's purpose is usually to inform the new donor about the organization's programs and its donor benefits and services.

2. Any copy that refers to the new member personally is likely to be vague and general; usually the charity knows too little to personalize the letter in any meaningful way. One important exception is the amount of the initial gift, which may be inserted in the cover letter if it's personalized, or noted on a gift receipt.

3. Some charities use the opportunity to request a second gift or even to suggest that a new donor join a giving club, such as a monthly sustainer program. But it's more common—and I think, more advisable—not to seek a gift with this package. For example, if you've decided that the best time to invite members to join a monthly pledge program is immediately after they join, I suggest you *first* mail them a welcome package and *then*, perhaps a week or ten days later, send the pledge invitation.

4. To introduce new donors to the organization's work, a recent issue of its magazine or newsletter is often enclosed. Sometimes brochures about its programs and services are included. Welcome packages are often heavy and expensive. They're an investment in future fundraising efforts.

5. Welcome packages frequently offer new donors multiple opportunities to respond—through surveys, requests for additional information, *member-get-a-member* programs, donor options, or other involvement devices.

## Six Reasons You Should Mail Welcome Packages

Let's take a look first at the many roles that a welcome package is created to play. Then we can review several possible elements you might consider including in your own welcome package or adding to your existing new donor acknowledgment.

It seems to me there are six reasons to go to the expense and trouble of sending new members a special, initial package that's more than a simple gift receipt or thank-you note.

1. All donors expect to be thanked for their support. A simple receipt is probably not enough to make them think you're being nice. And treating members well increases the chances they'll renew their annual

support. This is especially important if (like most other charities these days) your nonprofit has a very low first-year renewal rate.

2. Donors are most receptive to your message immediately after making their first gifts. This is the best time to approach them about such fund-raising options as monthly sustainer programs or *friend-get-a-friend* efforts. (However, it's not necessarily the best time to ask for a second gift.) If you can move a new member to take action right after joining—almost any action, in fact—you'll be well on your way to building a strong, mutually beneficial, long-term relationship. But timing is important here; receptivity fades fast, and donors can all too easily forget having contributed to a charity that's new to them.

3. Donors' first impression of your organization is likely to affect their views of all subsequent communications. A cheap thank-you, such as a postcard or an impersonal letter, may impress a few donors with its frugality, but far more donors are likely to be flattered by a carefully prepared, well-thought-out introductory package that underscores how very important their financial support is. I'm convinced most donors secretly think you're wasting money when you send fancy packages to other people but not when you spend money on them.

4. Donors are too often skeptical about how their contributions are put to use. They sometimes need to be persuaded that their gifts accomplish more than raise additional money. By describing your work in detail and offering opportunities for members to contribute more than money, a welcome package can drive home the message that your organization is lean, hard working, and cost-effective. This is true even when an individual member has no interest at all in contributing volunteer time. The offer and the opportunities communicate an important message.

5. New donors probably won't understand your organization and its programs unless yours is a local group that provides a single, direct, easily grasped service. Any nonprofit that's engaged in multiple projects—especially if it's a large, decentralized, complex nonprofit—will need a well-organized welcome package so donors will understand its work and the role they can play in it. Once donors do understand your organization well, they're much more likely to respond favorably when you ask for additional support.

6. Not all donors are created equal. Some may be delighted to send a small monthly contribution. Others may want to contribute only once per year. Still others might be interested in joining a high-dollar giving

club. The welcome package is an excellent opportunity to test their preferences on these and other fundraising questions by giving them a questionnaire or at least by clearly offering several different fundraising options and an easy way to request more information about them.

If your organization mails new donors more than a simple tax receipt or thank-you note, you may already be addressing some of the six opportunities I've just listed. But there may be a number of other ways you can accomplish a whole lot more. You might consider adding some enclosures to your thank-you letter or a full-fledged new donor welcome package.

---

### Possible Enclosures in Welcome Packages

- A small brochure or folder that catalogues membership services and benefits

- An involvement device that includes a brief new-member survey

- An explanation of how the organization works, either in a brochure or flyer or in copy in the cover letter

- A membership card, with an abbreviated listing of membership benefits on the reverse

- A brochure about your monthly sustainer program

- A brochure about your bequest and planned giving programs, if any

- A flyer that includes an order form for merchandise you sell, featuring a discount offer for new members

---

## Case Study: Global Fund for Women

On the CD-ROM provided with this book, you'll find two excellent examples of welcome packages, both developed for nonprofit membership organizations that offer members substantial benefits. But what sort of welcome package might a donor-based organization provide to newcomers? Without a hefty list of benefits, is there any way to craft a welcome package that will strengthen the relationship with donors?

The answer—you guessed it—is yes. Exhibits 11.2, 11.3, and 11.4 display the welcome package employed by the Global Fund for Women. As you can see, this simple package incorporates most of the elements routinely found in a welcome package—with just a few sheets of paper and without the need to dwell on extensive donor benefits. Witness:

- The letter is personalized and acknowledges the new donor's gift by amount and date.

- The reply device, which is printed on the same sheet as the letter and separated by a perforation, consists of a thank-you, a suggestion that the donor may enlist in the Global Fund's monthly giving program, and a detailed donor survey, which concludes with an ask for an additional contribution.

- The brochure sets the tone for the relationship between the organization and the new donor, reviews the case for giving, and lists several ways that donors may become involved in the work of the fund.

---

**EXHIBIT 11.2 a**

## New Donor Welcome Envelope, Global Fund for Women

the
**GLOBAL FUND**
for
**WOMEN**

1375 Sutter Street, Suite 400
San Francisco, CA 94109
*www.globalfundforwomen.org*

*Welcome!*

Ms. Jane Doe
GFW07YB/Ongoing/Pkg. 1: Low$ Welcome
123 Main Street
Anytown, AS 111111

RECYCLED & RECYCLABLE / PRINTED WITH SOY INK    6-YA3

---

**EXHIBIT 11.2 b**

## New Donor Welcome Letter, Global Fund for Women

**This is your tax receipt.**

*No goods or services were provided to the donor in consideration of this gift. The entire amount of this contribution to the Global Fund for Women is tax-deductible.*

**Global Fund for Women**

1375 Sutter Street, Suite 400
San Francisco, CA 94109
415-202-7640
*www.globalfundforwomen.org*

Ms. Jane Doe
GFW07YB/Ongoing/Pkg. 1: Low$ Welcome
123 Main Street
Anytown, AS 111111

Dear Ms. Doe,

Warm greetings from the Global Fund for Women! Thank you for your contribution of $35.00 on 05/15/07. I am excited to welcome you to our international network of women and men committed to gender equality, social justice, and peace.

I've enclosed a booklet for you that illustrates how your contribution supports women and girls around the world. Thank you again for embarking on a partnership with women on every continent who are standing up—often against the steepest odds—to bring a better future for women, girls, and their communities.

With sincere appreciation and best wishes,

*Kavita N Ramdas*

Kavita N. Ramdas
President and CEO

P.S.    We'd like to know more about what issues are important to you. If you can, please take a few
moments to fill out the information below. Thank you!

7-YA2W

**EXHIBIT 11.3**

# New Donor Welcome Reply Device, Global Fund for Women

Please take a moment to review and complete the following options. Please detach the survey from your tax receipt above and return your response in the enclosed postage–paid envelope.

**1. THANK YOU** for your recent contribution of $35.00. It is heartwarming to know you share our vision for a better world. Please consider becoming a supporter for ongoing change by making a monthly investment of in the power of women.

☐ YES. I authorize the Global Fund for Women to deduct the following amount each month from my checking account/credit card as indicated below. **I understand I can change the amount or cancel at any time.**

[ ]                              [ ] $_____

123456
WELS

Signature: _____

☐ Please deduct the amount indicated above from my checking account each month. I've enclosed a void check.

**OR**

☐ Please charge the amount indicated above to my credit card each month:
☐ Visa    ☐ MasterCard    ☐ American Express

Card # _____    Exp. Date: _____

## 2. DONOR SURVEY

Please complete this Donor Survey so that we can learn what issues are important to you and verify that our contact information for you is correct.

**a)** Name:    Ms. Jane Doe/GFW07YB/Ongoing/Pkg. 1: Low$ Welcome
**b)** Address:    123 Main Street
Anytown, AS 111111

**c)** Email:    _____
**d)** Home phone #:    (___)_____

**e)** How do you prefer to be addressed?
☐ Ms.    ☐ Mrs.    ☐ Miss    ☐ Mr.    ☐ Dr.    ☐ _____

**f)** Date of birth:  MONTH _____ DAY _____ YEAR _____

*Please see over* ▶

**EXHIBIT 11.3 (*Continued*)**

**g)** Do you have children?  ☐ YES  ☐ NO

**h)** Below is a list of issues facing women across the globe today. Please check those that are of greatest importance to you.

☐ Violence against women
☐ Access to economic opportunities
☐ Access to health care and sexual and reproductive rights
☐ Girls' access to education
☐ Trafficking and forced prostitution
☐ Political participation and legal rights
☐ Peace building and conflict resolution
☐ Traditional religious and cultural practices
☐ Other _____

**i)** What regions of the world are of particular interest to you?
☐ Africa              ☐ Middle East and North Africa
☐ Asia                ☐ Eastern Europe
☐ The Caribbean       ☐ Oceania
☐ Latin America       ☐ Other _____

**j)** If you read and speak a foreign language, please indicate which language(s): _____

**3. COMMUNICATION PREFERENCES**

The Global Fund for Women takes pride in respecting the wishes of our donors. Please take a moment to check only those boxes that are relevant to you.

**a)** All current donors receive our print newsletter.

I prefer not to receive this newsletter.  ☐

**b)** Donors with email addresses receive our bi-monthly e-bulletin with current updates.

I prefer not to receive this e-bulletin.  ☐

**c)** You can help us recruit new donors and expand our network by allowing us to exchange your name with other nonprofits we think may be of interest to you.

I do not wish to help in this way. Please do not share my name.  ☐

**4. PLEASE SEND ME** the following:

☐ How to spread my gift over the year (pre-arranged monthly giving)
☐ How to give a gift of stock
☐ How to leave a legacy by making a bequest
☐ How to volunteer my time
☐ How to host a House Party
☐ Annual Report
☐ Recent Global Fund for Women newsletter

**5. ADDITIONAL CONTRIBUTION**

I'd like to make an additional contribution to help women's groups protect and promote the rights of women and girls and build stronger communities around the world. Here is my gift of:

WEL

☐ **$25**    ☐ **$50**    ☐ **$75**    ☐ **$_____**

☐ I've enclosed a check payable to *Global Fund for Women*.

☐ I prefer to use my credit card.

Please charge my:  ☐ VISA   ☐ MasterCard   ☐ Amex

**Card Number** _____

**Exp. Date** _____ **Signature** _____

☐ I'd like to make this gift in honor/memory (please circle one) of:

_____

Please send a card acknowledging this gift to:

**Name** _____

**Address** _____

**City, State, Zip** _____

*Please return to:*     Global Fund for Women     1375 Sutter Street, Suite 400     San Francisco, CA 94109

**EXHIBIT 11.4**

# New Donor Welcome Brochure, Global Fund for Women

## Warm greetings!

Thank you for choosing to support the courageous efforts of women all over the world working to create communities free from poverty, violence and discrimination.

We are immensely grateful for your support and welcome you to our international network of women and men committed to equality, social justice and peace.

At the Global Fund for Women we believe philanthropy is an opportunity for each of us to participate in social change and to support the issues we believe in.

Unlike most nonprofits, we do not categorize our donors by gift amount. We see all of our supporters as equal partners in our work.

If you have any questions, please contact us. You'll find specific contact information on the back page. Thank you for your contribution, and welcome to our network!

*Kavita N Ramdas*

Kavita N. Ramdas
President and CEO

The Global Fund for Women is the largest grantmaking foundation in the world that focuses exclusively on women's rights globally.

We believe that women themselves know best how to determine their needs and propose solutions for lasting change. Our flexible grantmaking approach is designed to empower women at the local level.

Unlike most international funders, the Global Fund for Women accepts requests for funding in any format—handwritten, emailed or typed. We also accept requests in any language. This makes us truly accessible to even the most remote or underresourced groups.

All around the world, women and girls are taking the initiative to solve problems in their own communities. These inspiring, courageous leaders are not afraid to encounter opposition, and often risk their lives in pursuit of equality.

**EXHIBIT 11.4 (*Continued*)**

## Only 7.3% of US philanthropic dollars directly benefit women internationally.

### —Foundation Center

## We Invest Your Money Wisely

The way in which we do our work is as important as what we do. This philosophy is reflected in our respectful and responsive style of grantmaking and fundraising.

We award grants to women's organizations directly. We depend on the expertise and guidance of a global network of advisors from diverse backgrounds to inform our grantmaking decisions. Grantees provide specific feedback reports on what they have achieved with our grants.

## Since 1987, the Global Fund for Women has given away more than $56 million to seed, strengthen and link 3,300 women's groups in over 160 countries.

*"At this time, we at SWAA are humbled by the generosity and solidarity of all our partners. You are the ones who have made possible SWAA's efforts to ease the suffering of the people infected and affected by AIDS."*

*—Society for Women and AIDS in Africa, Sudan*

**EXHIBIT 11.4** (*Continued*)

The Global Fund for Women provides grants ranging from $500 to $20,000 to women's rights organizations around the world. We fund groups that focus on advancing the rights of women and girls by addressing critical issues, including:

- Economic independence
- Women's health and reproductive rights
- Access to education for women and girls
- Violence against women
- Harmful traditional practices
- The rights of women with disabilities
- Women's political participation
- Women in peace-building efforts
- Access to media, communications, technology and the Internet

**This work is only possible with the help of individuals like you. Thank you!**

PHOTOGRAPHS BY:
PETER ADAMS; TERRY LORANT;
MARK TUSCHMAN;
STINA KATCHADOURIAN;
REBECCA JANES.

"Women face violence, health care inequities, and educational barriers. And yet there's hope ... I know I'm affecting women's lives in a direct way."

—**Jennifer Weber**
**Global Fund for Women donor**

**EXHIBIT 11.4 (*Continued*)**

# Get Involved!

Your gift of money, resources or time is an opportunity to make a difference in the world. Here's how you can support the work of the Global Fund for Women:

## House Party

Organize a House Party and invite your friends and family to learn about the Global Fund for Women. Contact us for your free House Party kit.

## Monthly Gift

Provide a consistent contribution each month through our monthly giving program, the *Corazón Network*. Your pre-authorized monthly contribution will ensure we can continue to provide funds where and when needed.

## Celebration Gift

Celebrate Mother's Day, the lives of loved ones, birthdays, holidays and other events with a dedicated donation to the Global Fund for Women.

## Leave a Legacy

Leave a legacy that represents the things you believe in. Once you have taken care of your loved ones in your will, please consider including a bequest to the Global Fund for Women.

### We Invite You to Contact Us
### (415) 202-7640
www.globalfundforwomen.org

**Global Fund for Women**

1375 Sutter Street, Suite 400
San Francisco, CA 94109

RECYCLED & RECYCLABLE / SOY INK    7-YA5W

*Welcome to* the Global Fund for Women

# Chapter 12

# Appealing for Special Gifts
Bringing Your Case Down to Earth

**A SPECIAL APPEAL** urges donors or members to focus on one of the organization's individual programs, a specific issue, a season of the year, or a particular need or opportunity. Normally, the letter makes clear that funds contributed in response to a special appeal are undesignated—in other words, that they provide general operating support—even though the letter may heavily emphasize a single issue or project.

Exhibit 12.1 shows a response device representative of the thousands of special appeals mailed every year by nonprofit organizations to their previous donors. It could hardly be more obvious, with its request for a "special gift" during Lent "to help underwrite Bread for the World's efforts in 2007—as we work together . . ."

The distinguishing characteristics of this response device are typical of special appeals:

- Bread for the World is seeking support at a specific time significant to members of this faith-based organization: Lent. So, unlike an acquisition letter, this appeal cannot be continuously remailed. Special appeals are typically one-time (or annual) propositions.

- The open ask amount ("$_____") is appropriate for donors who have already established relationships with Bread for the World. Few fundraisers would venture an open ask with prospective donors, as that would likely yield lots of cost-inefficient $1 and $2 contributions.

- The only truly general description of Bread for the World's mission is to be found in the tagline in the lower right corner ("Seeking Justice. Ending Hunger."), although the letter (not displayed here) expands on that point with more general references to the organization's work. In any case, it's assumed that most readers of this appeal are familiar with the organization's purpose.

**EXHIBIT 12.1**

## Special Appeal Response Device, Bread for the World

# Lent 2007

☐ YES, I want to help underwrite Bread for the World's efforts in 2007—as we work together to help farmers and help end hunger. Enclosed is my special gift:

[ ] $_____

☐ Please send me _____ copies of Lenten Prayers for Hungry People free of charge. *Additional copies may also be ordered by visiting www.bread.org/lent.*

▶ *Please turn over for congressional contact instructions.*

> Mr. John Doe
> 123 Main Street
> Anytown, AS 00000
> BFW07AA/1-15-07/Pkg#3 All others

*Woodcut by Helen Siegl*

*If you wish to use your credit card to make a gift, please fill out the information on the reverse side.*

## Bread for the World
*Seeking Justice. Ending Hunger.*

50 F Street NW, Suite 500
Washington, DC 20001
1-800-822-7323   www.bread.org

RECYCLED & RECYCLABLE / PRINTED WITH SOY INK     7-AA2          07AADOEC   00000

---

Please charge a gift of $ _____

☐ Bread for the World   ☐ Bread for the World Institute

☐ Visa   ☐ MasterCard   ☐ Discover

Card # _____

Exp. date _____   Card security code* _____

Please print name on card _____

Signature _____

\* *For your protection, we are now required to request the 3 or 4 digit security code on the back of your credit card.*

**Please contact your members of Congress** to urge them to reform the U.S. farm bill so that it helps farmers and helps end hunger. Visit www.bread.org for more information about Bread for the World's 2007 legislative campaign. You'll also find the names of your senators and representatives.

**To contact your members of Congress:**
Capitol Switchboard: 202-224-3121

**To contact a U.S. Senator:**
The Honorable_____
U.S. Senate
Washington, DC 20510

**To contact a Representative:**
The Honorable_____
U.S. House of Representatives
Washington, DC 20515

### We use your contributions wisely and effectively

Gifts to Bread for the World are **not** tax-deductible since our members lobby Congress on behalf of poor and hungry people. If you prefer to make a **tax-deductible** contribution to support research and education efforts (such as the Hunger Report, the ONE Campaign, and research on trade), please make out your check to Bread for the World Institute. You are welcome to request a copy of our latest financial report by contacting: Bread for the World, 50 F Street NW, Suite 500, Washington, DC 20001-1565, (202) 639-9400 or 1-800-822-7323 or visit **www.bread.org**.

If you are a resident of one of the states below, you may obtain financial information directly from the state agency: **FLORIDA** — A COPY OF THE OFFICIAL REGISTRATION AND FINANCIAL INFORMATION MAY BE OBTAINED FROM THE DIVISION OF CONSUMER SERVICES BY CALLING TOLL-FREE, (800) 435-7352 WITHIN THE STATE. REGISTRATION DOES NOT IMPLY ENDORSEMENT, APPROVAL OR RECOMMENDATION BY THE STATE. (SC-05787)  **MARYLAND** — For the cost of copies and postage: Office of the Secretary of State, State House, Annapolis, MD 21401. **MISSISSIPPI** — The official registration and financial information of Bread for the World may be obtained from the Mississippi Secretary of State's office by calling 1-888-236-6167. Registration by the Secretary of State does not imply endorsement.  **NEW JERSEY** — INFORMATION FILED WITH THE ATTORNEY GENERAL CONCERNING THIS CHARITABLE SOLICITATION MAY BE OBTAINED FROM THE ATTORNEY GENERAL OF THE STATE OF NEW JERSEY BY CALLING (973) 504-6215. REGISTRATION WITH THE ATTORNEY GENERAL DOES NOT IMPLY ENDORSEMENT.  **NEW YORK** — Office of the Attorney General, Department of Law, Charities Bureau, 120 Broadway, New York, NY 10271. **NORTH CAROLINA** — Financial information about this organization and a copy of its license are available from the State Solicitation Licensing Branch at (919) 807-2214. The license is not an endorsement by the state. **PENNSYLVANIA** — The official registration and financial information of Bread for the World may be obtained from the Pennsylvania Department of State by calling toll-free, within Pennsylvania, (800) 732-0999. Registration does not imply endorsement.  **VIRGINIA** — State Division of Consumer Affairs, Department of Agricultural and Consumer Services, P.O. Box 1163, Richmond, VA 23218. **WASHINGTON** — Charities Division, Office of the Secretary of State, State of Washington, Olympia, WA 98504-0422; 1-800-332-4483.  **WEST VIRGINIA** — Residents may obtain a summary from: Secretary of State, State Capitol, Charleston, WV 25305.                    12/06

*Registration with any of these states does not imply endorsement, approval or recommendation by the state.*

## How Special Appeals Are Different from Other Fundraising Letters

Most special appeals share the following characteristics.

### Six Characteristics of Special Appeal Packages

1. They contain specific time references because special appeals are usually mailed only once, through a narrow window on the calendar. To emphasize their urgency and underline how different they are from other solicitations from the same charity, most special appeals refer to passing conditions or one-time opportunities or circumstances—or, as in the case illustrated here, a particular holiday or season.

2. The ask amount is (normally) variable. Usually, a special appeal is segmented; that is, different versions of the appeal are sent to distinct groups of donors. For example, those who've never contributed more than $50 at any one time might be asked for $75, and previous donors of between $200 and $499 would be urged to send a minimum of $500.

3. In most cases, there are specific program references. These are, after all, special appeals. More often than not, the funds requested are to support one particular project or program.

4. Special appeal letters are frequently short—just one or two pages. Many low-budget organizations, as well as some that are well heeled, include few inserts. The assumption is that proven donors are well acquainted with the charity's work and need few reminders about its value. This assumption is questionable, but it's common nonetheless. Also, inserts such as brochures or flyers may make a mailing seem less personal, blunting its effect. (There are many exceptional circumstances that justify such inserts, however. The dream catcher package from St. Joseph's Indian School, shown in Chapter Eight, is a good example. But even the letter in that package is a short one.)

5. A special appeal is far more likely than a donor acquisition mailing to be personalized. It's also more likely to include *live postage* (stamps) and use high-quality paper. The extra expense is often considerable, and it's magnified by the lower volume that's also typical of mailings to proven donors. But the resulting higher cost per unit tends to be justified by the response, which is customarily about five to seven times as great as that from a donor acquisition mailing.

6. The copy is likely to be warm and personal. It's built on individual donor histories. A charity knows a few things about its proven donors,

such as when they started giving, the sizes of their largest gifts, and the number of gifts they've sent. In a well-run fundraising program, those things are reflected in the frequent special appeals mailed in search of additional support.

## Case Study: Human Service Agency Special Appeal

Human Service Agency (not its actual name) was typical of many other local human service providers all across America in its dependence on government contracts (60 percent of its $3.6 million budget) and the relatively modest scope of its efforts to raise funds from individuals (accounting for just 12 to 15 percent of the budget).

When Human Service Agency contracted with me to edit the letter displayed in Exhibit 12.2, the agency's one-person development shop consisted of a development director; a simple, off-the-shelf database management program; and a laser printer. The donor and prospect database hovered around three thousand, with about seven hundred donors actually making a gift in any year. Appeals were produced in-house, allowing the agency to print donors' names and addresses directly on the envelope rather than use labels.

The relatively simple database program didn't let the director refer to past giving in his letters. In any case, he was reluctant to write separate letters for renewals and prospects because it was so time consuming.

In a typical appeal, the agency used one letter for the entire database, although all letters were personalized ("Dear Mr. and Mrs. Jones"). Each board member sent the letter over his or her signature to personal friends and business contacts, with a handwritten postscript. About nine hundred names in the database were linked to one board member or another. Of the remaining, unlinked solicitation pieces, all but five hundred went to people who had received at least one mailing in the past. Unlinked letters went out over the board chairman's signature and without a postscript. All signatures were handwritten. Linked letters were mailed first class with commemorative postage stamps. Unlinked letters were mailed nonprofit bulk rate in envelopes with a preprinted indicia square. A six-page agency newsletter was sent out at some point before the appeal.

In other words, each package the agency mailed was intended to serve double duty: as both a special appeal (to proven donors) and an acquisition letter (to prospective donors). In fact, one letter usually can't adequately meet both needs, presenting the *general* case for making a first gift and the *special* case for additional support. Nonetheless, many nonprofits feel forced by limitations in their budgets or the size of their mailings to send a single version of a fundraising letter to both donors and prospects. This was one of those cases.

The text of the letter I was sent to edit is reproduced as Exhibit 12.2. My edited version is shown in Exhibit 12.3. In the original, the names of the agency's board members were listed on the left side of the letterhead. The full package also contained a laser-addressed, closed-face outer envelope; a preprinted, wallet-flap remittance envelope; and copies of two editorials, printed on a single two-sided sheet.

## Critique of the Original Letter

The Human Service Agency had done an outstanding job of wordsmithing; the letter required few changes in wording. The agency's staff told an engaging story and made a strong case for supporting agency work. The lead was involving, and the closing tied the case and the story together. All good.

The only significant problem in the body of the letter was that it didn't directly ask for money. It's very important that a fundraising letter come clean on the subject of money—the earlier and the more straightforwardly, the better.

Ideally, of course, the agency would insert a specific, appropriate ask amount in each individual letter. (That amount might be 15 percent or 20 percent higher than the donor's gift last year, for example.) Unfortunately, that wasn't feasible in this project: it was prohibitively costly to insert a specific amount of money tied to the donor's previous support. But a second-best alternative comes to mind: to ask for gifts within a certain range (say, $150, $400, or $1,000 or more). There's a pitfall in this approach, though: you've got to be sure not to send the same letter to everyone. You don't want to ask donors for less money than they've given before.

A third-best alternative is to ask for "a generous gift" or something else nonspecific. But make sure there's no question you're asking for money.

A lesser problem, occasioned by the shortness of the letter, perhaps, was that there was no P.S. With only the rarest of exceptions, I include one in every fundraising letter. Typically, that involves singling out some aspect of the appeal with high reader interest. So I added a P.S., and transferred one of the strongest elements of the agency's case to that location. In the case of the linked letters, board members could easily add either a P.P.S. or an unlabeled personal note.

**EXHIBIT 12.2**

## Original Combination Special Appeal and Acquisition Letter, Human Service Agency

Date

Name

Address

City/zip

Dear xxxxx,

<u>Jeffrey is going to see his dad today and he is terrified.</u>

Jeffrey is seven and hasn't seen his dad in three years. His parents were divorced four years ago in a bitter fight. First Jeffrey lived with his mom, and his dad visited him every week. Then his dad stopped coming because "seeing his ex-wife was too difficult." Now Jeffrey has a new stepfather and a new last name. And his dad wants to see him again.

If Jeffrey is lucky, the court will order supervised visits at the Human Service Agency visitors' facility. It's a cheerful, home-like place where Jeffrey can feel safe as he and his dad get to know each other again.

Many families turn to Human Service Agency—for supervised visits in custody cases or treatment for sexually abused children. For hot meals for frail seniors or safe child care when parents work. And for counseling when lives are devastated by conflict and abuse.

That's why I'm asking you to help Human Service Agency now. During these difficult economic times, the demand for services

**EXHIBIT 12.2 (*Continued*)**

has exploded. In the last six months, for example, the number of people in counseling has increased 40% over the previous six months. And 89 cents out of every dollar contributed directly benefits the families who need a helping hand.

I know that if you could help just one child like Jeffrey, you would. You and I agree that families are the backbone of our society and that successful families build a healthy and strong community. Won't you join me in making sure that no family is turned away for lack of funds? Jeffrey and his dad are counting on us to give them a second chance.

Sincerely,

Avery I. Person

Board Chairman

---

**EXHIBIT 12.3**

## Edited Combination Special Appeal and Acquisition Letter, Human Service Agency

---

Date

Name

Address

City/zip

Dear xxxxx,

Jeffrey is going to see his Dad today—and he's <u>terrified.</u>

Jeffrey is seven and hasn't seen his Dad in three years. His parents were divorced four years ago in a bitter fight.

First Jeffrey lived with his Mom, and his Dad visited him every week. Then his Dad stopped coming because "seeing his ex-wife was too difficult."

Now Jeffrey has a new stepfather and a new last name. And his Dad wants to see him again.

If Jeffrey is lucky, the court will order supervised visits at the Human Service Agency visitors' facility. It's <u>a cheerful, homey place</u> where Jeffrey can feel safe while he and his Dad get to know each other again.

Many families turn to Human Service Agency—for supervised visits in custody cases or treatment for sexually abused children. For hot meals for frail seniors, safe child care when parents work, or counseling when lives are devastated by conflict and abuse.

**EXHIBIT 12.3 (*Continued*)**

Ironically, despite the current boom, the <u>demand for our services has exploded.</u> In the last six months, for example, the number of people in counseling has increased 40% over the previous six months.

That's why I'm asking you to help Human Service Agency today with a tax-deductible gift of $XXX or more.

<u>I know that if you could help just one child like Jeffrey, you would.</u> You and I agree that families are the backbone of our society and that successful families build a healthy and strong community.

Will you join me in making sure that no family is turned away for lack of funds? Jeffrey and his Dad are counting on us to give them a second chance.

With high hopes,

Avery I. Person

Board Chairman

P.S. Your support for the Human Service Agency will make a big difference here in [name of town]. <u>89 cents out of every dollar</u> contributed directly benefits the families who need a helping hand.

The original writer seems to have struggled to squeeze this letter onto a single sheet. To me, it's far more important to tell the story—and use the space necessary to do so—than to hold to some arbitrary length limit. In this case, that resulted in a two-page letter, with slightly broader margins. (Incidentally, since I know letter length is often a controversial question among people unfamiliar with fundraising practice, I sliced up my own edited version and reduced the letter to a single page again when I did the original work.)

## Format Changes

I'm going to repeat here what I said to the Human Service Agency at the time. It's what I say to almost every local and regional nonprofit organization that gives me the opportunity: listing the members of the board of directors on the side of a fundraising letter is a distraction. And unless your agency is very different from most others, the directors are not nearly so well known as you—or they themselves—might think they are. (I'm supremely confident about this statement because I reviewed mounds of public opinion polling data firsthand quite a number of times during years of full-time involvement in local politics.)

So if you don't have a closetful of letterhead and a high wall of political resistance to moving the listings off the letterhead (for fundraising letters only), you could list the board members on the back of a reply device or—in some other appeal—of a brochure. A fallback position is to place the listings more unobtrusively, at the *bottom* of the first page of the letter, in the smallest type you can get away with.

As for the format of the text, you'll note in my edited version that I eliminated italics, using a limited amount of underlining instead, indented every paragraph, and broke up the text into smaller paragraphs. I made all of these changes to enhance the readability of the copy and make the letter seem a little more personal and less institutional.

## Outer Envelope

I very much liked the use of laser addressing on a closed-face envelope, as the agency had planned to do. But I thought that using a postal indicia would detract from the personalized character of the envelope. I strongly recommend either first-class stamps or a postage meter (at least for prospects who aren't linked to board members but are past donors nonetheless). Another alternative, which I don't favor highly but think superior to an indicia, is to use precanceled, nonprofit bulk mail stamps.

## Remittance Envelope

I'm not a big fan of *bang-tail,* or *wallet flap,* remittance envelopes like the one the Human Service Agency was planning to use. These are envelopes with long, rectangular flaps on the back, usually printed both inside and out. Results are usually better with a detached, personalized reply device (so the donor doesn't have to write out all the information) and a business reply envelope that's big enough to hold the reply device without folding.

The best reply devices are involving. They affirm the donor's eagerness to help (usually by using the word YES!) and repeat and underline the principal reason or reasons given in the letter for supporting the agency at this time. You can't achieve that with preprinted remittance envelopes.

The agency talked about a "partnership level" on the remittance envelope but mentioned the concept nowhere else. Perhaps the agency had explained it in an earlier letter but left the copy on the envelope (another reason not to preprint remittance envelopes).

# Chapter 13

# Asking for Year-End Contributions
## Making the Most of the Holiday Spirit

**FOR THE OVERWHELMING** majority of Americans, the final weeks of the calendar year are a time for giving. It's no accident that a hugely dispro-portional share of the funds that nonprofit organizations raise each year are realized in the several weeks before New Year's. Nor is it coincidental that virtually every nonprofit organization that has its fundraising act together mails a year-end appeal to its donors or members.

The business end of most year-end appeals resembles the Bread for the World response device reproduced in Exhibit 13.1. At least four elements show that this is obviously a year-end appeal to donors:

- It says so. You can't mistake the words "a special year-end gift." No subtlety here (and none called for).

- The ask amounts are high enough to suggest that the people to whom this appeal was mailed have a history of support for Bread for the World. Few nondonors would seriously consider gifts so generous.

- The offer of a tax-deductible option (which appears in the fine print on the reverse of this reply device) is likely to be of special interest because the end of the tax year is approaching.

- The appeal is personalized. This package cost Bread for the World a sig-nificant amount of money for data processing. It's unlikely the group would spend as much on a fundraising appeal to nondonors.

## How Year-End Appeals Are Different from Other Fundraising Letters

The end of the year is a special time for most U.S. nonprofit organizations. A spirit of generosity holds sway, and donors turn to thoughts of tax deduc-tions, including charitable giving. In fact, many of the donor motivations described in Chapter One—loneliness, to cite just one example—are felt most strongly during the year-end holidays.

**EXHIBIT 13.1**

## Year-End Appeal Response Device, Bread for the World

### *R E P L Y   M E M O R A N D U M*

```
TO:      David Beckmann
         President
         Bread for the World
         Washington, D.C.

FROM:    Mr. John Doe
         123 Any Street
         Any Town, AS 00000
```

I'm pleased to make a <u>special</u> <u>year-end</u> <u>gift</u>. And I'll be pleased to join in Bread for the World's efforts in the new year to win even greater debt relief for the world's poorest countries and a "fair share" for U.S. families who suffer from hunger:

[ ] $1,000 [ ] $500    [ ] $250    [ ] $_____

[ ]   I prefer to make a tax-deductible contribution to support the research and education efforts of Bread for the World Institute, and I've made out my check accordingly.

## Bread for the World
*Seeking Justice. Ending Hunger.*

1100 Wayne Avenue, Suite 1000
Silver Spring, MD 20910
1-800-82-BREAD

156396
04DOE

*Bread for the World Institute welcomes gifts of stocks and securities. These gifts may result in tax savings. To arrange for tranfers, please contact Diane Hunt, Director of Development, at 301-608-2400, ext. 245.*

RECYCLED & RECYCLABLE / PRINTED WITH SOY INK

60042

---

**EXHIBIT 13.1 (*Continued*)**

---

*Contributions to **Bread for the World** are not tax-deductible since its members lobby Congress on behalf of hungry people. Tax-deductible gifts may be made to **Bread for the World Institute** to support research and education.*

You are welcome to request a copy of our latest financial report by contacting: Bread for the World, 1100 Wayne Avenue, Suite 1000, Silver Spring, MD 20910, (301) 608-2400.

If you are a resident of one of the states below, you may obtain financial information directly from the state agency: **FLORIDA** — A COPY OF THE OFFICIAL REGISTRATION AND FINANCIAL INFORMATION MAY BE OBTAINED FROM THE DIVISION OF CONSUMER SERVICES BY CALLING TOLL-FREE, (800) 435-7352 WITHIN THE STATE. REGISTRATION DOES NOT IMPLY ENDORSEMENT, APPROVAL OR RECOMMENDATION BY THE STATE. **MARYLAND** — For the cost of copies and postage: Office of the Secretary of State, State House, Annapolis, MD 21401. **NEW JERSEY** — Information filed with the Attorney General concerning this charitable solicitation may be obtained from the Attorney General of the State of New Jersey by calling (201) 504-6215. Registration with the Attorney General does not imply endorsement. **NEW YORK** — Office of the Attorney General, Department of Law, Charities Bureau, 120 Broadway, New York, NY 10271. **NORTH CAROLINA** — FINANCIAL INFORMATION ABOUT THIS ORGANIZATION AND A COPY OF ITS LICENSE ARE AVAILABLE FROM THE STATE SOLICITATION LICENSING BRANCH AT (919) 733-4510. THE LICENSE IS NOT AN ENDORSEMENT BY THE STATE. **PENNSYLVANIA** — The official registration and financial information of Bread for the World may be obtained from the Pennsylvania Department of State by calling toll-free, within Pennsylvania, (800) 732-0999. Registration does not imply endorsement. **VIRGINIA** — State Division of Consumer Affairs, Department of Agricultural and Consumer Services, P.O. Box 1163, Richmond, VA 23209. **WASHINGTON** — Charities Division, Office of the Secretary of State, State of Washington, Olympia, WA 98504-0422; 1-800-332-4483. **WEST VIRGINIA** — Residents may obtain a summary from: Secretary of State, State Capitol, Charleston, WV 25305.

Registration with any of these states does not imply endorsement, approval or recommendation by the state.

---

Year-end appeals are a major source of support for the nation's nonprofit organizations, because an estimated 40 percent of all charitable giving takes place during the final three months of the year. These appeals can be either annual (or membership) renewal mailings or special appeals (seeking gifts for earmarked purposes). But the fundraising letters that charities mail during this time tend to exhibit most of the following six characteristics.

### Six Characteristics of Year-End Packages

1. There are usually references to the season (particularly in letters from religious organizations). The benefits of year-end tax deductions are commonly mentioned too. Often the two are connected.

2. Ask amounts are usually variable. The generosity of year-end giving makes it possible for most groups to invest a little more in personalizing their appeals.

3. For the same reasons, many charities spend more on producing their year-end appeals than they do on fundraising letters mailed at other times of the year—not just on personalization but also on paper stock, ink colors, and premiums, such as holiday greeting cards.

4. A favored theme is "looking back, looking forward." The widespread tendency in the United States to think about New Year's resolutions lends itself to this Janus-like approach.

5. More often than at other times of the year, charities may launch multi-part appeals, consisting of a series of two or three letters, perhaps even combined with a telephone call.

6. Year-end appeals are often mailed to large proportions of the donor file.

## Case Study: Hebrew Women's League End-of-Year Appeal

The draft text of this straightforward year-end appeal is shown in Exhibits 13.2 and 13.3. My edited version follows in Exhibits 13.4 and 13.5. Look at both versions, and you'll grasp the essence of what I did to strengthen this appeal:

- Changed the emphasis from "we" to "you."

- Altered the look of the letter, adding subheads, underlining sparingly, and switching typefaces from Times Roman to Courier.

- Dropped the credit card payment option. At the time I edited this letter, I was not recommending that clients include such an option. Although results varied from one organization to another, tests often showed that a credit card option lowered response. I now believe that is no longer so likely to be the case.

- I also reinforced the seasonal connections. In the first paragraph of the revised reply device in Exhibit 13.5, above the string of ask amounts, note the words used there: "200Y"(a placeholder to be changed to the actual upcoming year), "tax-deductible," "year-end." With these few straightforward words and a few relatively subtle changes in the letter itself, what was originally a generic special appeal became a year-end appeal.

- You'll note the abbreviation "P.S." at the conclusion of the draft letter. That's exactly how it appeared when I received the text—implied but not written.

**EXHIBIT 13.2**
# Original Year-End Appeal Letter, Hebrew Women's League

"It's like a house of cards. Right now it is standing, but I feel like the slightest breath of wind, the merest breeze could knock down a wall, a room or the whole structure."

A mother of two young boys talking about balancing her work and family responsibilities.

December 200X

Dear HWL Member:

Every day more and more American families juggle the demands of work and family commitments. And, in family after family, it is women who bear the major burden of this task. In one out of _____ families, women are the only adult parent in the home. In one out of _____ families they care for children and aging relatives. In one out of _____ families they have children and hold down a job. In one out of _____ families, they work and care for a frail elderly relative.

When I think of these American families, I think about all the talk we hear these days about strengthening the family, about how much of it is just talk. And, I know the difference, because our organization—the Hebrew Women's League—knows the difference between talk and action for American families. After all, come _____ , we will have been acting on behalf of families for 100 years.

We help. We help parents of young children give those children the gift of the joy of learning. HWL's Learning Is for Kiddies (LIKE) Program has become a national force in the arena of preparing children to succeed in school. We are now serving 9,000 families in 17 states and new requests for LIKE are dramatically increasing. Children and their families, educators, legislators and HWL members are forming an educational partnership that has become a force for the future.

We care. We know how parents feel when they leave their little children in child care and go off to work. Our American Family Project and the projects it nurtured are trying to make sure that affordable, quality day care is there for families.

**EXHIBIT 13.2 (Continued)**

We lead by stimulating community action. It mobilizes communities to help employers assist their employees with their child and elder care needs.

We stand up for what American families need. On January 15, 200Y, in every HWL community across the country, you will take part in a coordinated advocacy event for American families. On HWL's Women at Work Day, mayors and governors across America will be presented with "Food for Thought" lunchboxes filled with action information to help families care for their young and oldest members.

As 200X draws to a close and you consider the charitable contributions you want to make, please make a tax-deductible contribution . . . To support HWL's work for families. (Use the enclosed card to tell us where you want your money to go).

This letter also brings you my best wishes for 200Y . . . our Centennial year.

With my warmest regards,

Marsha

P.S.

**EXHIBIT 13.3**

# Original Year-End Appeal Reply Device, Hebrew Women's League

Hebrew Women's League, 255 East Lexington Avenue, New York, NY 10001

Dear Marsha,

☐  Yes, you may have my vote to support HWL's Family Agenda

    ☐  $100   ☐  $75   ☐  $50   ☐  Other $

I want you to use my donation to increase HWL's work with:

☐  LIKE (Learning Is for Kiddies) Program

☐  Work/Family Project—Putting family values on America's Corporate Agenda.

☐  Women at Work Day . . . January 15, 200Y, when we draw national attention to the dependent care needs of working parents.

☐  HWL's Advocacy on behalf of legislation such as the Family and Medical Leave Act, the Violence Against Women Act, Women's Apprenticeship Bill and the Comprehensive Children's Initiative.

☐  You decide where it's most needed for HWL's Family Agenda.

Card # _____

☐  Visa  ☐  MasterCard  Expiration Date _____

Signature _____

Please make checks payable to Hebrew Women's League. Contributions may be charged to credit cards. Fill in your card number, expiration date and signature above. All contributions are tax-deductible to the extent allowed by law. Your canceled check is your receipt.

**EXHIBIT 13.4**

## Edited Year-End Appeal Letter, Hebrew Women's League

"It's like a house of cards. Right now it is standing, but I feel like the slightest breath of wind, the merest breeze could knock down a wall, a room or the whole structure."

—A mother of two young boys, talking about balancing her work and family responsibilities

December 200X

Dear Friend of American Families:

As a member of the Hebrew Women's League, you know the difference between talk and action when it comes to family values. Because you're already taking action.

** <u>You help.</u> **

Your membership support for HWL helps parents give their young children the joy of learning through the Learning Is for Kiddies Program (LIKE).

This model program has become a national force in the arena of preparing children to succeed in school. With your generous help, we're now serving over 9,000 families in 17 states—and new requests for LIKE are increasing dramatically.

Children and their families, educators, legislators and HWL members are forming an educational partnership that has become a force for a more hopeful future.

** <u>You care.</u> **

You know how parents feel when they leave their little children in inadequate child care arrangements and go off to work. Your American Family Project and the projects it nurtured are trying to make sure that affordable, quality care is there for families.

** <u>You lead.</u> **

As an HWL member, you're taking the lead by stimulating community action. Your Women at Work Project helps employers assist their employees with their child and elder care needs.

** <u>You're standing up for American families.</u> **

On January 15, 200Y, HWL members across the country will take part in a coordinated advocacy event for American families.

**EXHIBIT 13.4** (*Continued*)

On HWL's Women at Work Day, mayors and governors across America will be presented with "Food for Thought" lunchboxes filled with action information to help families care for their young and oldest members.

As 200X draws to a close and you consider how you'll direct your year-end charitable giving, please consider how much more you can do to help American families by sending a special, tax-deductible year-end gift to the Hebrew Women's League.

As you consider the size of your year-end gift, please think about the magnitude and the importance of the challenge you and I are facing:

Every day, more and more American families must juggle the demands of work and family commitments. And, in family after family, it is women who bear the major burden of this task.

In one out of xx families, a woman is the only adult parent in the home.

Women in one out of every xx families care for children and aging relatives, in one out of xx they have children and hold down jobs.

Please take a moment right now to write as generous a check as you can—and return it to me today in the enclosed self-addressed envelope.

As I look ahead to our Family Agenda for 200Y, I have to calculate how much funding will be available for each of our urgent and critical action programs. It will help so very much if I can have your year-end gift in hand by the 31st of December!

You may use the enclosed card to tell us which of the League's most urgent programs you want your gift to support.

With my warmest regards, and my best wishes for your health and happiness in 200Y,

[sign "Marsha"]

Marsha [Lastname]

P.S. Come 200Y the Hebrew Women's League will have been acting on behalf of American families for 100 years! To commemorate the beginning of our Centennial year, and give an extra boost to our Family Agenda for 200Y, will you consider a special, tax-deductible year-end gift of $100 or more?

**EXHIBIT 13.5**

# Edited Year-End Appeal Reply Device, Hebrew Women's League

*To Marsha [Lastname], Hebrew Women's League*

Dear Marsha,

Yes, you have my support for the Hebrew Women's League's Family Agenda for 200Y! To help meet the most urgent needs, I'm rushing you my special, tax-deductible year-end gift in the amount of:

☐ $100     ☐ $75     ☐ $50     ☐ Other $_____

Please use my gift to give an extra boost to your work on behalf of American families in the following area:

☐ Learning Is for Kiddies Program (LIKE)

☐ American Family Project (putting family values on America's corporate agenda)

☐ Women at Work Day, January 15, 200Y

☐ Advocacy (for legislation such as the Family and Medical Leave Act and the Violence Against Women Act)

☐ Please put my gift to work where it's most urgently needed.

*Please complete and return this form with your check by December 31st.*

*Please make your check payable to HWL and mail in the enclosed self-addressed envelope to: Hebrew Women's League, 255 East Lexington Avenue, New York, NY 10001. All contributions are tax-deductible to the extent allowed by law. Your cancelled check is your receipt. Thank you very much!*

# Chapter 14

# Recruiting Monthly Sustainers
## Offering Small Donors a Chance for Greater Impact

**FOR A GREAT MANY** donors, the option of making modest monthly contributions to a favored nonprofit organization is an attractive proposition. Some U.S. charities persuade 5 percent, 10 percent, or more of their donors to *convert* to this lucrative arrangement—lucrative because a monthly gift of $10 amounts to much more in the course of a year than infrequent gifts of $25. In much of the rest of the world, monthly (or *regular* or *committed* giving) is the rule rather than the exception. Even though there is much greater resistance to monthly giving here in the United States—due probably to our more complex banking system and to deeper distrust of nonprofit organizations—monthly gifts may still constitute one-third or more of a charity's small-donor income. Monthly contributors in the United States are typically called *sustainers* or *pledge donors.* They are often converted by a telephone call or mailing of the sort typified by the Bread for the World letter and response device reproduced in Exhibit 14.1. This is unquestionably a sustainer conversion mailing because

- The words "each month," "monthly gift," or "monthly giving" appear seven times on the front side of this appeal. It could hardly be more obvious.

- The copy dwells on the convenience and impact of monthly gifts rather than on the specific programs that constitute Bread for the World's work.

- The sustainer program has its own name, Baker's Dozen—itself clearly a sign of the monthly character of the program.

- The suggested gift amounts on the reply device are modest, even though joining this program will, in effect, make members into significant donors because of the cumulative impact of their gifts.

- The means of payment is unorthodox, requiring that members authorize their banks to transfer funds directly from their accounts into Bread for the World's account.

**EXHIBIT 14.1**

## Sustainer Invitation Letter and Response Device, Bread for the World

**Bread for the World**
*Seeking Justice. Ending Hunger.*

50 F Street NW, Suite 500
Washington, DC 20001
1-800-822-7323    www.bread.org

BFW07YA/Pkg. 5/New Member Follow-Up
Ms. Jane Doe
123 Main Street
Anytown, AS 11111

June 4, 2007

Dear Ms. Jane Doe,

You joined Bread for the World with a generous gift in January 2007. I'm grateful for your financial support and citizen action—you're making a real difference in the lives of hungry people.

I'm writing now to invite you to join the many other Bread for the World members who participate in our Baker's Dozen monthly giving program. By pre-authorizing your bank to send contributions each month, you ensure that your Bread for the World membership is automatically renewed—saving you time and trouble.

And because we save on paper and gift processing costs, <u>your</u> monthly contributions <u>will accomplish even more</u>—in effect, creating a 13<sup>th</sup> gift or a "baker's dozen." With just a small monthly gift (as little as $10), you will end up making a significant contribution in our effort to help end hunger.

Thank you again for your membership support—and for giving thought to this invitation.

Sincerely,

*Kari Bert*

Kari Bert
Development Assistant

Contributions to **Bread for the World** are not tax-deductible since its members lobby Congress on behalf of poor and hungry people. Contributions to **Bread for the World Institute** are tax-deductible and support research and education efforts.

## Join Baker's Dozen—and turn 12 gifts into 13!

When you pre-authorize your bank to send monthly contributions automatically, the money saved in gift processing over one year equals the value of a 13th gift— a baker's dozen.

☐ I'd like to join the Baker's Dozen. I've enclosed my first monthly gift and have signed the authorization below.

**Please direct my gifts to:** ☐ Bread for the World   ☐ BFW Institute

☐ **$30**   ☐ **$20**   ☐ **$15**   ☐ **$_____**

**Baker's Dozen**
*Monthly giving to end hunger*

BFW07YA/Pkg. 5/New Member Follow-Up
Ms. Jane Doe
123 Main Street
Anytown, AS 11111

44237708
BINV

Please see ▶
reverse side
for important
information.

**Signature** _____ **Date** _____
    *REQUIRED FOR BANK AUTHORIZATION*

RECYCLED & RECYCLABLE / SOY INK   7-YA2E

**EXHIBIT 14.1 (*Continued*)**

# Bread for the World's 2007 Campaign

In 2007, the U.S. Congress is expected to reauthorize—or renew—the farm bill. This piece of legislation will have an impact on everyone in this country—everyone who eats, and especially those who struggle to have enough to eat. Even people outside the United States feel its impact. The farm bill is only renewed every five years. This is an important moment and a critical opportunity to fight hunger in the United States and around the world.

Bread for the World's 2007 legislative campaign—*Seeds of Change: Help Farmers. End Hunger.*—will urge Congress to provide better and broader support for U.S. farmers, strengthen communities in rural America, help hungry people in this country afford a sufficient and nutritious diet, and support the efforts of small-scale farmers in developing countries to sell their crops and feed their families.

Please write or call your representative and senators in Washington, D.C. Urge them to improve our nation's farm policies to help farmers and rural communities here in the United States—as well as in Africa and other parts of the world that face the threat of hunger.

**How to contact your member of Congress:**

U.S. House of Representatives
Washington, D.C. 20515

U.S. Senate
Washington, D.C. 20510

Capitol Switchboard: **202-224-3121**

**Visit www.bread.org for updates about pending legislation and the names of your members of Congress.**

**If you have questions or concerns about your membership, please call 1-800-822-7323, ext. 132, M-F, 8:30-4:30 (Eastern Time) or e-mail memberservices@bread.org.**

## *How You Can Make a Bequest*

You may find the following wordings to be helpful. These brief descriptions are not intended as legal or financial advice; an attorney or other professional advisor should be consulted.

### ■ The General Bequest

"I give and bequeath to Bread for the World, Inc. (or Bread for the World Institute, Inc.) of 50 F Street NW, Suite 500, Washington, DC, 20001, the sum of $_____ (or a specific item of property, such as real estate, stocks or bonds, etc.) to be used as its board of directors determines."

### ■ Percentage Bequest

"I give and bequeath to Bread for the World, Inc. (or Bread for the World Institute, Inc.) of 50 F Street NW, Suite 500, Washington, DC, 20001, _____% (name a specific percentage) of the total value of my estate to be used as its board of directors determines."

### ■ Residual Bequest

You may leave the residue of your estate after you've provided for family members and other beneficiaries. "I give and bequeath to Bread for the World, Inc. (or Bread for the World Institute, Inc.) of 50 F Street NW, Suite 500, Washington, DC, 20001, the residue of my estate, to be used as its board of directors determines."

### ■ Income Only to be Used

"I give and bequeath to the Endowment of Bread for the World, Inc. (or Bread for the World Institute, Inc.) of 50 F Street NW, Suite 500, Washington, DC, 20001, the sum of $_____ to be invested and reinvested so that the income only may be used as its board of directors determines."

*For more information, please contact Molly Pearce or Steven Miller at 1-800-822-7323. All decisions to make charitable bequests are voluntary and revocable.*

# How Sustainer Invitations Are Different from Other Fundraising Letters

Joining the monthly sustainer program of a nonprofit organization requires a special commitment that relatively few donors demonstrate, and it's often difficult for a charity to convert its donors to this highly advantageous arrangement. Many organizations find that the response to direct mail conversion letters is not high enough to justify the cost. Telephone conversion is more typical—probably because prospects for monthly giving programs have many questions that can't necessarily be answered satisfactorily by mail. Still, some nonprofits continue to find conversion mailings cost-effective. These letters typically share some or all of the following six attributes.

### Six Characteristics of Sustainer Invitation Packages

1. Sustainer conversion mailings are rarely sent to all small donors. Normally, a nonprofit will select only those donors it believes show the greatest promise of accepting the invitation to join a sustainer program. They tend to be donors who (a) are of long standing and can thus be presumed to be committed to continuing their support and (b) consistently give small and frequent contributions. In some larger organizations, for example, only those donors who've shown a pattern of giving three or more gifts per year will be deemed strong prospects for monthly giving.

2. The emphasis tends to be on the prospect's relationship with the organization rather than on the issues or programs in which the organization is involved.

3. A principal argument for joining a monthly giving program is that it will allow a donor to achieve greater impact—partly because of the reliability and predictability of her gifts but also because the cumulative amount will allow her to become, in effect, a "major donor" despite the modest size of each contribution.

4. The letter (or the phone script) devotes as much attention as necessary to explaining the program's logistics, which often raise questions in donors' minds.

5. Unlike the example in Exhibit 14.1, most sustainer conversions emphasize that a monthly sustainer may opt out of the program at any time. This gives donors a sense that they remain in control even though payments will be made automatically.

6. There is frequently some incentive offered to donors to join a sustainer program. Sometimes the incentive is tangible—a coffee mug,

T-shirt, or lapel pin, for example—and sometimes it consists largely of convenience. In any event, a sustainer invitation will emphasize the personal benefits of joining the program.

## Case Study: People for the Environment Monthly Sustainer Invitation

The letter and reply device appearing in Exhibits 14.2 and 14.3 were parts of a monthly sustainer invitation package I wrote for an organization I'm calling People for the Environment (PFE). This package depicts what I believe is the single most important way to persuade donors to give more money: launching a monthly giving program.

Almost every nonprofit can benefit from a monthly giving program. As I mentioned earlier, for many charities that depend on small gifts from donors recruited through the mail, monthly giving or sustainer programs can bring in as much as one-third of their contributed income. But take care about using this letter as an example. Launching and managing such a program entails significant investment and continuing attention. It's not an effort to be undertaken lightly—certainly not as a short-term excuse to ask donors for larger gifts.

This package was conceived as an invitation from PFE's executive director to more than half of the organization's 80,000 members. Its purpose was to ask them to become charter members in the Friends of the Environment, a new monthly sustainer program featuring six categories or levels of support, from $10 per month to $50 per month. Those who "cannot join . . . as a Charter Member" were to have the option of making one-time gifts. These donors were to be encouraged to exceed their highest previous contribution (HPC) to PFE.

Eventually every level of membership in the program would offer unique benefits or services. Initially, the concrete benefits of charter membership at any level were to consist of just four items:

- A personalized certificate
- An "'insider's-only' newsletter" compiled by PFE staff and tentatively titled *PFE in Perspective*, which would be published at least six times per year
- Listing as a charter member in *PFE in Perspective*
- Automatic renewal of PFE membership—with freedom from regular and frequent fundraising letters (except the year-end appeal and any emergency package)

**EXHIBIT 14.2**

# Monthly Sustainer Invitation Letter, People for the Environment

DAY OF WEEK, DATE

NAME1
NAME2
ADDRESS 1
ADDRESS 2
ADDRESS 3

Dear SALU,

I get lots of questions from committed PFE members like you.

I'm often asked whether there's any way a PFE member can do more to help heal the earth. Something that a busy person without a whole lot of money can do—without changing jobs, or flying to Brazil, or going into debt.

Something that will really make a <u>difference</u>.

Concerned members like you also frequently ask me what we can do to reduce PFE's fundraising costs. Our fundraising program is already one of the most efficient, but I share your concern to make it even more efficient. So I, too, have asked whether there isn't some way to send fewer fundraising letters—and still raise enough money to meet PFE's growing budget.

These are questions we wrestle with all the time at PFE.

Now, finally, we've come up with an answer to both these important questions. It's a way for you to <u>multiply the impact</u> of your PFE membership—and help us save substantially on fundraising costs.

I'm writing you today because I want you to be among the first to know about this exciting opportunity.

The new program is called the PFE <u>Friends of the Environment</u>. I invite you to get in on the ground floor.

As a Charter Member of the Friends of the Environment, you'll receive special, <u>additional</u> membership benefits and privileges.

More important, though, your participation in this important new program will help sustain PFE's worldwide <u>leadership role</u> in protecting wildlife and the environment.

Here's what the Friends of the Environment is all about:

**EXHIBIT 14.2 (*Continued*)**

Whenever I need to raise money to support a crucial PFE program like saving the rainforests or countering threats to endangered species, I know I can count on you. PFE members are extremely generous. You've always come through in the past.

But raising money by mail takes time, so it's tough to assemble the necessary funds to respond quickly to a sudden, unexpected crisis.

For example, when [INSERT EXAMPLE OF EMERGENCY HERE], there wasn't time for me to send you a letter to ask for your financial support.

But there was no choice. I simply had to take action. I know you would've <u>insisted</u> I do!

Still, [THAT ACTION] took money. And, instead of taking your support for granted, I sure could've used a "ready-response" reserve fund.

Also, some PFE programs are long-term efforts, requiring years and years of dedicated work. But it's wasteful to write you when there's no new news.

Our work on the landmark [ENVIRONMENTAL LEGISLATION] is a perfect example. That bill included an innovative amendment—drafted by PFE—that will permanently [ACCOMPLISH SOMETHING VERY IMPRESSIVE].

But many <u>years</u> of work by PFE staff members preceded that crucial amendment. We had to fund their work, day in and day out, during times when public awareness of [THAT ISSUE] wasn't very high.

And that points to another important truth about our work: PFE programs sometimes just aren't very popular!

For instance, PFE played a leading role in [COMBATTING A MAJOR WORLDWIDE ENVIRONMENTAL PROBLEM].

But when PFE scientists began their work on [THAT PROBLEM] years earlier, the issue was hardly known outside scientific circles. And few people—except a handful of dedicated environmentalists such as you—were ready to step forward with financial support.

As you can see, the crux of the matter is this: PFE needs a stable, <u>dependable</u> source of funds. Money we can count on, month after month, through good times and bad.

- Page 2 -

**EXHIBIT 14.2 (*Continued*)**

We need the resources to help us <u>meet emergencies</u> and continue our work on a <u>broad range</u> of environmental issues—without interruption.

That's why we've decided to launch the Friends of the Environment. And that's why I'm turning to you again.

To become a Charter Member in the Partnership, what I need from you today is a commitment to make a small, monthly gift to PFE—as little as $10 per month.

Here's how the program will work:

o As soon as I receive your check in payment of your initial monthly gift, I'll see to it that your name is removed from the list of those PFE members who are sent regular, frequent fundraising appeals.

o You'll continue to receive the PFE newsletter. But I'll also see to it that you're mailed the premier issue—and every succeeding issue—of <u>PFE in Perspective</u>. This is a very special new "insiders-only" newsletter we'll be sending at least six times per year—exclusively to members of our Board of Trustees and a few others.

o Your name will appear in the Charter Membership Roll published in <u>PFE in Perspective</u>.

o And I'll inscribe and mail you a certificate of appreciation for enrolling as a Charter Member in the Friends of the Environment.

o Then, each month thereafter—unless you decide to cancel—you'll receive a reminder from us with a remittance envelope enclosed.

As you can see at a glance, the Friends of the Environment answers both the challenges I mentioned at the beginning of this letter:

(1) Your <u>reliable</u>, monthly support will help PFE continue—and expand—our worldwide leadership role in protecting the environment.

(2) You'll substantially <u>lower our fundraising costs</u>—and reduce our consumption of paper—by enabling us to mail you fewer solicitations.

- Page 3 -

**EXHIBIT 14.2 (*Continued*)**

I hope you'll accept this opportunity today to become a Charter Member of the Friends of the Environment.

Your dependable monthly gift of $50, $25, $20, $15, $12, or even $10 will multiply the impact of your membership in PFE manyfold.

I urge you to consider those gifts an investment in your future—and the future of your children and your children's children. They're an investment in the future of our planet.

Thank you sincerely for hearing me out.

In high hopes,


Barton Snodgrass
Executive Director


P.S. If you accept Charter Membership in the Friends of the Environment at the level of $20 per month or more, I'll be pleased to send you a copy of xxxx as a token of my appreciation. This magnificent volume . . .

- Page 4 -

**EXHIBIT 14.3**

# Monthly Sustainer Invitation Reply Device, People for the Environment

CHARTER MEMBERSHIP ENROLLMENT FORM
People for the Environment
Friends of the Environment

Prepared expressly for PFE Member(s):

NAME1

NAME2

ADDRESS 1

ADDRESS 2

ADDRESS 3

YES, I am pleased to accept Barton Snodgrass's invitation to join PFE's exciting new Friends of the Environment as a Charter Member.

I want to play an active, ongoing part in helping PFE sustain its leadership role over the long haul—and rapidly respond to new threats to the environment as soon as they arise.

☐ I'm enclosing my check in payment of my first monthly contribution, and I pledge to send the same amount each month. Please bill me. I understand I may cancel this arrangement at any time.

☐ $50   ☐ $25   ☐ $20   ☐ $15   ☐ $12   ☐ $10   ☐ $_____

_____         _____

Signature: NAME 1                                        Date signed

☐ I cannot join the Friends of the Environment as a Charter Member. But here's my special contribution to PFE in the amount of:

☐ $[HPC+50%]   ☐ $[HPC]   ☐ $_____

**EXHIBIT 14.3 (*Continued*)**

Friends of the Environment

Charter Membership Benefits

o  Help PFE sustain its worldwide leadership role in protecting the environment.

o  Help PFE reduce its fundraising costs.

o  Complimentary subscription to *PFE in Perspective,* a newsletter published at least six times per year exclusively for PFE's most loyal and involved supporters.

o  Your name removed from the list of those who are mailed regular and frequent fundraising letters.

o  Listing in the Charter Membership Roll in *PFE in Perspective.*

o  Automatic renewal of your PFE membership for as long as you remain a member of the Friends of the Environment.

o  Special certificate acknowledging your Charter Membership.

o  You may cancel your participation at any time.

And you'll continue to receive the PFE newsletter, and enjoy all the other benefits and privileges of your PFE membership.

Six Ways to join PFE's Friends of the Environment:

☐ Friend—$10 per month        ☐ Leader*—$20 per month

☐ Colleague—$12 per month     ☐ Patron*—$25 per month

☐ Associate—$15 month         ☐ Founder*—$50 per month

* If you accept Charter Membership in the Friends of the Environment at any of these levels, we will be pleased to send you as a token of our deep appreciation, a copy of xxxxxxxx. This magnificent, full-color volume is xxxxx and retails for $xxxxx.

In addition, anyone who joined at the level of at least $20 per month would receive a complimentary copy of a highly prized coffee-table book.

Here's a physical description of the full package sent to prospective sustainers (the letter and reply device are the ones shown in Exhibits 14.2 and 14.3):

1. *Outer envelope.* This was to be a Number 9 (slightly smaller than a standard business envelope), nonwindow (closed-face) envelope addressed by laser printer. The paper stock would be off-white (obviously recycled). Letters sent to the most loyal and generous members would bear first-class stamps; other prospects would receive their letters with bulk postage. In the upper-left-hand corner, the PFE name, logo, and return address would be printed in color, with the executive director's name typed above it. Lower, on the left, there was to be a bold teaser: **New Opportunity for PFE Members.**

2. *Letter.* The letter would be four pages long, printed in the format of standard PFE letterhead, with page 1 laser-personalized if possible. Text was to be printed in black, with the PFE logo and the signature on page 4 printed in dark blue. To fit the Number 9 envelope, the paper stock would be 8 by 10 inches, and it was to match the color and weight of the paper in the envelope.

3. *Reply device.* This form, headed "Charter Membership Enrollment Form," was to be laser-personalized and printed on 8-by-10-inch, tinted, recycled stock different from that of the letter and the carrier. (The form was to match the reply envelope.) It was to be printed in three colors: black text, plus the blue of the PFE logo, with a green "Friends of the Environment" name and logo. The list of membership benefits would appear on a perforated, detachable panel (to reduce the size of reply device so that it would fit neatly into the reply envelope). Only three specific ask amounts were to be offered to any individual member. Amounts would be assigned based on giving history.

4. *Reply envelope.* This was to be addressed to "Personal Attention: Barton Snodgrass [the executive director]." In letters sent to all active donors, the reply envelope would bear live postage (either two or three stamps or one commemorative stamp); others would receive business-reply envelopes instead. The reply envelope was to be a Number 6¾ or Number 7, with the paper stock matching that of the reply device. In either case, the "Friends" name and logo was to be printed on the left side.

This initial sustainer invitation package was to be followed up, within a month of the mail date, with telephone calls to at least the most promising segments of the file. It was also to be adapted into an invitation sent to every new member shortly after a welcome package was sent. This version of the sustainer conversion package was to be sent only to proven donors. The one sent to new donors was to be created later.

# Chapter 15

# Soliciting High-Dollar Gifts
## Framing the Case for Major Contributions

**DIRECT MAIL FUNDRAISING** typically attracts modest gifts, usually of less than $100. Within the last couple of decades, however, direct mail fundraisers have come to understand that similar techniques, carefully honed for greater impact on upscale donors, can generate gifts by mail of $500, $1,000, or more. The so-called high-dollar appeals that seek (and increasingly yield) such gifts are fast becoming a fixture in the pantheon of nonprofit fundraising.

Bread for the World used the reply device in Exhibit 15.1 in a high-dollar appeal that's typical of the genre in many ways:

- Clearly, this is a leadership appeal—a request that's far out of the ordinary, if only because it asks for unusually large sums of money. Bread for the World is asking John Doe to enroll in its Founder's Society by raising the total of his gifts for the year to $2,500.

- This appeal requests a gift of $1,500 or more—obviously untypical of direct mail fundraising letters.

- The importance of the $1,500 ask amount is highlighted by the final laser-printed line, which makes clear that gifts at this "leadership level" are recognized in the Bread for the World Annual Report.

- There are two donor options, which are infrequent in appeals to small donors because they may cause confusion (and thus delay). This is a special case, however. The Internal Revenue Service requires the disclosure that most gifts to Bread for the World are not tax deductible, because the group engages in lobbying on behalf of poor and hungry people. Gifts are tax-deductible only if made payable to the Bread for the World Institute. The organization offers this option knowing that the distinction is important to some donors.

**EXHIBIT 15.1**

## High-Dollar Appeal Reply Device, Bread for the World

### R E P L Y   M E M O R A N D U M

```
FROM:   Mr. John Doe
        123 Any Street
        Any Town, AS 00000


TO:     Diane Hunt
        Director of Development
        BREAD FOR THE WORLD
        Washington, D.C.


I'm pleased to renew my annual support of Bread for
the World at a leadership level.

[ ]   I wish to be a member of the Founder's Society,
      and I've enclosed a gift of $1,500 so that my
      total 1999 contributions are $2,500.

[ ]   At this time I prefer to make a special gift:

      [ ] $250      [ ] $100      [ ] $_____


[ ]   I wish to make a tax-deductible gift to support
      the research and education efforts of Bread for
      the World Institute, and I've made out my check
      accordingly.

[ ]   I prefer that my gift remain anonymous and not
      be recognized in the Annual Report.
```

### Bread for the World
*Seeking Justice. Ending Hunger.*
1100 Wayne Avenue, Suite 1000
Silver Spring, MD 20910
1-800-82-BREAD

```
                                              0
                                          01DOE
```

RECYCLED & RECYCLABLE / PRINTED WITH SOY INK    60012

---

**EXHIBIT 15.1** (*Continued*)

---

You are welcome to request a copy of our latest financial report by contacting:
Bread for the World, 1100 Wayne Avenue, Suite 1000, Silver Spring, MD 20910,
(301) 608-2400.

If you are a resident of one of the states below, you may obtain financial information directly
from the state agency:   **FLORIDA** — A COPY OF THE OFFICIAL REGISTRATION AND
FINANCIAL INFORMATION  MAY BE OBTAINED FROM THE DIVISION OF CONSUMER
SERVICES BY  CALLING TOLL-FREE, (800) 435-7352 WITHIN THE STATE. REGISTRATION
DOES NOT IMPLY ENDORSEMENT, APPROVAL OR RECOMMENDATION BY THE STATE.
**MARYLAND** — For the cost of copies and postage: Office of the Secretary of State, State
House, Annapolis, MD 21401.   **NEW JERSEY** — Information filed with the Attorney General
concerning this charitable solicitation may be obtained from the Attorney General of the
State of New Jersey by calling (201) 504-6215. Registration with the Attorney General does
not imply endorsement.   **NEW YORK** — Office of the Attorney General, Department of Law,
Charities Bureau, 120 Broadway, New York, NY 10271.   **NORTH CAROLINA** — FINANCIAL
INFORMATION ABOUT THIS ORGANIZATION AND A COPY OF ITS LICENSE ARE AVAIL-
ABLE FROM THE STATE SOLICITATION LICENSING BRANCH AT (919) 733-4510. THE
LICENSE IS NOT AN ENDORSEMENT BY THE STATE.   **PENNSYLVANIA** — The official
registration and financial information of Bread for the World may be obtained from the
Pennsylvania Department of State by calling toll-free, within Pennsylvania, (800) 732-0999.
Registration does not imply endorsement.   **VIRGINIA** — State Division of Consumer Affairs,
Department of Agricultural and Consumer Services, P.O. Box 1163, Richmond, VA 23209.
**WASHINGTON** — Charities Division, Office of the Secretary of State, State of Washington,
Olympia, WA 98504-0422; 1-800-332-4483. **WEST VIRGINIA** — Residents may obtain a
summary from: Secretary of State, State Capitol, Charleston, WV 25305.

Registration with any of these states does not imply endorsement, approval or
recommendation by the state.

**Questions or concerns about your membership?**
**Call 1-800-82-BREAD (1-800-822-7323)**

---

# How High-Dollar Appeals Are Different from Other Fundraising Letters

A high-dollar package may be used in the service of a great many fundraising purposes, even recruiting new donors. More typically, however, these high-cost efforts are directed at a nonprofit's most generous and responsive supporters—as special appeals or upgrade efforts, for example. But whether used in mailings to the *housefile* (the list of previous donors) or in acquisition mailings, high-dollar fundraising letters usually share at least five characteristics.

### Five Characteristics of High-Dollar Fundraising Packages

1. The ask amount is high. And that amount isn't just the highest in a string where the lowest suggested amounts let a donor off easy. If there's a choice of gift levels, every choice is a big number.

2. The packaging is often very expensive. These are upscale appeals, designed to communicate a feeling of exclusivity. High-dollar packages accomplish this aim by looking and feeling different from most other direct mail fundraising letters. Sometimes they're different in

size, shape, texture, and color as well as in their elegant design. High-dollar appeals embody what Hollywood calls *high production values.*

3. Almost always, high-dollar appeals are personalized, and often extensively so. Your chances of obtaining a $1,000 gift are slim with a letter beginning "Dear Friend."

4. The copy is often upscale in tone and approach. Many high-dollar fundraising letters are built around snob appeal or exclusivity (for example, offering invitations to "exclusive" or "intimate" events or societies).

5. Most important, a strong high-dollar appeal features a uniquely appropriate marketing concept: an offer to match the high-level ask. A genuine high-dollar letter doesn't just ask for a larger sum of money than other fundraising letters do; it supplies the donor with a special and credible reason to send the amount of money asked for. In other words, a high-dollar letter has a marketing concept all its own. (See Chapter Six for a detailed discussion of this concept.) And to reinforce the marketing concept, there may be only a single specified gift level. Often the offer involves a "gift club" or "giving society" that entails unique benefits or privileges.

## Case Study: Make-A-Wish Foundation High-Dollar Appeal

The fundraising package illustrated in Exhibits 15.2 to 15.5 is typical in several ways of the high-dollar packages my colleagues and I have been mailing for nearly thirty years:

- Like so many of those packages, it is mailed in an oversized (9-by-12-inch) carrier envelope bearing live postage stamps.

- The address is printed on a large, pressure-sensitive mailing label, affixed to the front of the carrier, rather than directly on the carrier itself.

- The contents of the package are held together with a paper clip, which betrays the hands-on treatment this appeal required.

- The letter is personalized—not just by virtue of its use of the name and address of the donor but also through the use in the text of the amount of the donor's most recent gift.

- The reply device is personalized.

- The enclosure—a "proposal"—is both personalized and prepared expressly for this particular mailing. There's no off-the-shelf brochure or flyer in this package!

What is atypical of this high-dollar package is the range of possible gift levels. Typically, a high-dollar package will focus on one giving level—most often, the minimum contribution required to join an annual giving club or society. In this case, the levels correspond with categories defined within that society. And the package makes no mention of the annual giving commitment that normally is associated with a high-dollar club.

---

**EXHIBIT 15.2**

## High-Dollar Appeal Address Label, Make-A-Wish Foundation

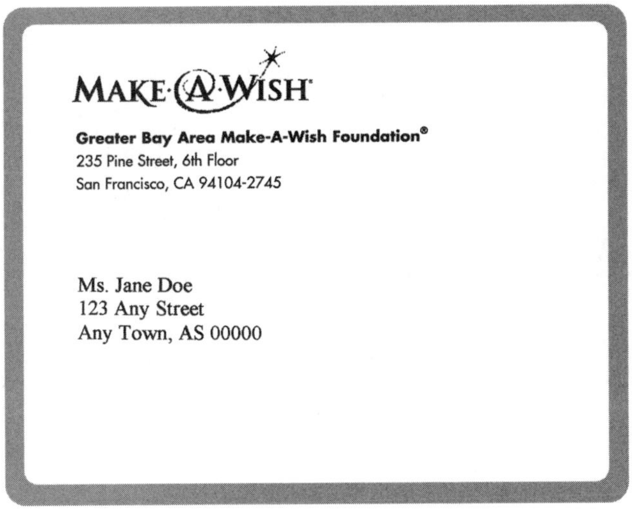

MAKE·(A)·WISH

**Greater Bay Area Make-A-Wish Foundation®**
235 Pine Street, 6th Floor
San Francisco, CA 94104-2745


Ms. Jane Doe
123 Any Street
Any Town, AS 00000

**EXHIBIT 15.3**

# High-Dollar Appeal Letter, Make-A-Wish Foundation

November 7, 2006

Ms. Jane Doe
123 Any Street
Any Town, AS 00000

Dear Ms. Doe,

Thank you for your continued support of the Greater Bay Area Make-A-Wish Foundation.

As one of our most loyal donors, your leadership giving helps make hundreds of special wishes come true every year. Thank you for making this possible.

As you can imagine, the awareness and success of Make-A-Wish is growing. And we're receiving more and more wish requests each year. On top of that, the average cost of a wish continues to increase.

That's why I'm writing today to ask you to consider the enclosed funding proposal —to invest in the Make-A-Wish Foundation, and to help ensure that our resources keep pace with children's wishes in the coming year.

Ms. Doe, your most generous gift of $100 was very thoughtful. I hope you'll consider increasing your support at this time with an additional gift of $250 to Make-A-Wish. Your gift will qualify you for membership in our **Well Wishers Circle** — and help guarantee that no child is turned away for lack of funds.

If a gift of that amount isn't possible for you at this time, please know that any gift you contribute today will make a difference to a child facing a life-threatening illness.

I know you understand what these kids are going through, and the importance of providing each child and their family with one magical experience in the midst of all their suffering.

In the enclosed proposal, I've included the stories of four children who've been touched by your past generosity—so that you can read first-hand how truly profound a

(over, please)

**Greater Bay Area Make-A-Wish Foundation®**

235 Pine Street, 6th Floor    San Francisco, CA 94104-2745    1-800-464-WISH (9474)    www.makewish.org

**EXHIBIT 15.3 (*Continued*)**

Page 2

simple wish can be to a child. I hope you'll take just a few minutes to read these stories and consider making as generous a gift as you can today.

And know that your compassion will bring a little joy to another child like . . .

. . . John, with Ewing's sarcoma, who wished to go to the World Cup in Germany . . .

. . . Simone, with leukemia, who wished to be a handbag designer . . .

. . . Derrick, with degenerative spinal disease, who wished to meet a famous meteorologist and be a storm chaser . . .

. . . Claudia, just age 4 and battling leukemia, who wished to have a shopping spree . . .

After you have had a chance to review the enclosed proposal and the stories of these four children, please consider making as generous a gift as you can to Make-A-Wish today. And help make wishes come true for many more children in the year ahead.

As a member of our **Well Wishers Circle,** you'll want to keep up on the special wishes granted because of your warm support. You'll receive periodic reports about children whose greatest wish was fulfilled, the Make-A-Wish newsletter, and invitations to Make-A-Wish events throughout the year.

But the most important benefit of the **Well Wishers Circle** is the good feeling you get from knowing you're doing something extra for young children in need.

Thank you for your extraordinary compassion and commitment to helping children in need. We simply could not continue this important work without you.

Sincerely,

*Patricia Wilson*

Patricia Wilson
Executive Director

P.S.   Every wish is as unique and magical as the children we help. Your gift today will help provide a special experience for a young child this coming year. Thank you.

EXHIBIT 15.4

# High-Dollar Appeal Reply Device, Make-A-Wish Foundation

## CREDIT CARD INSTRUCTIONS

Please charge my gift of $_____ to my:

☐ AMEX    ☐ Discover    ☐ VISA    ☐ MC

Card number _____

Exp. date _____

Signature _____

RECYCLED & RECYCLABLE / SOY INK

## MEMORANDUM OF ACCEPTANCE

TO:    Patricia Wilson
       Executive Director
       Greater Bay Area Make-A-Wish Foundation

FROM:  MAW06XA/11-2006/PKG 2
       Ms. Jane Doe                    06XADOEG
       123 Any Street                          0
       Any Town, AS 00000

**YES!** I accept your invitation to invest in the Make-A-Wish Foundation's important work in the year ahead and to help sustain the resources needed to make every child's wish come true.

Please enroll me as a member at the following level:

☐ Well Wisher **Friend** with my gift of $250
☐ Well Wisher **Sponsor** with my gift of $500
☐ Well Wisher **Patron** with my gift of $1,000
☐ Well Wisher **Benefactor** with my gift of $2,500
☐ Enclosed is my special gift of $_____

☐ I don't wish to become a member of the **Well Wishers Circle** at this time, but I would like to make a special gift of $_____.

☐ Please charge my gift to my credit card *(see other side of this form)*.

*Please make checks payable to Make-A-Wish. Your gift is fully tax-deductible.*

**MAKE·(A)·WISH®**

**Greater Bay Area Make-A-Wish Foundation®**
235 Pine Street, 6th Floor    San Francisco, CA 94104-2745
1-800-464-WISH (9474)    www.makewish.org

6-XA2

**EXHIBIT 15.5**

## High-Dollar Appeal Personalized Proposal, Make-A-Wish Foundation

*A proposal to*

Ms. Jane Doe

*We grant the wishes of children with life-threatening*

*medical conditions to enrich the human spirit*

*with hope, strength, and joy*

**Greater Bay Area Make-A-Wish Foundation®**
235 Pine Street, 6th Floor    San Francisco, CA 94104

# Chapter 16

# Going for Bigger Gifts
## Persuading Donors to Make an Extra Commitment

**MOST NONPROFIT** organizations slyly imply in their appeals to donors or members that a gift that's larger than the donor's previous gifts would be . . . well, better. They do this by suggesting gift amounts that are larger than the donors' earlier gifts by some prescribed amount—say, 25 percent or 50 percent or just $10 more.

However, there is a special class of fundraising appeal specifically designed to solicit an increased gift. These donor upgrade letters—sometimes special appeals or year-end appeals, sometimes membership or annual giving "renewal" letters—go out of their way to supply reasons why a donor's increased level of support will bring additional benefits. The Bread for the World response device reproduced in Exhibit 16.1 illustrates two of the elements commonly encountered in donor upgrade efforts:

- You can tell at a glance that its purpose is to upgrade John Doe's support. The appeal requests a gift of $100 or more—clearly a larger amount than Doe has ever contributed in the past—and offers him a special premium (a free copy of an important report) in exchange.

- Three gift amounts are suggested, with a fourth, open alternative, allowing Doe the opportunity to set the level most comfortable for him.

## How Donor Upgrade Appeals Are Different from Other Fundraising Letters

Fundraising letters of many types—including special appeals, renewals, and high-dollar appeals—frequently feature donor upgrade options, but those options are rarely emphasized. A true upgrade letter lays out a set of reasons that the donor should give more—and the argument to give more is a central theme in the copy, not an afterthought. This is the primary characteristic of an upgrade letter.

For example, a special appeal might seek gifts equal to or greater than the donor's highest previous contribution (HPC) to the charity. The reply

**EXHIBIT 16.1**

## Response Device for Donor Upgrade, Bread for the World

*Please renew your 1999 membership*

Yes, I want to renew my annual membership -- and help sustain Bread for the World for the next 25 years. Here's my anniversary membership gift:

[ ] $250      [ ] $100      [ ] $50      [ ] $_____

Mr. John Doe
123 Any Street
Any City AS 12345

| YOUR MEMBER NUMBER: | 99999 |
| DATE OF LAST GIFT: | 01/01/1998 |

☐ I've contributed $100 or more. Please send me a free copy of the *1999 Hunger Report: The Changing Politics of Hunger.*

R99DOE-A      99999

☐ I'm making a membership gift of $250 — and I'd also like to receive the special 25th anniversary lapel pin.

◀ **See reverse side for important information**

Mr. Doe —

Each year, at this time, we ask *all* Bread for the World members to renew their annual support -- to help provide the financial resources we need to launch our new Offering of Letters campaign.

Please consider renewing your membership with a gift of $50 -- to celebrate Bread for the World's 25th Anniversary and to lay the foundation for the *next* 25 years.

If you renew with a gift of $100 or more, you may request a free copy of the 1999 Hunger Report--*The Changing Politics of Hunger.* And with a membership renewal of $250 or more, you'll also receive the attractive Bread for the World 25th Anniversary lapel pin.

Whatever your renewal level, please send your gift today -- and save the time and expense of additional reminders. Thank you!

### To contact Bread for the World:

- David Beckmann, President
- Carole Southam, Vice President
- Dick Hoehn, Bread for the World Institute
- Barbara Howell, Government Relations
- Diane Hunt, Development and Membership
- Kathy Pomroy, Organizing
- Joel Underwood, Church Relations
- Lynora Williams, Communications

**Questions about your membership?**
**Comments or concerns?**
**Call toll-free: 1-800-82-BREAD  (1-800-822-7323).**

9-60972A

Your *25th Anniversary*
**Membership Card**

**Bread for the World**
1100 Wayne Avenue, Suite 1000
Silver Spring, MD 20910
Phone: 800/82-BREAD

Mr. John Doe

*IS A MEMBER IN GOOD STANDING*

*David Beckmann*

DAVID BECKMANN, PRESIDENT OF BREAD FOR THE WORLD

device might even offer three alternative giving levels: the HPC, the HPC plus 25 percent, and the HPC plus 50 percent. But that alone wouldn't make the letter an upgrade appeal. To qualify for that characterization, the letter would need to build a case for the increase in support. In inflationary times, that case might be to help the organization cope with steadily rising costs, and the letter might illustrate just how quickly costs were rising by giving concrete examples. Or the letter might spell out how much more the charity can accomplish if the donor sends a gift that's 25 percent or 50 percent larger than in the past. More commonly, however, an upgrade appeal is distinguished from a special appeal because it invites the donor to join a special group or giving category that requires significantly higher gifts. (That's the case with all the examples in this chapter.)

Three additional traits are shared by most upgrading efforts.

### Three Characteristics of Upgrade Packages

1. Upgrade letters customarily spotlight opportunities to join giving clubs or otherwise feature special benefits, premiums, or incentives for making the larger gifts requested. (Keep in mind that some or all of those benefits or incentives may be intangible.) In other words, there's a marketing concept appropriate to the request for a larger gift.

2. Upgrade efforts frequently offer two, three, or more alternative levels of support. Although this approach isn't universally used in upgrading efforts, it's common because the purpose of such efforts is usually to secure the largest possible gift—and the letter writer rarely knows how much that's likely to be.

3. Personalization and high-quality paper stock are often used in upgrade appeals—to match the ambitious request.

## Case Study: AIDS Project Los Angeles Upgrade Appeal

The package illustrated in Exhibits 16.1, 16.2, 16.3, and 16.4 is a simple straightforward upgrade appeal—in this case, an invitation to join the "Leadership Council" with a gift of $1,000 or more.

Often, appeals of this sort focus exclusively on one giving level, most often the lowest. In this example, however, donors are offered a choice of giving levels from $1,000 to $25,000 and above. Note the benefits offered at each of these levels: you'll see an abundance of special events (probably more typical of Los Angeles than of this particular organization!). Note also the multiple instances of personalization. Just imagine your chances of securing a gift of $1,000 or more with a "Dear Friend" letter!

**EXHIBIT 16.2**

## Upgrade Letter, APLA Leadership Council Appeal

LEADERSHIP COUNCIL

**APLA**
AIDS Project Los Angeles

The David Geffen Center
611 S. Kingsley Drive
Los Angeles CA 90005
www.apla.org

Thursday, February 8, 2007

APL07XA/01-2007/PKG 1: ALL
Ms. Jane Doe
123 Any Street
Any Town, AS 00000

Dear Ms. Doe,

Thank you for your generous support of AIDS Project Los Angeles.

As a donor of APLA since 2003, your support for our programs and services has been extraordinary. I am grateful for your partnership in helping people who are struggling with HIV/AIDS—and I hope you know the enormous difference you are making in our community.

Like you, perhaps, my initial involvement in APLA's work was deeply personal. I lost my twin brother, Greg, to AIDS in the summer of 1995.

Greg was just 34 years old when he died, and even though I was living in Chicago and couldn't be with him as much as I wanted to be, I know he wasn't alone. Thanks to AIDS Project Los Angeles, and the wonderful services they provide to people with AIDS, Greg received the care and attention he needed right 'til the very end.

APLA's Home Health program helped my brother live his final days in comfort.  Even more than that, APLA staff and volunteers helped him die with dignity. I'll never forget that.  It was then and there that I decided to become involved with APLA, and do everything I could to help them fulfill their mission on behalf of other people living with HIV/AIDS.

Ms. Doe, I'm writing to invite you to join me in becoming a member of APLA's Leadership Council with your gift of $1,000 or more.  I've just renewed my support for 2007, and I hope you won't think me presumptuous in asking you to do the same.

AIDS Project Los Angeles depends on the generosity of its *Leadership Council* to help underwrite their programs and services—so I urge you to take a moment now to consider supporting APLA at a higher level than you've ever given before.

Your gifts totaling $1,000 in 2006 were extremely helpful.

(Over, please)

**EXHIBIT 16.2 (*Continued*)**

Ms. Jane Doe
Page Two

Time and again, throughout the 12 years I've been involved with APLA, I've seen the people of Los Angeles step forward to help people living with HIV/AIDS.

Your support for APLA has been extraordinary, and it gives me the courage to make an extraordinary request of you. Will you consider making a gift of $1,000 or more—and joining APLA's *Leadership Council* today?

The *Leadership Council* provides the financial foundation for APLA's life-sustaining services and HIV prevention programs. By renewing your commitment at this time, you will help improve the lives of people struggling with AIDS, you will help protect a new generation from the scourge of HIV infection, and you will help advocate for fairer and more effective HIV-related public policy.

In short, you will help advance APLA's core mission on every level.

As a member of the *Leadership Council*, you will continue to receive special recognition and exclusive benefits. You'll be invited, for example, to attend gatherings reserved for Council members only, where you will have an opportunity to meet with APLA Executive Director Craig Thompson. You will also receive special briefings and be given VIP treatment at APLA events.

You will receive enduring recognition on the Donor Wall of Honor in The David Geffen Center, on the APLA website, and in the Annual Report published each spring.

Even more important, you'll be joining with other generous, caring, and compassionate friends whose annual gifts help to underwrite APLA's programs and services.

On behalf of the *Leadership Council*, I'm extremely grateful for your steadfast support, and I look forward to seeing you at one of our events in 2007.

With heartfelt thanks,

Jeff York
Member, APLA *Leadership Council*

P.S.    I'm increasingly mindful that it's the commitment of people like you and me—not the commitment of our government—that enables APLA to provide its life-saving programs. Please renew your leadership support today.

**EXHIBIT 16.3**

# Upgrade Reply Device, APLA Leadership Council Appeal

## MEMORANDUM *of* ACCEPTANCE

TO:     Jeff York, Member
        APLA Leadership Council

FROM:   APL07XA/01-2007/PKG 1: ALL
        Ms. Jane Doe
        123 Any Street
        Any Town, AS 00000

                                07XADOEB  5254    0

**YES,** I accept your invitation to become a Member of APLA's *Leadership Council.* I am honored to join with you in ensuring that AIDS Project Los Angeles has the resources to advance its life-saving mission. Please enroll me as a Member at the following level:

- ☐ I wish to become a *Member* with my gift of $1,000.
- ☐ I wish to become a *Friend* with my gift of $2,500.
- ☐ I wish to become a *Sponsor* with my gift of $5,000.
- ☐ I wish to become a *Patron* with my gift of $10,000.
- ☐ I wish to become a *Benefactor* with my gift of $25,000.

- ☐ I don't wish to become a Member of the *Leadership Council* at this time, but I'd like to make a special gift of $_____.

- ☐ Please list my/our name(s) on the Donor Wall of Honor, the APLA website, and in APLA's 2007 Annual Report as:
  _____

- ☐ I prefer my/our gift remain anonymous.

**LEADERSHIP COUNCIL**

**APLA**
AIDS Project Los Angeles

The David Geffen Center
611 S. Kingsley Drive
Los Angeles CA 90005
www.apla.org

*Your gift to AIDS Project Los Angeles is fully tax-deductible.*

**\* Please see reverse if you'd like to charge your *Leadership Council* gift to your credit card.**

---

☐ **I prefer to make my Leadership Council gift by:**

  ☐ VISA   ☐ MasterCard
  ☐ American Express

Amount: $ _____

Card Number: _____

Exp. date: _____

Signature: _____

☐ **I'd like to receive occassional email updates from APLA. My email address is:**
  _____

**Will your employer match your generous gift?**

☐ I have enclosed my employer's matching gift form.

RECYCLED & RECYCLABLE / PRINTED WITH SOY INK

7-XA2

EXHIBIT 16.4

# Upgrade Membership Benefits, APLA Leadership Council Appeal

LEADERSHIP COUNCIL

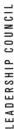**APLA**
AIDS Project Los Angeles

## BENEFITS OF MEMBERSHIP

The *APLA Leadership Council* is comprised of a group of leaders in our community who make a significant financial contribution on an annual basis to AIDS Project Los Angeles. Council members express their deep commitment to helping people affected by HIV disease, reducing the incidence of HIV infection, and advocating for effective HIV-related public policy through their generous annual gifts of $1,000 or more.

Council members receive exclusive benefits and enduring recognition. All members are invited to events reserved only for *APLA Leadership Council* members, for discussions with APLA Executive Director Craig E. Thompson and other prominent leaders involved in HIV/AIDS prevention. Council members also receive a complimentary subscription to APLA's quarterly newsletter, *The Optimist*, and other expressions of appreciation.

AIDS Project Los Angeles
The David Geffen Center · 611 S. Kingsley Drive · Los Angeles CA 90005
www.apla.org · 213-201-1564

## MEMBERSHIP LEVELS

**MEMBERS who make gifts of $1,000 to $2,499** are recognized in APLA's Annual Report, on APLA's website, and on the Wall of Honor in the main reception area of The David Geffen Center. They are invited to two major donor events each year and receive a subscription to *The Optimist*.

**FRIENDS who make gifts of $2,500 to $4,999** receive all of the benefits listed above and also receive advance invitations to all APLA functions and events, including a personal tour of APLA's offices.

**SPONSORS who make gifts of $5,000 to $9,999** receive all of the benefits listed above and also receive two invitations to the VIP breakfast preceding AIDS Walk Los Angeles, two invitations to APLA's Annual VIP Oscar Party, an opportunity to have dinner with a senior APLA staff member, and personal handling of requests and other VIP services.

**PATRONS who make gifts of $10,000 to $24,999** receive all of the benefits listed above and also receive four invitations to the VIP breakfast preceding AIDS Walk Los Angeles, four invitations to attend APLA's Annual VIP Oscar Party, and an opportunity to have dinner with APLA's Executive Director and Board Chair.

**BENEFACTORS who make gifts of $25,000 and above** receive all of the benefits listed above and also receive eight invitations to the VIP breakfast preceding AIDS Walk Los Angeles, six invitations to attend APLA's Annual VIP Oscar Party, VIP access to all APLA events, and special recognition opportunities for selected programs.

# Chapter 17

# Seeking Annual Gifts
## Building Long-Term Loyalty, One Year at a Time

**THE BACKBONE OF** most direct mail fundraising programs—indeed, of most fundraising programs generally—is an annual membership or "Annual Fund" program. Most such programs use a technique borrowed from the magazine subscription business to maximize donor participation: they mail a series of letters (or *notices*), stopping only when a member's gift is finally received. Smaller nonprofits may limit their *renewal series* to three or four such notices. Larger organizations with huge donor databases may send out ten notices or more (just as do major national magazines).

The Bread for the World membership renewal device reproduced in Exhibit 17.1 contains three elements that are both important and typical of the renewal notices used by nonprofits.

- This is clearly about renewing annual membership—since the headline says so!

- The form offers several different membership levels, so that the recipient may upgrade voluntarily.

- The message is extremely brief and focused almost exclusively on the relationship between the individual member and the organization.

## How Renewal Letters Are Different from Other Fundraising Appeals

Annual renewal efforts are of two general types: annual fund appeals (most commonly found at schools and colleges) and membership renewal series (which aren't limited to organizations with formal membership structures but are most frequently used by them). Both types usually share the following five characteristics.

### Five Characteristics of Annual Renewal Effort Packages

1. There are clear and explicit references to membership dues or the annual gift. In other words, it's unmistakably clear that the organization expects the donor's support, this year and every year.

**EXHIBIT 17.1**

## Annual Renewal Response Device, Bread for the World

### *Please Renew Your Annual Membership*

Yes, I want to renew my 2007 Bread for the World membership.
Enclosed is my annual gift of:

[ ] $300      [ ] $250      [ ] $100      [ ] $_____

Ms. Jane Doe
123 Any Street
Any Town AS 00000
BFW07RB/03-28-07/1: SECOND EFFORT RENEWAL

You've been a member since 2003. Please continue your support — and help strengthen our work to fight hunger, poverty, and disease.

Membership No.: 00000

*If you wish to use your credit card to make a gift, please fill out the information on the reverse side.*

BREAD FOR THE WORLD    ♦    50 F STREET NW, SUITE 500    ♦    WASHINGTON, DC 20001

07RBDOEA

## Bread for the World
*Seeking Justice. Ending Hunger.*

50 F Street NW, Suite 500
Washington, DC 20001
1-800-822-7323    www.bread.org

March 28, 2007

Dear Ms. Doe,

I'm writing to remind you to renew your Bread for the World membership.

If you recently sent your 2007 membership gift, please ignore this notice — and accept my sincere thanks for your continued support.

But if you haven't sent your gift, please take a moment right now to use the enclosed envelope to return your check.

Bread for the World's membership has grown dramatically in the last three years, and more and more college students and young adults have become involved in this citizens' movement to fight hunger, poverty, and disease.

Your membership contribution will help us turn all this growth and greater involvement into legislative victories for hungry people.

Thank you for taking time today to renew your membership.

David Beckmann, President

P.S.    Your membership gift of $300 — if possible — will be added to the contributions of many others, providing the financial foundation for all of our work to end hunger. Thank you for responding today.

*Please remember Bread for the World in your will—and help create a Legacy of Hope for hungry people.*

7-RB2

**EXHIBIT 17.1** (*Continued*)

Please charge my: ☐ Visa ☐ MasterCard ☐ Discover

Amount $_____

☐ Bread for the World ☐ Bread for the World Institute

Card #_____

Expiration date _____

Card security code _____

Signature _____

*(ALL FIELDS REQUIRED FOR AUTHORIZATION)*

**You may renew your membership and make a secure gift online, when you visit www.bread.org/renew.**

## We use your contributions wisely

Gifts to Bread for the World are **not** tax-deductible since our members lobby Congress on behalf of poor and hungry people. If you prefer to make a **tax-deductible** contribution to support research and education efforts (such as the Hunger Report, the ONE Campaign, and research on trade), please make out your check to Bread for the World Institute. You are welcome to request a copy of our latest financial report by contacting: Bread for the World, 50 F Street NW, Suite 500, Washington, DC 20001-1565, (202) 639-9400 or 1-800-822-7323 or visit **www.bread.org.**

If you are a resident of one of the states below, you may obtain financial information directly from the state agency: **FLORIDA** — A COPY OF THE OFFICIAL REGISTRATION AND FINANCIAL INFORMATION MAY BE OBTAINED FROM THE DIVISION OF CONSUMER SERVICES BY CALLING TOLL-FREE, (800) 435-7352 WITHIN THE STATE. REGISTRATION DOES NOT IMPLY ENDORSEMENT, APPROVAL OR RECOMMENDATION BY THE STATE. (SC-05787) **MARYLAND** — For the cost of copies and postage: Office of the Secretary of State, State House, Annapolis, MD 21401. **MISSISSIPPI** — The official registration and financial information of Bread for the World may be obtained from the Mississippi Secretary of State's office by calling 1-888-236-6167. Registration by the Secretary of State does not imply endorsement. **NEW JERSEY** — INFORMATION FILED WITH THE ATTORNEY GENERAL CONCERNING THIS CHARITABLE SOLICITATION MAY BE OBTAINED FROM THE ATTORNEY GENERAL OF THE STATE OF NEW JERSEY BY CALLING (973) 504-6215. REGISTRATION WITH THE ATTORNEY GENERAL DOES NOT IMPLY ENDORSEMENT. **NEW YORK** — Office of the Attorney General, Department of Law, Charities Bureau, 120 Broadway, New York, NY 10271. **NORTH CAROLINA** — **Financial information about this organization and a copy of its license are available from the State Solicitation Licensing Branch at (919) 807-2214. The license is not an endorsement by the state. PENNSYLVANIA** — The official registration and financial information of Bread for the World may be obtained from the Pennsylvania Department of State by calling toll-free, within Pennsylvania, (800) 732-0999. Registration does not imply endorsement. **VIRGINIA** — State Division of Consumer Affairs, Department of Agricultural and Consumer Services, P.O. Box 1163, Richmond, VA 23218. **WASHINGTON** — Charities Division, Office of the Secretary of State, State of Washington, Olympia, WA 98504-0422; 1-800-332-4483. **WEST VIRGINIA** — Residents may obtain a summary from: Secretary of State, State Capitol, Charleston, WV 25305. 1/03

*Registration with any of these states does not imply endorsement, approval or recommendation by the state.*

# Bread for the World's 2007 Campaign

Please write or call your representative and senators in Washington, D.C. Urge them to improve our nation's farm policies to help farmers and strengthen rural communities here in the United States— as well as in Africa and other parts of the world that face the threat of hunger.

For the names of your members of Congress and for more information about Bread's 2007 legislative campaign—*Seeds of Change: Help Farmers. End Hunger.* —visit **www.bread.org.**

RECYCLED & RECYCLABLE / PRINTED WITH SOY INK

2. The letter focuses on the process of renewal, repeating an action taken last year (and maybe for many years past).

3. The case is usually made in general and institutional terms rather than focusing on a particular program or special need. An annual gift, after all, represents support for the institution, not for some limited aspect of its work.

4. Renewal letters are typically short. The most important point to make in such letters is "please renew"—and that may be all you really need to say.

5. The element of time and its limits is always at least implicit: "this year's dues," "your expiration date," "the deadline for renewing."

## Case Study: Corporate Accountability International's Annual Membership Renewal Series

Exhibits 17.2 through 17.5 show the outer envelopes of the four efforts in Corporate Accountability International's membership renewal series, just to give you a sense of the changing character of these reminder notices as time goes by. The full packages are shown in color on the accompanying CD-ROM.

Here's how a renewal series typically works:

- All of last year's active members, plus many of those whose membership has lapsed, are mailed the first effort in the series. Those who respond with gifts are then immediately thanked and cycled into a sequence of special appeals. They will not receive any subsequent renewal notices.

- Nonresponders to the first effort will receive the second some four to six weeks later. If they respond to the second renewal effort, they will be removed from the renewal process, and included in any special appeals the organization may subsequently send.

- The later efforts, numbers three and four in this case, will function in an identical manner, mailed at intervals of approximately one month. Through this process, by the time the entire series has been mailed, a substantial proportion of the organization's members will have renewed.

- However, some members ignore renewals and respond only to special appeals. Those mailings, which take place only once the renewal series is well underway, serve to reactivate an additional number of members. (In many organizations, there is no meaningful distinction made between "members" and "donors.")

For a great many nonprofit organizations, the renewal series is the backbone of the small-donor fundraising program. Renewals often account for a huge proportion of the revenue from direct mail, telephone, and online fundraising programs.

**EXHIBIT 17.2**

**First Membership Renewal Effort Outer Envelope, Corporate Accountability International**

CORPORATE ACCOUNTABILITY INTERNATIONAL
CHALLENGING ABUSE, PROTECTING PEOPLE
*formerly* **Infact**

46 Plympton Street
Boston, MA 02118-2425

U.S. POSTAGE
0.00

It's Time to Renew for 2006!

RECYCLED & RECYCLABLE / PRINTED WITH SOY INK    6-RA3

**EXHIBIT 17.3**

**Second Membership Renewal Effort Outer Envelope, Corporate Accountability International**

Ms Jane Doe
123 Any Street
Any Town AS 00000
CAI06RB/4-24-06/PKG.A:ALL

**EXHIBIT 17.4**

## Third Membership Renewal Effort Outer Envelope, Corporate Accountability International

**CORPORATE ACCOUNTABILITY INTERNATIONAL**
CHALLENGING ABUSE, PROTECTING PEOPLE
*formerly* **Infact**

46 Plympton Street
Boston, MA 02118-2425

NONPROFIT ORG
MAILED FROM ZIP CODE
95374
U.S. POSTAGE
$0.00
P.B. METER
673474A

We're Counting on You: **2006 Renewal Reminder**

RECYCLED & RECYCLABLE / PRINTED WITH SOY INK    6-RC3

---

**EXHIBIT 17.5**

## Fourth Membership Renewal Effort Outer Envelope, Corporate Accountability International

**MEMBERSHIP SERVICES**
Corporate Accountability International
46 Plympton Street
Boston, MA 02118-2425

RECYCLED & RECYCLABLE / SOY INK    6-RD3

# Chapter 18

# Thanking Your Donors
## Friend-Raising Before Fundraising

**YOU PROBABLY FIGURED** this out a long time ago: writing fundraising letters is no way for your organization to make a quick buck. Raising money by mail, like fundraising conducted by any other means, is a long-term process. The fundraising letters you mail as that process unfolds may differ dramatically from one another because your relationships with donors change over time. You know much more about your donors in the later stages of the process than you do at the earlier, and your letters will reflect that knowledge in ways that are both obvious and profound. But there's one element all effective fundraising letters share: they show appreciation.

Even when you're writing a prospective donor who's known to you only as a name on a list, it's sound practice to find a way to compliment her while you make your case for a gift—and then to thank her in advance for agreeing to help. It's the *polite* thing to do.

When you write to a proven donor to solicit additional support, it's important to reinforce her goodwill (and her memory) by thanking her for her past generosity. It's not only polite to do that; it's sure to make your letter work better.

And when you're asking a donor to make an extra special effort to upgrade her support—by joining a high-dollar club or a monthly sustainer program, for example—you'll get the best results when you include repeated, heartfelt thanks in your letter. After all, the donors you select to include in most upgrade campaigns are very special people who've already given you more money or given more frequently or for a longer period of time than all the rest of your supporters. It's polite, effective, and natural to thank them in an upgrade appeal.

In other words, every fundraising letter is a thank-you.

Even so, that's not enough. The savviest fundraisers learn early on that they need to mail special letters dedicated exclusively to thanking their donors.

# How Thank-You Letters Are Different from Other Fundraising Letters

The Bread for the World acknowledgment letter reproduced in Exhibit 18.1 is an excellent example. This letter displays five elements that clearly set it apart as a thank-you and nothing more.

### Five Characteristics of Thank-You Letters

- In three straightforward paragraphs, the message here is consistently "thank you!"

- The letter specifically refers to the date and amount of the gift.

- The second paragraph clearly implies that membership in Bread for the World is much more than a checkbook relationship for the donor. The donor is invited to engage in Bread for the World's program work.

- The message is brief and to the point, so as not to muddy the thank-you theme.

- Although this letter includes a response device that contains an ask, many thank-yous do not. In fact, I tend to frown on asking for additional contributions in acknowledgment letters. Even this ask appears only on the reply device and not in the letter, "softening" it in effect.

## Why You Need to Write Thank-Yous

Focus group research consistently turns up comments like the following:

"I sent them some money over a year ago, but I never got a thank-you. Well, never again!"

"I've been giving to them for years, twenty, twenty-five bucks at a time. They got a hundred bucks from me recently—and all they sent back was the same preprinted postcard they always send. How much do you think they're going to get the next time around?"

"The thing that burns me up is getting a thank-you about two months after I send a check—after they've already asked me for more money! I won't give to a group that's that disorganized . . . or rude."

Why do comments like these so commonly turn up in focus group research? Because so many charities defy what I call the Golden Rule of Donor Acknowledgments: thank your donors promptly!

Consider my alter ego—whom I call the Phantom Donor. This generous soul sends $15, $20, or $25 gifts once or twice a year to some of the nation's top nonprofit organizations—and studies the mail that comes in return.

**EXHIBIT 18.1**

# Thank-You Letter, Bread for the World

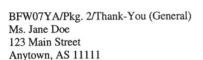

Bread for the World
Bread for the World Institute

50 F Street, NW, Suite 500
Washington, DC 20001
1-800-822-7323    www.bread.org

BFW07YA/Pkg. 2/Thank-You (General)
Ms. Jane Doe
123 Main Street
Anytown, AS 11111

March 5, 2007

Dear Ms. Jane Doe,

Thank you for your gift of $50 to Bread for the World, received on January 25, 2007.

Your financial support is especially helpful right now as we launch our 2007 legislative campaign – *Seeds of Change: Help Farmers. End Hunger.* Visit www.bread.org to find out how you can participate in this crucial effort to reform U.S. farm policies. You'll also find information about the June 2007 Gathering, which will include an interfaith convocation and a forum of presidential candidates.

Your generosity and involvement are creating hope and opportunity for hungry people – here in the United States and around the world. Thank you!

Sincerely,

*David Beckmann*

David Beckmann
President

## If you'd like to make another gift...

Your extra contribution will help sustain our work together to bring hope and opportunity to hungry people in the U.S. and overseas. Thank you!

☐ **$100**    ☐ **$50**    ☐ **$25**    ☐ **$_____**

☐ Please send me information about the Baker's Dozen monthly giving program.

☐ I'd like to begin receiving the *Legacy of Hope* newsletter with information about charitable bequests and other planned gifts.

☐ Please start my free subscription to *Hunger Sunday,* the Bread for the World newsletter designed for churches and faith communities.

BFW07YA/Pkg. 2/Thank-You (General)
Ms. Jane Doe
123 Main Street
Anytown, AS 11111

1764528
THNK

Bread for the World
Bread for the World Institute

50 F Street, NW, Suite 500
Washington, DC 20001
1-800-822-7323    www.bread.org

◄ *Please see reverse side for important information.*

RECYCLED & RECYCLABLE / SOY INK    7-YA2B

Several years ago, the Phantom paid special attention to the donor acknowledgment practices of some favorite charities. The experience was sobering. The Phantom mailed a round of $15 checks to twenty organizations, all on the same day and accompanying the most recent reply device and reply envelope received from each of the mailers. Eight weeks later, the Phantom Donor had been thanked by only fifteen of the twenty groups. One of them, the American Red Cross, got out a thank-you (admittedly only a postcard) within less than one week. But few others arrived within the first month. The typical response time was five to seven weeks.

That performance was pathetic. And we're not talking about the mom-and-pop charity down on the corner. These were some of the most successful nonprofit mailers in America—groups such as the Humane Society of the United States, Common Cause, and the Christian Appalachian Project. In fact, most direct mail fundraisers do a downright poor job of thanking their donors. The donor acknowledgment practices of those big charities simply mirror what goes on throughout the independent sector.

Charities that cut costs by refraining from mailing thank-yous or by sending such cut-rate items as preprinted postcards are all missing the boat, because they can do so much better. But even worse is to defy the Golden Rule of Donor Acknowledgments.

The most heartwarming and informative thank-you copy will be wasted on a donor who may already have forgotten that he sent you a check. (If you doubt donors react this way, run a couple of focus groups, and ask donors what they think.) In fact, I'm so concerned about the widespread failure to heed the Golden Rule of Donor Acknowledgments that I'll offer a corollary: Send even a "bad" (that is, impersonal) thank-you if you can get it into the mail much faster than a "good" (that is, personal and specific) one!

Here, now, are a few other pointers for effective donor acknowledgments.

## Pointers for Effective Donor Acknowledgments

- Reassure your donors that it was a good idea to send a gift. Don't let them suffer from buyer's remorse. Reinforce their original belief that your group is effective, caring, and worthy of their support.

- Be warm and friendly. If they're new donors, welcome them to the "family."

- Praise their generosity. Tell them how, by joining with other supporters, they're having a significant impact on your work.

- Reaffirm your gratitude at the end of the letter or in a P.S.

- Give examples of recent organizational successes donors can feel proud of.

Most fundraisers believe it's advisable to suggest another gift in a thank-you package—and I agree with them when it's a "soft" ask that no one could possibly interpret as arm-twisting. There are circumstances in which I don't think such an approach is advisable—the Bread for the World thank-you letter reproduced in Exhibit 18.1 is an excellent example—but it's often worth considering. For example, in emergencies and with important deadlines approaching, it might be unnatural not to ask for additional support. In any case, it's almost always a good idea to enclose a reply envelope, even if you're not soliciting an additional gift.

To explore some of the numerous possibilities opened up by thank-you packages, let's take a look at the diverse styles and approaches followed by those fifteen mailers who (eventually) thanked the Phantom Donor.

## How Some of the Country's Top Fundraising Mailers Thank Their Donors

A Number 10 window envelope was far and away the preferred choice of the fifteen mailers who responded to the Phantom's unsolicited contributions. Not a single one used a closed-face (nonwindow) envelope, although CARE opted for a self-contained *fast-tab* envelope. There were also two postcards (from the American Red Cross and from the National Organization for Women).

Of the envelope packages received, nearly half featured teasers. Nothing flashy, just a simple "thank you" in five out of the six cases. The sixth got fancier: "A special note of thanks."

Some direct mail pros argue that a thank-you is the best time to solicit another contribution—a "get 'em while they're hot" mentality. All the thank-you packages sent to the Phantom (except the two postcards) included a return envelope to be used for subsequent gifts. However, only seven of these thirteen mailers directly pitched for funds by including reply devices. The most aggressive approach was the attempt to seek an immediate upgrade through membership in a monthly giving club. Two environmental groups opted for this stratagem: Greenpeace USA and the National Audubon Society. Significantly, in both cases letter copy emphasized the long-term commitment needed in the day-to-day battle to save our environment.

Most of the packages consisted of copy that was short and to the point. Aside from the two postcards, the Phantom received six short-form receipts, one of which also incorporated a membership card. Of the seven actual letters, five were of the one-page variety. The exceptions were the two monthly sustainer packages: Greenpeace used a two-page letter, Audubon a three-pager.

One intriguing point about the two longer pieces was that these were the only letters that were not personalized. Both instead used a variation on the "Dear Supporter" salutation—ironically, a rather impersonal way to elicit a substantial upgrade.

Almost all the acknowledgments straightforwardly and profusely thanked the Phantom—from a simple "your gift makes a difference" to the gushy "you are special to us and we hold you in our hearts and minds." Religiously oriented groups were likely to add a "God bless you."

Generally, the message was upbeat and gracious, reminding the Phantom Donor of the good work being accomplished by the group (to make her—or him—feel better about parting with fifteen bucks). Occasionally, though, the tone was more downbeat, and the Phantom was treated to a lecture on the ills faced by the organization. The Republican National Committee, for example, was up in arms about the "Clinton/Democrat tax and spend frenzy," while the World Wildlife Fund informed the Phantom that many species "are on the brink of extinction."

Four of the thirteen letter packages contained inserts. What was particularly striking was that all four were on the subject of planned giving. Each of these inserts incorporated a return coupon for requesting additional information. In two other instances—where a planned giving brochure was not enclosed—a checkoff box was included on the reply device for requesting further material.

Most of the Phantom's charities avoided sending premiums. The Billy Graham Evangelistic Association was a notable exception. As in previous acknowledgment packages, the Graham organization included a 300-page paperback book and a reprint from its monthly magazine. Only two other groups mailed premiums, apart from the Nature Conservancy's membership card. St. Joseph's Indian School sent a prayer card, and Father Flanagan's Boys' Home included an excerpt from a book by its executive director. The latter also enclosed a "handy" wallet calendar that was "made in our own print shop."

Father Flanagan's Boys' Home also alerted the Phantom to be on the lookout for a future premium. The personalized copy declared, "In my next letter, because you are one of our family, I'm sending you an honorary certificate of citizenship." Two weeks later the certificate arrived—with another appeal for funds.

Despite bells and whistles and occasional high-pressure requests for additional donations, few donor acknowledgments generate even enough revenue to cover their costs. Nevertheless, savvy (if far from speedy) fundraising mailers go to all this trouble and expense not just because it's thoughtful and polite to send thank-yous but also for the following three reasons. The first two are obvious and easily confirmed by testing; the third presents a more fundamental reason to invest in timely and appropriate donor acknowledgments.

---

### Three Reasons to Send Thank-Yous

1. Thank-yous increase response to subsequent appeals.

2. Thank-yous increase donor loyalty.

3. Thank-yous help build long-term relationships with donors.

---

To give you a better sense of what I mean, I'm going to guide you through a thank-you package from another major fundraising mailer—one not on the Phantom's charity list.

## Case Study: An Example of a Great Thank-You Letter

The Southern Poverty Law Center, in Montgomery, Alabama, sent out a masterful donor acknowledgment package that consisted of an outer envelope and two notebook-sized pages, printed on one side only (see Exhibits 18.2 and 18.3). Many fundraisers insist you should include a self-addressed reply envelope in every communication with your donors, but there was none in this package (much less a personalized reply device that might generate a bounce-back gift). I'll bet, though, that this warm, informative acknowledgment generated gifts at least an order of magnitude greater than the few, paltry bounce-back contributions that might have resulted if the package had included a reply envelope.

This package was mailed first class. Had it been mailed bulk rate instead (to save on postage), the Southern Poverty Law Center couldn't have used Bobby Person's name and address as the return address on the outer envelope. (Under postal regulations still in force in the United States at this writing, a nonprofit organization must correctly identify itself on the outer envelope to qualify for the nonprofit postal discount.) Why mail first class? With a first-class letter from a person unknown to the recipient, the package had an air of mystery about it and unquestionably received high readership—far higher, in all likelihood, than a letter identified as coming from the center would have garnered.

Clearly, the Southern Poverty Law Center chose to invest in its future relationships with donors by spending a modest sum on thank-yous like these. You'd be well advised to consider whether this technique makes sense for your own organization. It probably does, because the revenue generated from future appeals to new donors is likely to dwarf the investment you've made in acquiring and converting first-time donors to loyal donors through such techniques as this. And far more of your new donors are likely to respond to those future appeals (and more generously so) if they feel you've treated them like part of the family.

It's really that simple. Treat every one of your donors like Grandma or Uncle Paul, and your organization will reap the rewards for many years to come.

---

**EXHIBIT 18.2**

## Thank-You Outer Envelope, Southern Poverty Law Center

Bobby Person
Route 1, Box 407
West End, North Carolina 27376

**EXHIBIT 18.3**

# Thank-You Letter, Southern Poverty Law Center

Bobby Person
Route 1, Box 190
West End, North Carolina 27376

October 15, 1993

Ms. ⌷⌷⌷⌷⌷⌷⌷ ⌷⌷⌷ ⌷
⌷⌷⌷ ⌷⌷⌷⌷⌷⌷ ⌷⌷⌷⌷
⌷⌷⌷⌷⌷, ⌷A 947⌷⌷

Dear Ms. ⌷⌷⌷⌷ ⌷ ,

I understand from my friends at the Southern
Poverty Law Center and its Klanwatch Project in
Montgomery that you recently sent a gift to help in
their work.

I wanted to show some appreciation for the work
the Center did for me and I wrote them a letter of
thanks. They asked if I would share my feelings
with you so that you might better understand that
their work touches the lives of real people in a
meaningful way. I was more than glad to help by
writing you directly.

When I needed their help to protect me from
harassment from members of the Ku Klux Klan, they
spent hundreds of hours and several thousand
dollars to protect my family and me.

Let me tell you about my case.

I am a black person living in a small rural
North Carolina community and work as a guard at a
state prison. I wanted to advance myself and asked
my supervisor for permission to take the sergeant's
examination. No black man had ever been sergeant
of the prison guard.

I did not know at the time that one of the
white guards was a Klansman. That night, a Klan
cross was burned in the dirt road in front of my
house. My wife and children were terrified. A few
nights later, several Klansmen wearing sheets and
paramilitary uniforms, and carrying guns, drove up
in front of my home and threatened to kill me. My
children were so frightened that they did not sleep
well for months. Later, shots were fired at the
guard tower at night from cars passing on the road.

**EXHIBIT 18.3 (*Continued*)**

The lawyers from the Southern Poverty Law Center filed suit against three Klansmen suspected of this harassment.  They also filed suit to stop the Carolina Knights of the KKK from operating their paramilitary army.  After a few months, they received a court order stopping the Klan paramilitary training.  The three Klansmen who harassed me and my family also stood trial and were ordered to stop.

Since the Center came to my aid, I am proud to tell you that I won the promotion to sergeant.

You may have heard of some of the big cases the Center has handled.  Many of these cases receive national publicity and many have made significant advances in human rights.  My case is not very important in the long run and you may not ever have heard about it, but it was important to my family and me to be able to call on a group of lawyers who had the money to go after the Klan and who are experts in how to stop Klan terrorism.  Funds were available to help me only with help from people like yourself.

Now the Center has expanded its work with a new educational project to encourage the teaching of tolerance in our schools.

For the first time in history, an organization exists that is not only fighting the Klan in the courtroom, but also in the classroom by helping teach children the value of tolerance.

Please continue your financial support of the Center.  This is a long, hard fight that needs people like yourself committed to working for a future when all people live in peace and harmony.

My family and I want to thank you personally for the generous gift that you gave the Center.

Sincerely,

*Bobby Person*

# Chapter 19

# Promoting Legacy Gifts
## Seeking the Ultimate Commitment

DIRECT MAIL FUNDRAISING—indeed, all direct response fundraising, including telemarketing and e-philanthropy—works because lots of people contribute small gifts, and many of them continue to do so, year after year. Most people who specialize in other aspects of fundraising deal in gifts that are substantially larger than the typical direct response gift, sometimes running into hundreds of thousands or millions of dollars. Viewed from one perspective, legacy fundraising is a bridge between the direct marketers who typically traffic in small contributions and the traditional fundraisers who are often discontent if the gifts they secure don't run into five, six, seven figures, or more. That's because legacy gifts in the United States tend to be comparable in size to the major gifts, foundation grants, and corporate contributions that constitute the bread and butter of traditional fundraisers.

Legacy fundraising is most advantageously viewed as an offshoot of direct mail fundraising for three reasons.

---

### Why Promote Legacy Fundraising by Mail?

1. The overwhelming majority of legacy gifts are in the form of bequests, which typically consist of a sentence or two in an individual's will, living trust, or estate plan. Research shows that direct mail is the most effective way to market legacy giving through bequests.

2. So-called planned giving officers, for reasons of their own, tend to concentrate on wealthy individual prospects who may be candidates for multimillion-dollar legacy gifts (often in the form of complex tax-avoidance trusts that require lawyers, accountants, and other high-priced help to establish). But the vast majority of legacy gifts come from individuals who are not rich—the very same people who normally relate to and support charities primarily through the mail.

3. The tools used by sophisticated direct mail fundraisers, statistical analysis and segmentation, are by far the most cost-effective way to identify prospective legacy donors.

---

**EXHIBIT 19.1**

**Legacy Response Device, Bread for the World**

*A Legacy of Hope*

☐ Please send more information, without obligation, about:
    ☐ How IRAs can be used for charitable gifts
    ☐ Charitable gift annuities
    ☐ Charitable lead and remainder trusts
☐ I would like more information on remembering Bread for the World in my will.
☐ I've established a charitable bequest to Bread for the World or Bread for the World Institute. Please add my (our) name(s) to the Legacy of Hope display:

_____

PLEASE PRINT YOUR NAME(S) AS YOU WISH IT (THEM) TO APPEAR.

Mr. John Doe
123 Anv Street
Any Town AS 00000
BFW07LA/2-13-07/Others

Phone _____ / _____
    0
    07LA

*All information about charitable bequests and other planned gifts is held in the strictest confidence.*

    **1**   07LA B

*Bread for the World Institute welcomes gifts of stocks and securities. To arrange transfers, please contact Molly Pearce at 1-800-822-7323, ext. 137.*

**Bread for the World**
*Seeking Justice. Ending Hunger.*
50 F Street NW, Suite 500    Washington, DC 20001-1567
1-800-822-7323    www.bread.org

The Bread for the World renewal device shown in Exhibit 19.1 illustrates several of the characteristics that are commonly found in direct mail promotions for legacy giving:

- There's no mistaking the fact that this mailing is about legacy giving, since the headline makes it clear at the outset.

- The options offered donors include opportunities both to declare a bequest previously arranged and to inquire about legacy giving possibilities. This reflects the reality that a large proportion of legacy gifts are never disclosed to the charity they benefit until after the will is probated.

- The form emphasizes in bold print (on the right-hand side) that any response will be "held in the strictest confidence." This is a matter of considerable importance to most legacy givers.

## How Legacy Promotion Letters Are Different from Other Fundraising Appeals

Nonprofit organizations may promote legacy giving through a variety of forms and techniques. Among these are special newsletters mailed periodically both to declared legacy donors and to prospects, occasional letters specifically promoting bequests sent to the most likely legacy donors, legacy clubs or societies that celebrate donors who commit to leaving legacies, information about legacy giving (sometimes including special software to calculate tax benefits) on the charity's Web site, and recognition at special events and in annual reports. However, the most effective promotional efforts, regardless of the medium employed, display the following four features.

### Four Characteristics of Effective Legacy Promotion Packages

1. They emphasize bequests rather than planned gifts of the sort that are usually of interest only to wealthy donors.

2. They dwell on the organization's vision and mission, not on the mechanics involved in leaving a legacy. Legal and accounting information is, at best, only marginally interesting to most donors. Many regard it as a turnoff.

3. The request to declare a legacy gift typically notes that going public shows leadership by providing an example to other donors.

4. The primary purpose of most legacy giving promotions is not to secure a legacy commitment by return mail (or on the phone or by e-mail): it is to engage the donor in a dialogue that, at length, may result in such a commitment. Leaving a legacy requires a major commitment—psychologically as well as financially. Many donors take a long time to think about the prospect.

## Case Study: Project Bread Bequest Promotion Letter

Exhibits 19.2 to 19.6 show the full contents of a straightforward legacy promotion mailing to selected donors of Project Bread, a Boston-based antihunger organization. There are several noteworthy aspects of this mailing:

- The letter was mailed in a closed-face envelope (rather than a window). Since this mailing was generic (nonpersonalized), the donor will have to supply her name and address on the reply form. Obviously, Project Bread could have afforded to use personalization in this mailing. Instead, though, the organization opted to underline the confidentiality of the appeal by including no personalized elements inside the package.

- The letter is short and very much to the point: "establishing a charitable bequest." And there's no doubt how the money will be used: "to provide life's most basic necessity—food—to all our neighbors in need."

- The brochure was developed exclusively for this mailing. It's no off-the-shelf general promotional brochure. Rather, it dwells on the topic at hand: creating "a legacy of hope and opportunity for hungry families in Massachusetts."

- The reply form is headlined "Confidential." Its purpose is not to secure a commitment but rather to initiate a conversation with the donor, probably by telephone.

- The reply envelope, also marked "Confidential," is directed to a single, dedicated individual. This presumably will increase donors' confidence in the confidentiality of the process.

With this chapter, we come to the end of Part Three. In Part Four, we'll venture into cyberspace and explore the creative challenges of communicating with donors and prospects on line, through e-mail and the World Wide Web.

---

**EXHIBIT 19.2**

# Legacy Outer Envelope, Project Bread

Project Bread™
*Feeding people,
nourishing hope*

145 Border Street
East Boston, Massachusetts 02128

Mr. John Doe
123 Any Street
Any Town AS 00000

RECYCLED & RECYCLABLE / PRINTED WITH SOY INK    6-LA3

**EXHIBIT 19.3**

## Legacy Promotion Letter, Project Bread

Project
Bread℠
*Feeding people,
nourishing hope*

Dear Friend,

Your generous and faithful support of Project Bread has made a profound difference in the lives of hungry people in Massachusetts.  Thank you.

Despite our accomplishments, over 400,000 people in Massachusetts are struggling to feed themselves and their families.  Right now, thousands of hard-working families are being forced to choose between paying ever higher heating bills, providing medical care for their children—or putting food on the table.

Emergency services are a vital part of Project Bread's goal to alleviate hunger in the Commonwealth.  However—if we are to finally end hunger in our state—emergency services must be complemented by preventative efforts.  Our work to prevent hunger is based on the premise that hunger has become a public health crisis in Massachusetts— one that involves both physical and emotional trauma.  For children especially, hunger threatens their ability to grow and learn.

That's why I hope you will consider continuing your support of our work by making a planned gift to Project Bread—The Walk for Hunger, Inc.

Specifically, by establishing a charitable bequest that benefits Project Bread, you will reaffirm your commitment to ensuring that families have enough to eat.  Legacy gifts provide financial support for hundreds of food pantries and soup kitchens.  These planned gifts also enable Project Bread to develop and implement hunger prevention programs that protect the state's most vulnerable citizens—children and the elderly—from hunger.

I hope you will decide to include Project Bread in your estate plans.  Taking this small step now will have a big impact for years to come.  Your bequest will also inspire others to join you in supporting our efforts to end hunger in Massachusetts.

Thank you for all you do to provide life's most basic necessity—food—to all our neighbors in need.

Sincerely,

Lori Miller
Director of Individual Giving

145 Border Street • East Boston, MA  02128 • Tel 617-723-5000 • Fax 617-248-8877
www.projectbread.org • info@projectbread.org

6-LA1

EXHIBIT 19.4 a

# Legacy Promotion Brochure Exterior, Project Bread

## A Commonwealth ...where everyone is free from hunger

### Other Creative Ways to Help

You can also designate Project Bread as the beneficiary of insurance policies or retirement plans. In some cases, you or your heirs may also realize significant tax savings. Project Bread also accepts gifts of securities (stocks and bonds). To discuss these and other possibilities, please contact Lori Miller at 617-239-2560 or via e-mail at lori_miller@projectbread.org.

When you remember Project Bread in your will or living trust, you create a legacy of hope and opportunity for hungry families in Massachusetts. For more information on making a bequest or other legacy gifts to Project Bread, please contact Lori Miller at 617-239-2560 or via e-mail at lori_miller@projectbread.org.

Project Bread's tax identification number is 04-2931195.

Project Bread™
Feeding people,
nourishing hope

145 Border Street
East Boston, MA 02128
617-723-5000
FoodSource Hotline at 1-800-645-8333
www.projectbread.org

RECYCLED & RECYCLABLE / SOY INK    6-UAS

**EXHIBIT 19.4 b**

**Legacy Promotion Brochure Interior, Project Bread**

# Continue your legacy of feeding the hungry in Massachusetts.

For nearly 40 years, Project Bread – The Walk for Hunger has worked to create solutions to the problem of hunger in our midst. The progress we've made has been possible because of thousands of compassionate volunteers, walkers, and donors. Together, we have raised more than $59 million to help hungry families. In 2005, Project Bread supported over 400 soup kitchens and food pantries that served 40 million meals. In addition, through collaboration with civic leaders and community groups, Project Bread has played a leadership role in developing public policies that address hunger and nutrition, especially among children.

Now, you have the opportunity to assist hungry families for years to come. By including Project Bread in your estate plan, you can leave an enduring legacy of support for efforts that feed people and nourish hope.

## The Legacy of Compassion and Good Health

You don't need to be wealthy to make a gift that will have an impact on future generations. A charitable bequest to Project Bread in your will or living trust will serve as a powerful testimony to your conviction that no one should have to struggle to provide food for themselves or their families in Massachusetts.

No matter how modest your assets, establishing a will or living trust can ensure your estate is settled quickly—and with fewer complications for your family and loved ones.

## You Can Make a Bequest

You may find the following wordings to be helpful. These brief descriptions are not intended as legal or financial advice. Please consult your attorney or financial planner.

- **TO MAKE A SIMPLE BEQUEST**

"I give and bequeath to Project Bread – The Walk for Hunger, Inc., of 145 Border Street, East Boston, Massachusetts, 02128, the sum of $_____ (or a specific item of property, such as real estate, stocks or bonds, automobile, etc.) to be used as the organization determines."

- **TO MAKE A RESIDUAL BEQUEST**

You may choose to leave the residue of your estate after you have provided for family members and other beneficiaries. "I give and bequeath to Project Bread – The Walk for Hunger, Inc., of 145 Border Street, East Boston, Massachusetts, 02128, the residue of my estate, to be used as the organization determines."

- **TO MAKE A PERCENTAGE BEQUEST**

"I give and bequeath to Project Bread – The Walk for Hunger, Inc., of 145 Border Street, East Boston, Massachusetts, 02128, _____% (name a specific percentage) of the total value of my estate to be used as the organization determines."

**EXHIBIT 19.5**

## Legacy Promotion Reply Device, Project Bread

CONFIDENTIAL REPLY

☐ I'm considering including Project Bread in my estate plan. Please send me additional information about leaving a charitable bequest or other planned gift.

☐ I have already included Project Bread in my estate plans.

☐ I prefer that my charitable plans remain anonymous.

Project Bread
Feeding people, nourishing hope

145 Border Street
East Boston, MA  02128
Tel 617-723-5000
www.projectbread.org

PLEASE PRINT:

Name _____

Address _____

City _____ Zip _____

Email address (optional) _____

Phone: _____ - _____

☐ Please call me. The best time to reach me is:
   ☐ morning   ☐ afternoon   ☐ evening

*Please be assured that there is no obligation, and that all information about charitable gifts and bequests will be held in the strictest confidence.*

6-LA2

---

**EXHIBIT 19.6**

## Legacy Promotion Reply Envelope, Project Bread

Project Bread
Feeding people,
nourishing hope

PLEASE
PLACE
STAMP
HERE

Confidential:
Please Route to Lori Miller

Project Bread
145 Border Street
East Boston, MA 02128-1903

RECYCLED & RECYCLABLE / SOY INK   6-LA6

# Part Four

# Using E-Mail and the Internet

**HERE'S WHERE WE** venture outside the realm of classical direct mail fundraising and peek into the emerging field of raising money on line. Though far from the panacea for the high costs of direct mail that many optimists were hoping for, online fundraising has emerged as a useful adjunct to the fundraiser's toolbox—and it's been growing consistently, by at least 35 percent annually, for several years. All of which justifies our taking a close-up look at

- What's different (and what's not) between writing direct mail and writing Internet and e-mail appeals

- The anatomy of a successful e-mail appeal

- How to create an effective electronic newsletter (e-newsletter)

- Twenty ways to involve your donors on line

# Chapter 20

# Writing Online Appeals
## Harnessing the Power of the Internet

**GET OUT YOUR** pencil and notebook now. It's time for a pop quiz.
Question: Which one of the following statements is true?

a. The most important thing for raising money on line is the capacity to accept donations on your Web site.

b. E-mail costs so much less than direct mail that it is rapidly replacing it as a fundraising medium of choice.

c. Nonprofit organizations in the United States are raising more than 10 percent of their revenue on line, and that proportion is expected to rise to 50 percent by 2013.

d. The way to raise money on line is to take your direct mail letters and send them out by e-mail to all your donors.

e. Almost everyone in the United States is now on line, so it's only a matter of time before nonprofits can expect their donor lists to grow exponentially through an influx of younger donors who will join through the World Wide Web.

Careful now—that was a trick question.

Have you got it? You figured out that *not one* of these answers is true? Go to the head of the class! But if you're unsure about whether these statements reflect current reality, listen up. Fundraising on line is a highly promising field, but it's a world in itself, with its own rules, quirks, and culture. If you plunge in blindly, heedless of the idiosyncrasies and challenges of communications on line, you may find that fundraising via e-mail and the Internet is anything but cheap.

For starters, here are a few of the things you can (and can't) expect from online fundraising:

• E-mail, not the Web, is the key to raising money on line. A strong Web site is absolutely necessary, but it's far from sufficient. If you build it and just let it sit there, they *won't* come.

• Online fundraising revenue is growing at an astounding rate—an estimated 35 to 40 percent annually—but it's building on a very small base.

The most reliable estimates I can find indicate that e-mail and the Web yielded approximately 1 percent of total philanthropic revenue in the United States in 2006, or a little more than 1 percent of giving by individual donors. Even if we assume straight-line growth at the rate of 37 percent per year (which is not a safe assumption), we'll have to wait until 2014 before online fundraising accounts for even 10 percent of philanthropic giving.

• Online fundraising techniques don't work equally well for all non-profit organizations. Those engaged in emergency humanitarian relief are the biggest beneficiaries—and those organizations with well-known brands, such as the Red Cross, the Salvation Army, and UNICEF, are the biggest of all. Prominent advocacy organizations such as Amnesty International and the Human Rights Campaign have also gained in major ways from the Internet, largely because they deal in hot-button issues that dominate the headlines. (The issues that have attracted the most attention are personal and civil liberties, environmental protection, and human rights.) High-profile political campaigns have benefited too. Although organizations in other fields have sometimes managed to build significant online donor files, they tend to be the exception, not the rule. Not yet, anyway.

• Despite the hype about the Internet's big fundraising success stories, relatively few donors have given on line. However, those who do make contributions on line give significantly more money on average than do direct mail donors.

• The Internet's competitive advantage against all other media is speed. In your direct mail fundraising program, you may allow months to elapse between conception and the mailbox. That would lead to utter failure on line. It's no accident that the most successful online fundraisers are disaster relief agencies, advocacy organizations, and political campaigns—because all of them rise or fall with breaking news. To make the Internet work for you as a fundraising tool, you'll need to find some way to introduce a strong sense of urgency into your appeals.

• The demographics of Web users reflect a lower median age than that of direct mail respondents. After all, the median direct mail donor for most nonprofits tends to be fifty-five or older, and for some organizations the median age can reach into the seventies. But the fact that teenagers and twenty-somethings have grown up with the Internet and can often be found in cyberspace at any hour of the day or night doesn't mean that they're now rushing into philanthropy. Yes, online donors tend to be younger than direct mail donors, typically in their forties and fifties rather than their sixties or seventies. But online communications reach older folks as well as youngsters—and it's the older ones who disproportionately respond to appeals for money.

• Decades of research into the habits and expectations of direct mail donors have given us considerable insight into what's likely to work in the mail, and what isn't. (Even so, our best guesses are wrong far too often!) Research into the minds of online donors is, by comparison, in its infancy. At this writing, the Web is celebrating its fifteenth anniversary, and fundraising on line on any meaningful scale dates only to the late 1990s. Bluntly put, there's a whole lot more that we don't know than that we do know about raising money on line.

• One thing we know for certain, though: much of what works in the mail most assuredly does not work on line. There are profound differences in style, format, and approach between the two media. If your Web site features brochures and direct mail appeals transposed intact, you've probably already discovered how ineffective they can be.

• Oh, one last point: The technical demands of raising money on line can be daunting. Chances are, unless you or a member of your staff is a dyed-in-the-wool geek with a broad knowledge of what works on line, you'll find your organization's performance on the Internet to be limited if you try going it alone. For starters, you'll need to sign up with an online service provider, such as Convio or Kintera, to manage the technical aspects of maintaining your list, sending out e-mail messages and e-newsletters, and hosting your Web site. You're also likely to find it advisable to hire one of the growing number of online fundraising consultants. Let the consultant keep up with the proliferation of online opportunities on your behalf— and stick to raising money yourself.

To explore this high-potential medium and how to make the most of it, let's first take a look at the structure and contents of a typical e-mail appeal.

## Anatomy of an E-Mail Appeal

The appeal displayed in Exhibit 20.1 won the Package of the Year Award from the Direct Marketing Fundraisers Association for 2006 because of the unusually strong results it yielded. From top to bottom this e-mail message is a whole different species from any direct mail fundraising letter. Consider each of these elements:

*From.* Direct mail testing often shows that the identity of a letter signer may have little or no impact on the results of a mailing. Not so in e-mail.

**EXHIBIT 20.1**

## Award-Winning E-Mail Appeal, MoveOn.org

**From:** Nita Chaudhary, MoveOn.org Political Action [mailto:moveon-help@list.moveon.org]

**Sent:** Thursday, April 26, 2007 1:52 PM

**To:** Madeline

**Subject:** This is a brave man

George Bush keeps saying that he's the one who supports the troops and those of us who want to end the war don't. Someone has to take him on for that. And John Bruhns—who served in Iraq as a sergeant—is the man to do it.

MoveOn members chose John to be the subject of a TV ad by Oliver Stone as part of our VideoVets project. After coming home, John decided he could no longer remain silent. He says keeping our troops in Iraq without end is "wrong, immoral, and irresponsible." He's brave and patriotic, and his first-hand truth is an essential antidote to the administration's lies.

**Can you chip in $25 so we can get John's story on TV and spread it across the internet?** Click below to watch the video and contribute:

https://pol.moveon.org/donate/videovets2.html?id=10248-8035350-IQPyZs&t=4

We talked to John this morning, and he's really moved by this whole experience. Here's a note he asked us to pass on to MoveOn members:

> *I'm overwhelmed by the statements of those who saw my video. I can't put into words how honored I am that people were so moved by it. For so long I felt so helpless—in a sense that there was nothing I could do to make a difference in regards to ending the war and educating the American people on the reality of the situation. I made a promise to myself in Iraq that if I was lucky enough to make it home I would do everything in my power to help transition us out of the war. Thank you all so very much for giving me this tremendous opportunity. I am very grateful.*

Oliver Stone and his team are working on the ad as we speak. And John is getting ready to get on a plane and go work with them. We want to make sure as many people as possible hear John's message about the real cost of war.

Can you chip in $25 to help get John's message out there through a big online and TV ad campaign?

https://pol.moveon.org/donate/videovets2.html?id=10248-8035350-IQPyZs&t=5

The president is accusing Congress of playing politics with our troops because they want a plan that starts a responsible redeployment this year. John's video—along with the interviews of all the VideoVets participants—prove that supporting our troops does NOT mean supporting the president's reckless policy in Iraq.

The truth is that it's President Bush and his Republican allies who have not supported the troops. Our brave men and women are stranded in the middle of a civil war, with inadequate protection and resources—and the president wants to send more still.

Supporting our troops is more than a catch phrase. The way to support our troops is to listen to them and their families. Folks like John have stepped up to get the truth out there.

**EXHIBIT 20.1 (*Continued*)**

Please help us get John's story out to counter the administration's spin on Iraq.

https://pol.moveon.org/donate/videovets2.html?id=10248-8035350-IQPyZs&t=6

Oliver Stone did a special interview with us about why he chose to get involved. Click below to watch it:

http://pol.moveon.org/videovets?id=10248-8035350-IQPyZs&t=7

Thanks for all you do,

-Nita, Laura, Karin, Patrick and the MoveOn.org Political Action Team

Thursday, April 26th, 2007

P.S. One thing John makes clear is the need to safely redeploy our troops. The fight to end the war is heating up in Congress right now. We thought you might enjoy this note from Senator Feingold. Click below to read it:

http://www.moveon.org/r?r=2538&id=10248-8035350-IQPyZs&t=8

**Support our member-driven organization:** MoveOn.org Political Action is entirely funded by our 3.2 million members. We have no corporate contributors, no foundation grants, no money from unions. Our tiny staff ensures that small contributions go a long way. If you'd like to support our work, you can give now at:

http://political.moveon.org/donate/emailhtml?id=10248-8035350-IQPyZs&t=9

PAID FOR BY MOVEON.ORG POLITICAL ACTION, http://pol.moveon.org/
Not authorized by any candidate or candidate's committee.

**Subscription Management:**
This is a message from MoveOn.org Political Action. To change your email address, update your contact info, or remove yourself (Madeline) from this list, please visit our subscription management page at:
http://moveon.org/s?i=10248-8035350-IQPyZs

If the "From" line at the top of your e-mail doesn't reflect someone or something familiar to your supporters—your organization's name, the name most familiar to your supporters (probably that of your executive director), a celebrity name, or some combination of those elements—the odds are great that your message will go straight into the trash.

*Subject.* The subject line, equivalent to a headline in a space ad, is probably the single most important element in the text of an e-mail appeal. Someday, books will be written about subject lines and how to craft them. Nowadays, you'll have to be content knowing that the subject line must tease the recipient (but not so much that she chuckles and trashes the message) and offer a benefit (but without triggering spam filters). However, teasing can backfire when you're seeking an annual renewal or a year-end gift.

*Lead.* In a direct mail fundraising appeal, you might well lead with a story about how some hapless individual's life has been turned around by the miraculous service your organization has provided. Not in e-mail—unless that story is highly emotional and very short. The first few lines of your message may be all that the recipient ever sees—because he's probably viewing your e-mail through a *preview pane.* A wordy or unclear lead will guarantee that a message goes straight into the trash. The direct mail device known as the *Johnson's Box*—a sentence or two of copy that appears above the salutation—can be put to work in e-mail, too. Sometimes response will rise significantly if you place your most dramatic and compelling sentence at the very top of the message—because it's certain to be read, even through a preview pane.

*Graphic.* Most fundraising appeals incorporate graphics—that is, they're HTML messages. However, controversy is raging among the denizens of cyberspace as to whether graphic images such as the one shown here reduce the deliverability of e-mail. Many e-mail delivery services work hard to ensure their messages, including graphics, avoid the spam filters at Hotmail, Yahoo, AOL, Comcast, and the other big e-mail providers. To work effectively with them, however, you'll probably need to contract for the services of a qualified Internet service provider such as Convio or Kintera.

*Links.* The rule of thumb in raising money by e-mail is to include three click-through links to a donation page on your Web site—one near the beginning, one in the middle, and one toward the end of the message. These links should lead to a separate *landing page,* which is a donation page custom-tailored to that particular appeal. (Rather than construct an individual landing page for each link, I recommend that you embed a unique source code within the link. That way, you can track which link draws the most traffic.)

*Unsubscribe.* Include instructions on how to get off your list ("unsubscribe") in every message. In fact, most e-mail delivery services hardwire this into their systems. If people don't want your messages, make it easy for them to stop, and for you to avoid accusations of spamming.

*Landing page.* When a donor clicks on one of the links you've embedded in your appeal, she will be transported to a specified landing page on your Web site. Smaller organizations tend to link donors to a generic donation page, but I don't recommend that. In direct mail, it's almost always important to enclose a separate reply device that matches the letter in theme, tone, and appearance. The landing page should do that too. See Exhibit 20.2 for an example.

**EXHIBIT 20.2**

# Landing Page for Award-Winning Online Appeal, MoveOn.org

 POLITICAL ACTION®

CAMPAIGNS | SUCCESS STORIES | DONATE | SIGN UP | ABOUT

## Help get John Bruhns' story out there

George Bush keeps saying that he's the one who supports the troops and those of us who want to end the war don't. Someone has to take him on for that. And former Sergeant John Bruhns—who served in Iraq—is the man to do it. He's the subject of a new ad by Oliver Stone. Your contribution will help us spread his story—and those of the other VideoVets participants—far and wide through a big TV and online advertising campaign. **Can you contribute?** Complete the form below to contribute.

No video? Click here.

**1 YOUR INFORMATION**

Your Name

E-mail

Billing Address

City

State

Billing Zip

* Occupation

* Employer

**2 SELECT AN AMOUNT**

○ $25    ○ $100    ○ $500    ○ $2000

○ $50    ○ $250    ○ $1000    Other $

**3 CREDIT CARD INFORMATION**

Credit Card Number (VISA/MC/AMEX)

Verification #    Expiration Date (mo/year)

**4 CONTRIBUTION RULES**

By checking the box below I confirm that the following statements are true and accurate: 1) I am a United States citizen or a permanent resident alien. 2) This contribution is not made from the general treasury funds of a corporation, labor organization or national bank. 3) This contribution is not made from the treasury of an entity or person who is a federal contractor. 4) The funds I am donating are not being provided to me by another person or entity for the purpose of making this contribution. 5) If under 18: I am contributing knowingly and voluntarily with my own funds.

* ☐ I have read all of the rules above and I certify that I comply with each of them.

☐ Remember my data (except credit card information) for next time.

 **Submit Contribution »**

* Required by federal law

The landing page is the business end of an online appeal, equivalent to the reply device in direct mail. How you design and write this form can be critical to the success of your e-mail appeal. The landing page must look and feel like the appeal itself. It's wise to limit, or even eliminate, links to other pages on your site. Be certain the ask is clear and that you've restated the creative, or marketing, concept of the appeal, repeating the language in the appeal, just as you would in direct mail. Offer several giving options. Use a one-column format (rather than two) where you ask for personal information. (Testing has shown the one-column approach outpulls the two-column format.) And, above all, keep this form simple.

With the possible exception of a graphic image, every e-mail appeal you send should absolutely, positively include every one of the foregoing elements. And each of them is worth every bit of attention you can pay to ensure that you've got them all just right.

One more important point about e-mail appeals: In direct mail fund-raising, we sometimes lamely urge our donors to "pass along to a friend, colleague, or family member" any duplicate appeal they receive. Naturally, you can probably count on the fingers of one hand the number of times this has actually happened. But on line, it's a different story. The capacity for *viral* messaging, in which one donor forwards an appeal from you to twenty friends, or two hundred, is one of the advantages of the Internet. You're unlikely to raise a lot of money that way or recruit a large number of new donors, but there may be some—and it's practically free anyway. So it's a mistake not to offer your donors an opportunity to "pass along" your appeal to others. However, the proper place to make that request is not in the solicitation itself but on the landing page or in the thank-you message you send upon receipt of the gift.

## How Writing On Line Is Different from Putting Words on Paper

Take, for example, the typical special appeal illustrated in Exhibit 20.3. There's nothing out of the ordinary in this direct mail letter sent by AIDS Project Los Angeles (APLA) unless you count the generic approach (rather than a personalized one) to previous supporters. Just try, though, to e-mail an appeal structured like this one to your supporters, and you'll see quickly enough that what works in the mail falls flat on line.

To gain a sense of the specific differences between the online and printed approaches, take a look at the same appeal *repurposed* in an online format and shown in Exhibit 20.4. (This repurposed appeal was prepared for this

**EXHIBIT 20.3**

## Direct Mail Fundraising Appeal, APLA

AIDS Project Los Angeles

The David Geffen Center
611 S. Kingsley Drive
Los Angeles, CA 90005
www.apla.org

Ms. Jane Doe
123 Any Street
Any Town AS 00000
APL07AC/6-12-07/MATCHING GRANT APPEAL

*INSIDE:*

*Special Matching Gift Offer Will Double Your Gift!*

RECYCLED & RECYCLABLE / SOY INK    7-AC3    1

book and was not sent. If it had been e-mailed, "unsubscribe" language would have appeared below the image shown.)

The appeals shown in Exhibits 20.3 and 20.4 convey almost exactly the same message. But the e-mail version isn't just the original letter transposed into e-mail—it's truly repurposed. Note the significant differences between the two versions:

- The e-mail appeal is shorter—much shorter. That reflects the more limited attention span of e-mail recipients. Research estimates that you've got an average of eight seconds to grab the attention of a direct mail recipient and induce her to read the letter. On line, you'd be lucky for a recipient to scan your message for half that time. Many e-mail recipients simply highlight all incoming messages, preparing them for deletion—and then preserve the few they really want to read by removing the highlighting. It's a cruel world out there in cyberspace!

- The e-mail appeal gets right to the point. Note the headline and the caption above the photo on the right-hand side. Then read the first sentence of the e-mail appeal and compare it with the lead of the direct mail letter. There's no mistaking the point of this electronic appeal, even when only its top portion is viewed through a preview pane.

- Clearly, this HTML appeal—the format in which the overwhelming majority of e-mail messages are sent these days—features graphic elements that would appear intrusive in a direct mail format. Sure, some

**EXHIBIT 20.3 (*Continued*)**

The David Geffen Center
611 S. Kingsley Drive
Los Angeles, CA 90005
www.apla.org

June 5, 2007

Dear Friend and Supporter,

I'm writing to you today with some wonderful news for AIDS Project Los Angeles and for people in our community living with HIV/AIDS.

At a time when many other AIDS service organizations are seeing diminishing support from corporations, APLA continues to receive an annual $100,000 Matching Gift offer from Wells Fargo Bank.

> For the next 100 days, Wells Fargo Bank will match all contributions from current APLA members—dollar for dollar—up to $100,000. For a limited time, you can <u>double the impact</u> of your gift through the Wells Fargo Matching Gift offer.

This is tremendous news—and we are appealing to our core donors like you to step forward and participate in this generous offer. Unlike many other challenge grants with specific program guidelines, the Wells Fargo offer will allow APLA to use the $100,000 in matching funds wherever the need is greatest.

That means we'll be able to increase our funding this summer to increase the HIV prevention and outreach efforts taking place in neighborhoods that have been hardest hit by AIDS. We'll be able to expand our Home Health Services to provide bedside care for people who are seriously ill with AIDS. And we'll be able to meet the growing needs of low-income clients who count on APLA each week for groceries and other necessities of life.

These are challenging times for AIDS service organizations across the country. This week marks the 26th anniversary of the first reported case of AIDS and we are reminded that more than 25 million people around the world have already died of AIDS—including 30,000 people living right here in Los Angeles.

I feel privileged to live and work in Los Angeles where we have steadfast supporters like you to help us get through these challenging times. And to continue serving our clients in the year ahead, we need the matching gift support of our core donors this summer.

As you may know, government support for our services is decreasing. Federal funding through the Ryan White CARE Act is again being threatened—and Los Angeles County just

**EXHIBIT 20.3 (*Continued*)**

can't count on receiving the same amount of HIV prevention education funding this year as we received last year.

There are over one million Americans living with HIV, and more than 59,000 of them live right here in Los Angeles County. Many of these individuals turn to APLA for help each year—and only through our partnership with friends like you and Wells Fargo Bank are we able to meet this growing need for our services.

> If you are able to send a $25 contribution to APLA today,
> it will be matched immediately and APLA will have $50
> to help someone in our community living with HIV/AIDS.
> Your gift of $100 will become $200, and will go twice as
> far in providing groceries to APLA clients at one of our food
> distribution centers. Your $500 gift will actually enable
> APLA to provide $1,000 worth of home health care visits
> to persons who are too ill to leave their homes.

Please know that I'm personally grateful to you for your compassion, your confidence in APLA, and your continuing support for persons living with HIV/AIDS.

I urge you to help us take advantage of this extraordinarily generous offer by Wells Fargo Bank and help APLA qualify for every dollar of the $100,000 grant. I can assure you that your gift will be matched, but the difference you make in the life of someone struggling with AIDS will be unequaled.

Thank you, once again, for staying with us.

With high hopes,

*Craig E. Thompson*

Craig E. Thompson
Executive Director

P.S.    As you may know, Wells Fargo Bank has a proud history of supporting APLA and giving back to the community. APLA has been a grateful beneficiary of Wells Fargo gifts for several years, and I hope you'll join us this year by sending in a gift of $25, $50, $100, $500, or more within the next 100 days and help us reach our $100,000 goal. For more information on Wells Fargo and their charitable giving, please visit their website, www.wellsfargo.com. Thank you.

**EXHIBIT 20.3 (*Continued*)**

## $100,000 Wells Fargo Matching Gift Campaign

**TO:**    Craig E. Thompson, Executive Director
AIDS PROJECT LOS ANGELES

**FROM:**    Ms. Jane Doe
123 Any Street
Any Town AS 00000
APL07AC/6-12-07/MATCHING GRANT APPEAL        07ACDOEA
0
5254

**ABOUT:**    <u>Doubling</u> <u>My</u> <u>Support</u> <u>for</u> <u>APLA's</u> <u>Programs</u> <u>and</u> <u>Services</u>

<u>YES</u>, I wish to take advantage of Wells Fargo's Matching Gift offer and double the amount of my gift to AIDS PROJECT LOS ANGELES. I understand my gift will be matched dollar for dollar. Enclosed is my special contribution of:

[ ] **$100 — turning my gift into a $200 contribution to APLA**
[ ] **$200 — turning my gift into a $400 contribution to APLA**
[ ] **$_____**

**Do you prefer to make your gift by credit card?**

☐ VISA        ☐ MasterCard        ☐ American Express

Name on card: _____

Account number: _____

Exp. Date: _____    Gift Amount: _____

Signature: _____

*To contribute online via our secure server, please visit:* ***www.apla.org.*** *Your gift to AIDS Project Los Angeles is fully tax-deductible.*

**APLA**
AIDS Project Los Angeles

The David Geffen Center
611 S. Kingsley Drive
Los Angeles CA 90005
www.apla.org

RECYCLED & RECYCLABLE / SOY INK        7-AC2

1

---

**APLA**
AIDS Project Los Angeles

7-AC6

<u>ATTN</u>: Special Wells Fargo Matching Gift

||| ||

**AIDS PROJECT LOS ANGELES**
GIFT PROCESSING CENTER
2550 NINTH STREET  SUITE 1059
BERKELEY  CA  94710-2551

||||||||||||||||||||||||||||||||||||||

**EXHIBIT 20.4**

## Repurposed Online Version of Direct Mail Appeal, APLA

 **Double Your Impact**
for people living with HIV/AIDS

Wells Fargo is matching all donations to APLA up to $100,000 through DATE.

▶ **Have your gift matched today!**

Dear Friend,

At a time when many other AIDS service organizations are seeing diminishing funding from the government and corporations, AIDS Project Los Angeles has a critical opportunity to increase support for the 59,000 people in our community living with HIV/AIDS.

**For the next 100 days, Wells Fargo Bank will match all contributions to APLA – dollar for dollar – up to $100,000.**

<u>**Please, have your gift matched today**</u>!

This opportunity is especially exciting because, unlike many other challenge grants with specific program guidelines, Wells Fargo is allowing APLA to use the matching funds wherever the need is greatest.

This means that – if we meet our goal of $100,000 – we'll be able to:

Bring our HIV prevention and outreach efforts to neighborhoods that have been hardest hit by AIDS.

Expand our Home Health Services to provide bedside care for people who are seriously ill with AIDS.

Meet the growing needs of low-income people who count on APLA each week for groceries and other necessities of life.

With government support decreasing and federal funding through the Ryan White CARE Act being threatened — Los Angeles County just can't count on receiving the same amount of HIV prevention education funding this year as we received last year.

**If we want to continue bringing our services to the people who need them in the year ahead, we need the matching gift support of our donors this summer. <u>Please have your gift matched today</u>!**

While the dollars you donate will be doubled, the difference you make in the life of someone struggling with AIDS will be unequaled.

<u>**I hope you'll take this opportunity to make that difference.**</u> Thank you in advance for your generous contribution, and thank you, once again, for staying with us.

With high hopes,

*Craig E. Thompson*

Craig E. Thompson
Executive Director

 *leadership in prevention, advocacy & service*

611 South Kingsley Drive
Los Angeles, CA 90005
213.201.1600 Main line
213.201.1500 Clientline

mailers use headlines and photos in their letters. However, such graphic elements are likely to look out of place in most direct mail appeals. As you have probably deduced from the earlier chapters in this book, I use graphics very sparingly in direct mail letters. My tendency is to do so on line as well—and there is a growing body of evidence that's calling into question the wisdom of loading up e-mail messages with graphics. The jury is still out.

- There are three asks in the letter. Even in the much shorter e-mail message, there are three asks too. Each of the three underlined passages links to a giving page on the organization's Web site.

Those are specific differences. As you can see, though, the difference in the look and feel of the two versions is greater than the sum of these parts. E-mail is an entirely different medium from print—and if that contrast doesn't show in your e-mail appeals, you'll find your online campaigns falling far short of their goals.

## The Cardinal Rules of Writing E-Mail Appeals

It's premature to lay down the law about writing on line because so much is yet unknown. Fundraisers and commercial marketers alike are evaluating their efforts and gaining new insight all the time. However, there are certain basic guidelines that are worth observing and are unlikely to be overturned by later experience.

---

### Some Basic Guidelines for Writing E-Mail Appeals

- The "From" address should be consistent in all your e-mail appeals. Use your organization's name on that line rather than the name of an individual person or a department.

- Avoid using the recipient's name in the "Subject" line, since that will make your message appear to be spam.

- Make sure that the top two to four inches of your appeal—the portion that will show through a preview pane—is compelling enough to induce readers to open the message and read it all.

- Limit the length of your lines to 50 to 60 characters. (That's about 4½ inches if you're using 12-point Courier type.)

- Just as in direct mail, make sure there's plenty of white space on all sides and between paragraphs.

- Limit paragraphs to no more than five lines.

- Don't overload your message with Web links. Include only those you must: the landing page (perhaps three times) and the home page, plus a contact link and an opt-out link at the bottom.

- Minimize your use of asterisks, stars, and other typographical devices (they may trigger spam filters).

- Test each message before sending it.

---

Keep in mind that timeliness is one of the keys to success on line. This doesn't just mean you must respond to headline-grabbing events within hours, if possible—it also means you need to send appeals to newly acquired online supporters within thirty days. Click-through rates drop after that point, and much more dramatically after sixty days.

### Eight Ways Writing E-mail Appeals Is the Same as Writing Direct Mail Letters

1. Donors respond to the same lofty goals and aspirations on line as they do in direct mail. Your organization's vision and mission are the most important motivators. While techniques such as challenge grants, premiums, thermometers (or other symbols of a campaign's promise), or clever campaign concepts may work a little better on line than they do in the mail—so long as they are absolutely clear at a glance—contributions on line come from the same space in our hearts, minds, and spirits as they do in direct mail. (If you need a refresher course in the fundamentals of donor motivation, check out the motivational hierarchy developed by Abraham Maslow.)

2. A direct mail appeal will fall flat if its marketing, or creative, concept isn't absolutely clear without a second look. The same is true of an e-mail appeal. From the subject line to the lead to the language on the landing page, the marketing concept must ring true. At no point in the process should you muddy the waters by introducing ideas that are inconsistent with the marketing concept.

3. Successful fundraising on line is no less dependent than fundraising by mail on making it easy for the donor to give. You go to great lengths to prepare a response device that is tightly connected, thematically and visually, to the main letter. You should devote no less attention to the landing page where people actually use their credit cards to donate.

4. Just as your direct mail letters must come across as personal, one-to-one communications, so too must your e-mail appeals. Use "I" and "you" as liberally as possible.

5. Direct mail offers abundant opportunities to boost response and increase cost-effectiveness through segmentation. The same is true on line. At first, you may want to limit yourself to appeals that are identical for all your donors. However, as you build a database of response data—far more detailed and intricate than you could ever build through the mail—you'll find that the possibilities for segmentation on line appear endless. It's worth learning how to fine-tune your e-mail fundraising

program with variable copy and ask amounts. But don't get carried away: as in direct mail, the most broadly useful segmentation is based on a donor's highest previous contribution (HPC).

6. In direct mail, the major factors influencing the success of an appeal are the list, the offer, and the format. That's no less the case with e-mail. One major difference is that although renting or exchanging donor, member, subscriber, or activist lists or demographically defined lists is normal in direct mail marketing, you generally can't rent donor lists from other nonprofit organizations or publications because of privacy and permission issues. The lists generally available for rental don't work for fundraising and will also subject you to complaints that you are spamming, even if the names are allegedly on an *opt-in* list, meaning people have given permission for their use.

7. Urgency is a critical element in direct mail. Unless your appeal conveys a sense that it really makes a difference for the donor to respond right away, chances are high that he'll simply put your letter aside intending to "get to it later"—which of course happens infrequently. (Siegfried Vögele, about whose work I wrote in Chapter Two, estimated that about half these responses will be lost.) In e-mail urgency is even more the name of the game. If your organization can e-mail a relevant message about a headline event within a couple of hours of the event, or a day at most, you may generate many times more revenue than you would if you had waited an extra day or two. One of the prime virtues of online communication is its speed. You need to make the most of it.

8. True fundraising—not those one-off gifts that come from donor acquisition campaigns but the renewal and special appeal gifts that stiffen the backbone of the development process—depends on involving donors. In direct mail, a form of involvement can come from a device as simple as a survey or petition or as substantial as a phone conversation with a legacy-giving officer in a follow-up to a letter. In electronic communications, the possibilities of involvement are much more numerous. The most common of the involvement techniques is the e-newsletter.

## Creating an Effective E-Newsletter

Building relationships in the ephemeral world of online communications is a challenge. If your donors find it easy to discard your direct mail appeals unopened, they can delete your e-mail appeals even more easily. Paradoxically, though, relationships grow strong over time only if the frequency of contact is high—once monthly at a minimum. Today's most successful online fundraisers e-mail their supporters much more frequently—weekly, two or three times weekly, or even daily. But if your organization is small, thinly budgeted, or able to craft a credible appeal only infrequently, then an e-newsletter may be a useful tool for building interest among your online supporters and advancing the process of involving them in your organization. One such product is pictured in Exhibit 20.5.

Most e-newsletters are published in HTML format, like the sample in Exhibit 20.5. That way, you can include graphics and photos as well as Web links shrunk to manageable size ("Click here," for example). A few organizations—a shrinking number—still use plain text. (A handful of organizations send their newsletters as Adobe PDF attachments, but these

**EXHIBIT 20.5**

## Sample E-Newsletter, Sierra Club

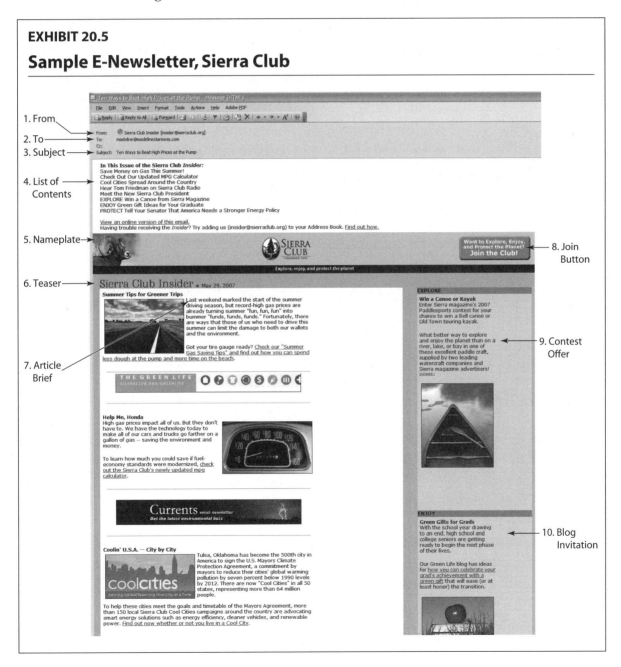

**EXHIBIT 20.5 (Continued)**

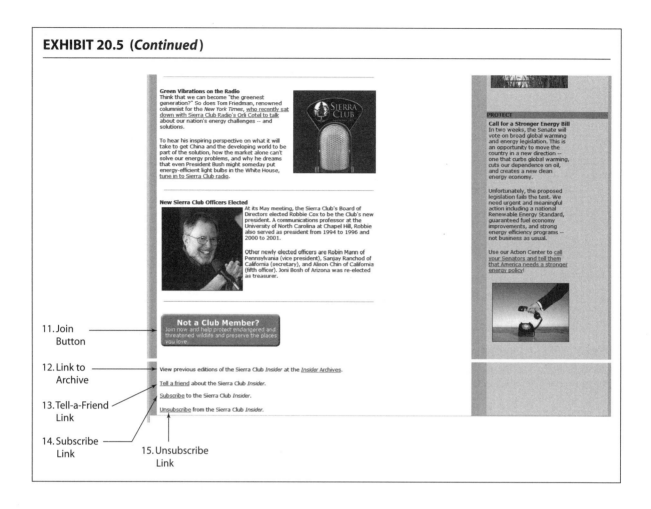

11. Join Button

12. Link to Archive

13. Tell-a-Friend Link

14. Subscribe Link

15. Unsubscribe Link

are likely to be treated as spam.) However, most publishers offer a plain text version as an option.

Then there are the formatting questions that arise about the newsletter's layout. Some publishers insist that a long form is best—one that includes the full text of each article in sequence. Others maintain that readership increases when the e-newsletter itself contains only a one- or two-paragraph summary of each article, followed by a link to the full text on another Web site. Still others say that such long summaries are distracting and a single sentence plus a link to the Web site will suffice. There is no conclusive evidence yet available that one of these approaches consistently works better than the others. However, my own experience suggests that because brevity works better on line than wordiness, a newsletter that appears shorter is more likely to gain and keep readers than one that goes on for page after page of text.

Keep in mind that an electronic communication—like any message sent to supporters—needs to be interesting, substantive, and written in a lively style. Most e-newsletters are boring. Ideally, a newsletter should include news. Short of that, it ought to include enough human interest and colorful information that your supporters will want to read it.

What structural elements should you include in an e-newsletter? The possibilities are endless, of course. However, I strongly recommend that you publish shorter newsletters relatively often rather than longer ones infrequently, and that you consider incorporating at least the following elements into each issue.

---

## Recommended Elements of a E-Newsletter

- *List of contents.* Not all e-newsletters lead with this abbreviated listing of articles, but experience on line seems to suggest that this approach increases readership—so long as the entries are brief and the language is clear. Perhaps that's because at least some of the list of contents will show through on a preview screen—and one of the several articles listed may be a greater incentive to open and read the newsletter than the opening lines of a single article.

- *Limited number of articles.* Some e-newsletters are jam-packed with contents—ten, twelve, or even fifteen articles—but I don't recommend it. I believe that the more digestible your newsletter, the more it will be read. I would opt for a daily newsletter that includes a single article more readily than a weekly newsletter containing seven. And I most assuredly would not wait until I'd accumulated a critical mass of articles—fifteen, twenty, or more—and then publish a monthly issue. A hefty print newsletter might—I say *might*—be more attractive than a flimsy one. On line, though, it will discourage readership.

- *Appeal for funds—sometimes, not in every issue.* Some direct marketers advocate asking for money at every opportunity. I don't. Your readers are expecting content from you (interesting, useful information) not an appeal for funds at every turn. Fundraising efforts are more effective when they're interspersed with substantive material, not a predictable and inevitable part of every communication. In any case, newsletter appeals don't usually generate a lot of donations unless your list is very large.

- *Pass-along option.* The most effective location for an invitation to pass along your newsletter is at the very top of each issue. It's intrusive of course, and may be esthetically undesirable. Many publishers relegate this link to the bottom of the issue.

- *Call to action or other involvement opportunity.* Though I believe requests for money ought to be sent sparingly, I feel very different about requests for action. The biggest and most responsive e-mail lists are those built through such devices as grassroots lobbying and consumer-generated content (material written by supporters rather than you or your staff). The more involving you can make your newsletter, the more likely it is your subscribers will open it regularly. And make no mistake—the frontline challenge in e-mail is similar to that in direct mail: getting the recipient merely to open your message. Typical open rates nowadays are in the range of 10 to 20 percent, with rates between 20 and 30 percent qualifying as above average, and rates north of 30 percent being exceptionally good.

- *Unsubscribe option.* I regard it as a cardinal sin to e-mail an electronic newsletter without including a link to a site where the recipient may opt out of her subscription. It's not just bad practice to omit an unsubscribe option—it may someday be illegal, given the rush of legislative interest in combating spam. (It's already illegal for for-profits under the CAN-Spam Act.)

- *Copyright and publisher information.* It's wise to include both a current copyright notice and the name and contact information of your organization. These elements signal an element of professionalism and thus heighten the credibility of an e-newsletter.

One more word of advice: just as I've urged you to write your fundraising letters in an informal, conversational style, I implore you to do so in your e-newsletters. Not only do online readers trend younger, they're also accustomed to the greater informality of the Web.

## Eighteen More Techniques to Involve Your Donors On Line

Cyberspace is a direct marketer's dream. The possibilities for dialogue and involvement are unlimited, and new technologies that increase the options appear to be coming on line almost monthly. Here are just some of the possibilities that come to mind at this writing. Some are well tested, others just now coming into view. They're all worth your consideration as donor involvement devices as well as list-building efforts if you want to develop an innovative online fundraising program.

1. *Activism*. If your organization engages in lobbying of any sort . . . if your mission includes public education . . . if you are seeking to change public opinion about a high-profile issue (or one whose profile you want to raise) . . . then online activism may provide you with an opportunity to advance your mission while involving supporters on line. Just as direct mail letters sometimes include action devices such as petitions or postcards, you can incorporate action devices into your online appeals and e-newsletters. Activism is the single most effective way to build a large database of online supporters.

2. *Quiz*. A quick-and-dirty quiz that consists of no more than half a dozen questions relevant to your organization's work can do double duty as a clever way to attract traffic to your Web site and as a way to educate the public about the issues you address.

3. *Survey*. There are many types of surveys—everything from an informal questionnaire included in your electronic newsletter to an online survey directed at a statistically valid sample of your e-mail list. If your primary goal is to promote involvement, an informal survey may be a winner. If you are seeking actionable data about your online prospects, then you probably need to hire a third-party supplier with a large screening panel that will permit statistically valid results. Short of that, surveymonkey.com and other sources of inexpensive software make it easy for you to manage the survey process.

4. *Poll*. Like surveys, polls can be conducted either informally or formally. For instance, you can structure an informal poll that serves to attract new visitors to your site and to give your existing supporters an opportunity to become involved. You might ask visitors to "vote" on a yes or

no question (or several questions), and report the results in real time on your site. Polls of this type are popular and appear to remain effective as involvement devices—especially if you offer voters a chance to add comments that will be posted on line.

5. *Game.* Some well-heeled and venturesome nonprofits have invested large sums of money in developing professional-quality games that have helped them gain a foothold on the World Wide Web. See, for example, the United Nations World Food Programme's Web site for its game Food Force, at http://www.food-force.com. Exhibit 20.6 reproduces the home page.

6. *Video.* Video can bring life to an e-mail appeal or a Web page. A testimonial from a celebrity, an up-to-the-minute report from a program officer in the field, an update from the executive director—any of these, and many more, can deepen a supporter's experience of your organization. It might also increase response, although some organizations have found it doesn't. What's more, you can post the video on YouTube and reach more people at no cost. There's a catch, however. Experience shows that only short videos generally work well on line. That eight-to-ten-minute video your organization has produced to introduce your organization's work at house parties

**EXHIBIT 20.6**

**Food Force Home Page, United Nations World Food Programme**

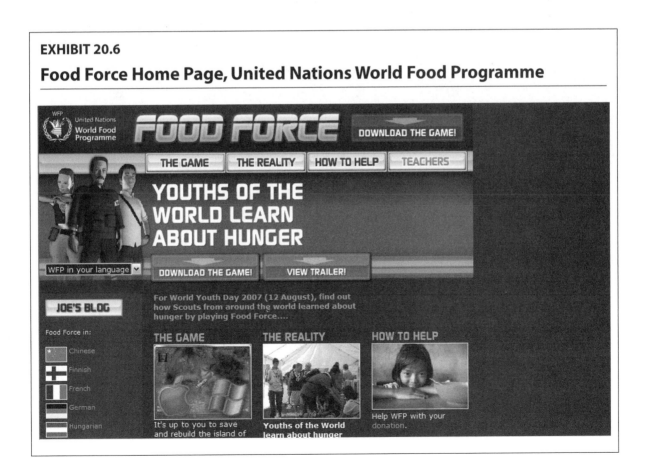

will likely fall flat on line. Think two-minute productions, or three at most. Many viewers tune out after no more than one minute.

7. *Animation.* Animation using Flash software is often cute, sometimes funny, and—every once in a while—genuinely effective. At its best, a truly clever animated short can induce your donors to send it along to all their friends, triggering a viral-marketing success story. But it can also come across as amateurish and silly. It is exceedingly difficult to produce an animated video that will work on line (no matter how clever or hilarious you may think it is). Use animation sparingly, and only if you know what you're doing (or have hired someone who does).

8. *Podcast.* Many people like downloading audio podcasts to their iPods or other devices. They're much easier to make than a video, but you'll still need to find an interesting subject and a good speaker and do a professional job on the recording. Then you can include a link to your podcast in an appeal or an e-newsletter for your activists, donors, or prospects.

9. *Contest.* Some of direct mail's biggest successes have been built on the back of a sweepstakes offer or other contest. In e-mail it's easier. "The first 50 donors to this campaign will receive a free [something-or-other]." Or: "As a supporter of this cause, your e-mail address will be entered into a drawing. You could be one of the 100 lucky donors who will win a free [something-or-other]." Or: "Your winning 50-word essay may be selected for posting right here on our Web site along with nine other lucky winners." However, if you launch a campaign of this sort with any significant scope, you may run afoul of state laws that require registration and limit your options in a variety of ways.

10. *Q&A.* One way to ensure a growing body of content on your Web site while involving your supporters as well is to offer quick answers to people's questions about the field or issue your organization addresses. In each issue of your e-newsletter, you can highlight this service by offering a link to the Q&A page of your site and featuring an especially interesting, recent question and answer. The growing archive of these Q&A's will become an attraction in its own right, drawing more attention to your organization.

11. *Testimonials.* Studies in word-of-mouth marketing show that testimonials—whether from rank-and-file donors or buyers or from experts or celebrities—are regarded as highly credible by the public. A well-crafted testimonial from one of your donors might be substantially more persuasive to an ambivalent donor than a message from you. And donors (like most people!) are often pleased to endorse a service or an organization that pleases them. All you have to do is ask—in your e-newsletter, for

example. Then, if you wish, you can feature these testimonials both in your e-newsletter and on your Web site. The prominence given donor testimonials is likely to attract others to offer their own.

12. *Friend-get-a-friend*. Asking donors to recruit friends, neighbors, coworkers, or relatives is a technique that surely predates direct mail. Properly framed, it works, sometimes very well. It's ordinarily one of the cheapest ways to prospect for new donors. On line the possibilities for friend-get-a-friend campaigns are numerous. The simplest approach is simply a request in every e-newsletter for the reader to pass along a copy—ideally, by entering the names and e-mail addresses of one or more prospects on a landing page on your Web site, thus triggering e-mail messages to them that incorporate the same content as that of the newsletter. You might also attempt a purer form of viral marketing by sending a video or animated short to your supporters and suggesting they share it with all their friends. Or you could take the process a step further and offer some form of prize or other incentive to those donors who recruit the largest number of new donors, activists, or e-newsletter subscribers. However, the most successful friend-to-friend efforts in online fundraising revolve around special events such as walkathons, bikeathons, and the like.

13. *User-generated show-and-tell*. Animal welfare organizations have involved and energized thousands of supporters by encouraging them to post photos of their pets on line. You may not be able to make such a beguiling offer, but some variation on this show-and-tell technique could work for you. For example, you might ask supporters to post their own personal stories, with or without photos. You could ask them to post their photos and explain why they feel the issue you're addressing is important, then post their entries on a Google map to show your supporter base across the nation or the world.

14. *Personalized landing pages*. If your online vendor is up to the task, you can embed personal data in the landing page for a link included in an e-mail appeal or e-newsletter. This way you can build an individualized ask just as you might do in a direct mail appeal.

These fourteen online involvement devices are relatively straightforward and technically undemanding. New technologies—what geeks call collectively Web. 2.0—offer abundant new possibilities for involvement. Many of these are much less straightforward. Here are just a few examples:

15. *Blogs*. With an estimated fifty million blogs on line as I write, you might feel left out if your organization doesn't offer your supporters at

least one. But make sure you know what you're getting into. It's easy and cheap to create a blog, but it's quite another thing to maintain it on a daily basis. It's also easy (at least for some people) to write thousands of words. It's harder to write in a colorful, uniquely personal, and hard-hitting style that will engage readers and keep them coming back for more.

16. *Social networking sites.* Most well-informed individuals are aware that people under, say, thirty years of age can frequently be found on such sites as MySpace and Facebook, sharing secrets about themselves and clustering together in communities of shared interest. It's less well known that some similar sites attract people in their thirties, forties, and even older. Many nonprofit organizations are creating pages on these sites, offering visitors music, animations, and other digital widgets to download, and trying to figure out how to use their "friends" to build their supporter base.

17. *Virtual worlds.* Apparently, as a wise and eloquent man once wrote, "the world is too much with us." What else might explain why so many millions of people seek refuge in virtual worlds on line? If you've never experienced alternate reality, check out Second Life (www.secondlife.com), home (some of the time) to eight million people. Increasingly, nonprofit organizations are setting up shop there—though they're raising only very modest amounts of money. It's hard to know whether these virtual worlds will prove to be a momentary fad—or a compelling phenomenon over the long haul.

18. *Do it yourself.* One of the newest trends—and it may eventually become the most important—is giving your supporters online tools that enable them to become fundraisers for you. This method has been used for a decade for events like the American Cancer Society's Relay for Life, where runners create *personal pages* on line and send their friends and colleagues there to donate. Now organizations are creating *charity badges* and other widgets that supporters can place on their MySpace and Facebook pages or on their blogs, inviting visitors to donate. Donation totals are updated in real time, and the organization can also update news content on the badges.

## The Immediate Future of Online Appeals

Online fundraising has brought millions of new donors into the world of philanthropy thanks to fundraising campaigns for humanitarian relief following the South Asian tsunami and Hurricanes Katrina and Rita. Leading advocacy organizations have enlisted hundreds of thousands, even millions of supporters on line. In political fundraising too, the impact of the Internet has been substantial, especially in the 2004 and 2008 U.S. presidential campaigns. (One candidate, U.S. Senator Barack Obama, enrolled 150,000 donors on line in the second quarter of 2007 alone. He could never have identified them cost-effectively by mail or phone.) Other nonprofits have gained footholds on line through significant investments in marketing. For all these organizations, online techniques are locating new donors who are not responsive to other communications media. The most successful U.S. nonprofits have 10 percent or even 15 percent of their small donors giving on line—and typically giving much higher average gifts than direct mail donors—and those numbers are growing while direct mail returns for these nonprofits may be flat or declining. Clearly, for some nonprofit organizations, the advent of the Internet has been a major boost.

Still, for the overwhelming majority of nonprofits—those not involved in emergency relief, high-profile advocacy, or politics—online fundraising has yet to live up to the extravagant promise trumpeted by "experts" in the heady, early days of the Web after its debut in 1992. I remain optimistic that electronic communications will someday figure far more prominently in our work as fundraisers. I'm convinced that an investment of time, effort, and money in learning the techniques of online fundraising will eventually pay off handsomely.

For the immediate future, though—at least a decade and probably two—the more traditional direct marketing channels of mail and the telephone will continue to dominate the quest for individual contributions in the nonprofit sector. Direct mail is, and will remain for some time to come, the workhorse in your annual fund, annual campaign, or membership program—and the likely source of the overwhelming majority of later major and legacy gifts.

• • •

That wraps up the main body of this book. But some people think the best part is at the back, following this chapter. It's Part Five, "The Letter Writer's Toolbox." There you'll find a collection of practical tools you can put to immediate use as you craft your own fundraising letters.

# Part Five

# The Letter Writer's Toolbox

**THIS IS THE PART** where I invite you to steal my ideas as you might see fit. The resources that follow lay out for your unregulated use a bag full of treatments for the dread disease of writer's block:

- Sixty successful outer-envelope teasers
- Fifty-four strong leads for fundraising letters
- Ninety ways to use the word "you" in a fundraising letter
- Sixty-three ways to handle awkward copywriting transitions
- Forty-one powerful ways to end a fundraising letter
- Fifty-eight ways to start a P.S. in a fundraising letter
- Fifteen ways how *not* to get results
- Books and other resources to help you write successful fundraising letters

There are two ways to use these resources: (1) as an amusing assortment of copywriting ideas that will reassure you because they're so many and varied or (2) as a crutch you can lean on as you start writing an especially troublesome appeal.

# Appendix A

# Sixty Successful Outer-Envelope Teasers

**IT'S HARD TO MAKE** general statements about outer-envelope teasers, much less lay down rules and regulations about how to write them. Instead, I'll do three things in this chapter: (1) list some of the many different kinds of teasers and show an example of each, (2) tell you about thirty of the teasers that have impressed me the most, and (3) list thirty all-time favorite teasers from five of my peers in the practice of raising money by mail. My hope in approaching the subject this way is to tickle your imagination. Perhaps I'll help lead you to write a few all-time favorite teasers for your own fundraising letters!

## What You Can Accomplish with a Strong Teaser

To increase the likelihood the reader will open your appeal, you might write a teaser to fill any one of a number of needs—for example:

| Function | Example |
|---|---|
| Describe the contents | *Membership Card Enclosed* |
| Establish urgency | *Your response needed within 10 days.* |
| Hint at advantages | *R.S.V.P.* |
| Flag the importance of the contents | *Membership Survey* |
| Start a story | *She was only 11 years old. She was as old as the hills.* |
| Offer a benefit | *Your Free Gift Enclosed* |
| Ask a question | *Would you spend $1 a day to save the life of a child?* |
| Pique curiosity | *What do these people have in common?* |
| Challenge the reader | *Take this simple quiz to learn your Health I.Q.* |

There are both advantages and pitfalls in every one of these approaches. For example, the reader might answer a loud NO! to the question you pose, be totally unconvinced by your effort to establish urgency, or be miffed by the offer of a free gift. In other words, none of these approaches is guaranteed to work.

Nevertheless, teasers can deliver. Let's take a close look now at thirty of them that really do—at least as far as I'm concerned.

## Thirty of My Own Favorite Teasers

My own all-time favorite outer-envelope teaser from the fundraising field was one I didn't write. It's pictured at the top of Exhibit A.1. Judge for yourself whether it inspires you. It certainly intrigued a lot of other people. That teaser has been remailed for many years and has helped recruit hundreds of thousands of members for Handgun Control, Inc.

The best teaser I've ever written myself was the one that appears at the bottom of Exhibit A.1. It worked well, I believe, because the letter (which I

---

**EXHIBIT A. 1**

**Exemplary Outer-Envelope Teasers**

**ENCLOSED:**
**Your first real chance to tell the National Rifle Association to go to hell! . . .**

Copyright © Handgun Control, Inc. Used by permission of Handgun Control, Inc.

---

Nellie Red Owl wants a piece of your mind . . .

didn't write) asked readers to do precisely what the envelope copy implied: to "give Nellie Red Owl a piece of their minds"—by jotting down a greeting or comment that could be read on the air of the Native American–run radio station that was the beneficiary of this appeal. In other words—and this is key, I believe—the teaser didn't just sucker readers into opening the envelope. It delivered.

Here are a few of my other recent favorites:

- PRE-PAID FEDERAL EXPRESS ENVELOPE ENCLOSED

  *From the National Republican Senatorial Committee (Washington, D.C.), rubber-stamped in red ink on an 11½-by-14½-inch brown kraft envelope bearing six postage stamps.*

- Open Carefully . . . You may unleash a powerful spirit

  *From the Smithsonian Institution (Washington, D.C.)—typeset in red ink on a white 6-by-9-inch window carrier next to a full-color illustration of a Native American ceremonial mask.*

- "I read your <u>State of the World</u> every year."—Bill Clinton

  Maybe you should too . . .

  *From Worldwatch Institute (Washington, D.C.)—in large blue type dominating a white Number 10 window envelope.*

- NOTICE OF ENROLLMENT:

  Membership card enclosed.

  Confirmation requested.

  *From KQED (San Francisco)—printed in blue and black ink on a 3⅞-by-7½-inch white window envelope.*

- Because many people who sell alcohol think pennies are more important than human lives . . .

  *From MADD (Mothers Against Drunk Driving, Irving, Texas)— typeset in red ink on a white Number 10 window envelope next to a second window through which a real penny shows.*

- Bill Moyers

  *From the Southern Poverty Law Center (Montgomery, Alabama)— typeset in bold black type in the corner card of a brown kraft Number 11 window carrier.*

- "We believe every American has the right to be different and not be punished for it." <u>Don't open this envelope unless you agree!</u>

  *From the American Civil Liberties Union (New York)—typeset in black ink on a tan Number 10 window envelope, with the word "Don't" underlined in bold red.*

- Critical that you read this today. W.B.W.

     URGENT: SOMALIA UPDATE

  *From Project HOPE (Millwood, Virginia)—a note handwritten in black ink above a headline in a broad yellow band stretching across the bottom of a 4-by-8-inch white window envelope.*

- DO NOT FORWARD

     CRITICAL INFORMATION PREPARED FOR:

     [my name and address]

     PETITIONS ENCLOSED FOR:

     PRESIDENT GEORGE BUSH

     SENATE MAJORITY LEADER GEORGE MITCHELL

     HOUSE SPEAKER TOM FOLEY

     IMMEDIATE RETURN REQUESTED BY:

     [date]

  *From Common Cause (Washington, D.C.)—alternately typeset and laser-printed in blue, black, and red ink on a white personalized packet 9¼ by 13½ inches.*

- OK, THE ELECTION WENT OUR WAY. **NOW WHAT?**

     AN IMMODEST PROPOSAL ENCLOSED FOR:

     [my name and address]

  *From the Victory Fund (Washington, D.C.)—printed in blue and red on a white Number 10 window envelope.*

- Your Sierra Club membership EXPIRES THIS MONTH!

  *From the Sierra Club (San Francisco)—typeset in bold black and blue on a white Number 10 carrier.*

- Would <u>you</u> go to jail to keep a puppy from being tortured?

     WE ARE!

  *From Last Chance for Animals (Tarzana, California)—typeset in black and red ink above and below a photograph of a pathetic puppy showing through a large second window on a white Number 10 envelope.*

- The Favor of a Reply is Requested . . .

  *From the American Association of University Women (Washington, D.C.)—the latest example of an old chestnut that seems to work so often, typeset in an elegant face across the top of a window on a cream-colored Number 10 carrier.*

- FREE SEEDS ENCLOSED

    This miracle tree could mean a new life for the world's poor . . .

    NOTE: If no seeds are visible, tip the envelope.

  *From the New Forests Project (Washington, D.C.)—typeset in white and red type within and below a broad band of dark green across the front of a two-window Number 10 outer envelope (with seeds showing through the second window).*

- CHANGE THE FACE OF TELEVISION!

    THIS AIN'T NO MICKEY MOUSE CLUB

  *From In the Life/Media Network (New York)—printed in purple and gold across the front of a white Number 10 window envelope, alongside playful drawings and a shieldlike circular emblem featuring a Mickey Mouse hat.*

- Would you give $10 . . . just $10 . . . to help save a child's life?

  *From St. Jude Children's Research Hospital (Memphis, Tennessee)— handwritten in dark blue ink on the back of a white 3⅞-by-7½-inch window carrier.*

- PULL HERE FOR YOUR FREE BACKPACK

    (details inside)

  *From the National Audubon Society (New York)—set inside a band of red and blue on a perforated strip outlined in dashes above a personalized membership card that appears in an odd-sized window at the center of a 6-by-9-inch white outer envelope.*

- A personal reminder

  *From the Sierra Club Legal Defense Fund (San Francisco)—handwritten and underlined with a scrawl in dark blue ink across the face of a gray 4-by-7½-inch window envelope.*

- Have you heard about Bill Clinton's NEW TAX? Details Inside . . .

  *From Americans for a Balanced Budget (Falls Church, Virginia)—handwritten above the window on a white Number 10 envelope.*

- What would you do with 500,000 pounds of BEANS?

  *From Feed the Children (Oklahoma City)—handwritten in red ink in the upper-left-hand corner of a white Number 10 window outer envelope.*

- RELAX!

    Both of you.

    (A $10 nest egg will do it.)

    (Do not fold. Bumper sticker enclosed.)

  *From the Nature Conservancy (Arlington, Virginia)—on one of the most unusual and celebrated membership acquisition packages of recent years: printed in black ink in several different typefaces and at different angles, alongside fingers pointing to a full-color portrait of a startled-looking ostrich and my name and address showing through the window of a white 6-by-9-inch outer envelope.*

- Bill Clinton

    430 South Capitol Street, SE

    Washington, DC 20003

    VIA AIR MAIL

  *From the Democratic National Committee (Washington, D.C.)—"typed" upper left in black and printed in dark blue on the right on what appears to be a standard bluish Number 10 airmail envelope (with red and blue stripes around the perimeter).*

- IMPORTANT SURVEY ON GUN CONTROL ENCLOSED

  *From the Coalition to Stop Gun Violence (Washington, D.C.)—typeset in huge red letters on a self-contained, 11-by-15-inch "doormat" package beneath an official-looking address section that includes a personalized "Registered Survey Number."*

- Christmas Card Enclosed . . .

  *From Habitat for Humanity International (Americus, Georgia)—typeset above the window on a bright red 6-by-9-inch outer envelope beneath a corner card reading only, "Rosalynn Carter."*

- Here's <u>your</u> chance to help stop filth on television.

  *From the American Family Association (Tupelo, Mississippi)—printed in large blue letters across the face of a Number 11 white window envelope.*

- Enclosed: Important Information Regarding U.S. Government Grants

  *From World Vision (Monrovia, California)—typeset in black in the upper-left-hand corner of a closed-face white 5¾-by-8⅜-inch envelope.*

- STEP INSIDE FOR A TASTE OF

  The Good Life

  YOUR FREE TICKETS FOR A PRIVATE TOUR ARE ENCLOSED

  *From the Oakland Museum/Museum of California Foundation (Oakland, California)—set in contrasting typefaces in red and green inks on the front of a Number 10 white window outer envelope embellished with nonspecific but elegant-looking designs in pale pink and continued on the back in simple red block letters.*

- Do you want to lose the Property Tax Exemption for your home?

  *From the People's Advocate, Inc. (Sacramento, California)—printed in black above the window on a white Number 10 outer envelope.*

## Another Thirty All-Time Favorite Teasers

Taste in teasers is a function of style as well as the character and circumstances of the charities that use them. To give you a broader range of examples than my own files and taste will permit, I turned for help to my colleagues in the Association of Direct Response Fundraising Counsel (ADRFCO), the trade association for companies that provide direct mail fundraising services to nonprofit organizations. Several firms responded to my call for nominees for the All-Time Favorite Fundraising Envelope Teasers.

I received eighteen nominees from Charlene Divoky (Divoky & Associates). The following are the ones that teased me the most:

- P.S. We named the duck Harold.

  *Community Service Society of New York*

- Why don't woodpeckers get headaches?

  *Boston Public Library Foundation*

- The committee's decision is official . . . your Kind Human Award is enclosed.

  *Northeast Animal Shelter*

- Me? Sleep in a subway station?

  *Community Service Society of New York*

- Enclosed: The Life or Death Seed Catalog

  *U.S. Committee for UNICEF*

- She finally allowed herself to be rescued.

  *Northeast Animal Shelter*

Michael P. Scholl (Direct Mail Decision Makers, Inc.) sent me twenty-five teaser candidates. Here are the ones I liked the most:

- How Sister Alice became GRANDMA

  *Missionary Sisters of the Immaculate Conception*

- Father Carl . . . brutally murdered

  *Passionist Missions*

- One of the hardest letters I've ever had to write

  *Missionary Servant of the Most Blessed Trinity*

- Fr. Bob is an Alcoholic and he's going through a private hell!

  *Guest House*

- Rejoice with me . . .

  *Old Saint Mary's Church, San Francisco*

- She arrived at the Grotto with tears in her eyes

  *Missionary Sisters of the Immaculate Conception*

Here are a few of the best teasers I received from Wendy Fisher (Mailworks):

- <u>FACT</u>: At 91, Emily Smithtown doesn't have a friend in the world. Not even one.

  *Little Brothers/Friends of the Elderly*

- Think kids are safer at home than on the street? <u>Think again.</u>

  *Night Ministry/Youth Shelter Network*

- FACT: Last year we distributed over 22 million pounds of food to hungry people.

    FACT: It wasn't enough.

  *Greater Chicago Food Depository*

- Will you be killed by a handgun in the next 23 minutes?

    [BACK FLAP]: Someone will be.

  *Illinois Citizens for Handgun Control*

- Come. Step with me for a minute into Emily's apartment.

  *Little Brothers/Friends of the Elderly*

- She dared to have a dream—that one day her beloved mountain gorillas would be safe.

  Safe to roam their Viruna mountains in search of food . . . safe to give birth . . . rear their young . . . safe—so that their species can survive.

  Dian Fossey nurtured her dream . . . she died with that dream . . .

  But her beloved gorillas are still not safe.

  *Dian Fossey Gorilla Fund*

Here are some verbal letter openers from Robert E. Hoagland (L. W. Robbins Associates):

- They Were the Last Words Lisa's Parents Expected to Hear . . . And They Changed Her World Forever!

  *Joslin Diabetes Center*

- What Has No Wings, Flies, and Is Called an Angel?

  *Arkansas Children's Hospital Foundation*

- "When it Comes to Courage, This Kid Is an All-Star!"

  *Dana-Farber Cancer Institute/The Jimmy Fund*

- Your Personal Emergency Relief Kit

  Open to Activate

  *American Red Cross of Massachusetts Bay*

- The Cat Licked Her Face. And for a Moment, the Woman and the World Were Young Again.

  *Bide-a-Wee Home Association*

Here are some of the teasers suggested by my colleague Bill Rehm (Mal Warwick & Associates):

- They're at it again!

  California telephone customer alert

  *Toward Utility Rate Normalization*

- My son was 29 years old when he died.

  *Hyacinth Foundation*

- [HANDWRITTEN:] I need to know what <u>YOU</u> think.

  *Wellstone Alliance*

- Can you remember where you were on June 5, 1981?

  *Shanti Project*

- IMPORTANT NOTICE about your telephone bill

    Please read before paying

  *Toward Utility Rate Normalization*

- ARE YOU PREPARED FOR FIRE?

    Checklist enclosed

  *American Red Cross/Bay Area*

- WELCOME BACK!

  *Toward Utility Rate Normalization*

# Appendix B

# Fifty-Four Strong Leads for Fundraising Letters

1. Thank you . . . !
2. I'm writing you today . . .
3. You are among the first . . .
4. You may be surprised to learn . . .
5. Did you know that . . . ?
6. Don't you wish . . . ?
7. It's no secret that . . .
8. You've probably said to yourself . . .
9. Think about it for a moment.
10. Let's face it.
11. If you sincerely want to . . .
12. I wish you could have been with me when . . .
13. I was sure you'd want to know that . . .
14. I can't get the image out of my mind . . .
15. I still wake up in the middle of the night . . .
16. I've just returned from . . .
17. I need to hear from you this week about . . .
18. I don't want to waste words or paper . . .
19. I don't usually write such long letters . . .
20. We tried to reach you by phone . . .
21. According to our records, your membership has lapsed.
22. Will you please take a moment right now to renew your membership?
23. I want to tell you a story about . . .
24. You won't believe it.
25. As I was passing through _____ recently, I . . .
26. I've just returned from . . .

27. I want to tell you about a remarkable . . .

28. I'm writing to invite you . . .

29. I'd like to take just a few moments of your time to . . .

30. I hope you'll take a moment right now to . . .

31. Because you've been so generous . . .

32. I'm writing you this urgent letter today because . . .

33. It's been awhile since I heard from you . . .

34. I have exciting news for you!

35. I'm writing you today because _____ is [are] in grave danger.

36. Have you ever wondered . . . ?

37. Do you ever feel . . . ?

38. I want to share a recent experience with you.

39. I want to give you the latest information on . . .

40. I hope you'll be as excited as I am to learn . . .

41. Have you ever wanted to be part of . . . ?

42. Have you ever said to yourself . . . ?

43. If you've always wanted to . . .

44. Haven't you wondered how you could help . . . ?

45. It's no surprise that . . .

46. It's hard to believe, but . . .

47. I know you'll be interested to know that . . .

48. I know you'll want to be a part of this . . .

49. Let's be frank.

50. I have a secret.

51. You've been chosen . . .

52. If you've seen the recent headlines, you're well aware . . .

53. Someone you know . . .

54. I'd like to say it isn't so.

# Ninety Ways to Use the Word "You" in a Fundraising Letter

1. Thank you for . . .

2. Thank you very much for . . .

3. Thank you again for . . .

4. As you know . . .

5. I'm writing you today . . .

6. I'm sure you'll agree that . . .

7. With your generous support,

8. Because you helped,

9. You are among the first . . .

10. You're the kind of person who . . .

11. I know that you . . .

12. Would you believe that . . . ?

13. As I wrote to you recently,

14. Did you know that . . . ?

15. I don't know about you, but I . . .

16. Will you spend just pennies a day to . . . ?

17. How many times have you said to yourself . . . ?

18. You're among the few I can count on to . . .

19. I was delighted to hear from you.

20. You're among our most generous supporters.

21. Now, at last, you can . . .

22. You're in for a pleasant surprise.

23. Have you ever wondered . . . ?

24. . . . may astonish you.

25. You may never forgive yourself if . . .

26. The benefits to you are substantial.

27. You can rely on . . .

28. You'll be joining the ranks of . . .

29. None of this would be possible without your generous help.

30. You owe it to yourself to explore this opportunity.

31. You've helped in the past, and your generosity . . .

32. Your membership gift . . .

33. You're one of our most generous supporters . . .

34. You've been with us for a long time, and . . .

35. As one of our newest members, you . . .

36. I want to tell you about . . .

37. It's people like you who . . .

38. I know, like me, you must feel . . .

39. You're such an important friend . . .

40. Through the years, you've been . . .

41. You've shown just how much you are . . .

42. You may be shocked . . .

43. You may be surprised . . .

44. I've noticed you haven't . . .

45. Working together, you and I . . .

46. You're one of the few people who truly understand . . .

47. You should be proud of what we've accomplished together.

48. With your special gift, _____ can . . .

49. Your gift can make the difference between . . .

50. You can help them [grow strong, live a better life] . . .

51. You helped prevent . . .

52. When _____ happened, you were there.

53. Have you ever felt as if . . . ?

54. Have you ever wished you . . . ?

55. Please believe me—you can . . .

56. Like me, you may . . .

57. I can tell you from my own experience . . .

58. I've seen firsthand how you . . .

59. When you join . . .

60. I'll be pleased to send you . . .

61. I need to hear from you by _____ . . .

62. I'll keep you informed . . .

63. I'll want to keep you involved . . .

64. It may seem to you . . .

65. You've helped so many people with . . . !

66. Now you can play a leadership role . . .

67. Can you believe . . . ?

68. Have you seen . . . ?

69. What would you think if . . . ?

70. Because of people like you . . .

71. You're just the kind of person who . . .

72. How can you, as a _____ , . . . ?

73. You and others like you are _____ 's only hope!

74. Have you ever noticed . . . ?

75. Can I rely on you to . . . ?

76. I hope you'll consider . . .

77. You're someone who . . .

78. You can rest assured that . . .

79. You may never again have an opportunity to . . .

80. You're not someone to stand by while . . .

81. Your gift really will make a difference.

82. What can you do? These __*[number of]*__ things:

83. You too can be part of this project.

84. I want you by my side (again) at this critical time.

85. This is all possible because of you.

86. You probably had no idea . . .

87. Find out for yourself.

88. Here's a new opportunity for you.

89. For you, free of charge.

90. Reserved for you:

# Appendix D

# Sixty-Three Ways to Handle Awkward Copywriting Transitions

1. As I'm sure you'll understand,
2. But that's not all.
3. [Use subheads.]
4. But now, for the first time,
5. Today, more than ever,
6. Best of all,
7. Here's why:
8. Think of it:
9. One thing's for sure:
10. The truth is,
11. To show you what I mean,
12. I'm hoping you'll agree.
13. And there's more:
14. It's that simple!
15. It's now or never.
16. There's never been a better time.
17. Am I claiming too much? I don't think so.
18. That's why I'm writing you today.
19. In addition,
20. Not only that, but . . .
21. And . . .
22. Now,
23. Next,
24. [Indent paragraph]

25. Before I tell you . . .

26. As you can see,

27. Because it's people like you who . . .

28. Because there's no time to lose.

29. But wait, that's not all.

30. Why am I so concerned? Because . . .

31. Let me explain . . .

32. In a moment I'll tell you more about _____. But first . . .

33. And, most important of all,

34. That's what _____ is all about.

35. It may seem hard to believe, but . . .

36. There's so much at stake!

37. Let me tell you more.

38. That's why I'm asking you to do three things right now.

39. The recent news from _____ is shocking, but I'm sure you know . . .

40. To clarify what I mean . . .

41. Now is the time to . . .

42. But wait: there's more.

43. Just imagine:

44. Consider the consequences:

45. In other words,

46. Put yourself in their place:

47. Time is of the essence.

48. Can you think of a better way to . . . ?

49. It's sad but true:

50. I know how you feel about _____ because you . . .

51. Will you help?

52. Are you willing to take the next step to . . . ?

53. Why wait?

54. It's clear that . . .

55. Despite the lack of media attention . . .

56. I think you'll agree that . . .

57. The truth hurts.

58. I know this isn't pleasant . . .

59. As you know very well . . .

60. Act now, and we'll . . .

61. If you really think about it . . .

62. Ask yourself:

63. Now that you know . . .

# Forty-One Powerful Ways to End a Fundraising Letter

1. Thank you for caring so very much!

2. You may not know their names, but they'll carry thanks in their hearts for your kindness and generosity.

3. From the bottom of my heart, thank you!

4. Your investment will bear dividends for years to come.

5. I'm sure you'll be glad you did.

6. Isn't that what life is really all about?

7. So you can't lose!

8. Don't miss this unique opportunity!

9. It's up to you.

10. May I hear from you soon?

11. The future is in your hands.

12. And that can make all the difference in the world!

13. I'm counting on you!

14. In return, you'll have the satisfaction of knowing that . . .

15. Together, we will . . .

16. With your help, we'll . . .

17. The satisfaction you'll receive is indescribable.

18. Thank you for joining me in this . . .

19. I'm looking forward to hearing from you very soon.

20. Together, I know we can . . .

21. When you look back at this moment in history . . .

22. Please, if you feel the way I do,

23. I can't think of a better gift to give our children and grandchildren than . . .

24. Thank you for your compassion.

25. I know you won't be disappointed.

26. Please, send your gift today.

27. And I promise to send you _____ just as soon as . . .

28. Thank you for taking the time to help.

29. I know I can count on you!

30. My warmest wishes to you.

31. You'll be so glad you decided to help!

32. You'll be proud to be part of . . . !

33. The _____ are depending on you!

34. _____ won't forget you!

35. I can't thank you enough.

36. I believe you'll make the right choice.

37. Please act today!

38. This is your chance to . . .

39. With your help, _____ will have a chance to . . .

40. Please show them they're not alone!

41. The future of your children and your children's children hangs in the balance.

# Appendix F

# Fifty-Eight Ways to Start a P.S. in a Fundraising Letter

1. Thank you again for . . .

2. If you respond within the next X days, you'll receive . . .

3. If you send $ _____ or more, you'll receive . . .

4. There's not much time.

5. The enclosed _____ are yours to keep—our gift to you.

6. Please use the enclosed _____ to . . .

7. If $ _____ is too much for you to give at this time, will you consider a gift of $ _____ or $ _____ ?

8. We need to _____ by _____, so please send your gift today.

9. Your gift of $ _____ makes it possible for . . .

10. Please don't set this letter aside.

11. Remember, if you respond by . . .

12. Please take a look at the _____ I've enclosed for you.

13. As a special benefit for the first _____ people who respond, I'll . . .

14. And remember, your gift is tax deductible.

15. I've always regarded you as one of our strongest supporters, so . . .

16. Please don't wait.

17. Every day that goes by . . .

18. I hope I can count on receiving your gift in the next _____ days.

19. Please, as always, feel free to contact me at [telephone number] if you have any questions about . . .

20. If you decide not to join us in this crucial effort, I hope you'll take a moment to write and tell me why.

21. Just as soon as I return from _____, I'll let you know how . . .

22. I need to send that shipment of _____ in the next _____ days, so . . .

23. Don't forget:

24. You've come through so many times in the past, and I hope I can count on you again now.

25. _____ need[s] your help today.

26. Did you know that . . . ?

27. If you act by . . .

28. Your gift of $ _____ will make it possible for _____ to get _____.

29. $ _____ is just _____ per day!

30. For less than a cup of coffee a day,

31. I promised _____ that . . .

32. When I look into the eyes of . . .

33. Unless you and I act immediately,

34. Please know that your gift is _____ 's only hope for _____.

35. Without your help, _____ doesn't stand a chance.

36. Won't you please take out your checkbook now and . . .

37. I hope I can count on you to respond by . . .

38. Take a moment right now to look at the enclosed _____. I'm sure you'll feel the same as I do:

39. I hope you'll enjoy—and use—the enclosed _____.

40. Remember, to reach our goal by _____, we need . . .

41. I can't stress enough how much your support will mean to us!

42. Without your support, I can't . . .

43. It's members like you who . . .

44. There's no better time to . . .

45. Don't miss this chance to . . .

46. I'd like to hear your thoughts about . . .

47. Don't delay.

48. If your check and this letter have crossed in the mail,

49. What may seem a small gift to you can . . .

50. I know it's hard to imagine _____, but . . .

51. Put yourself in _____ 's place for a moment.

52. All it takes to _____ is $ _____!

53. If you and I don't do something right now,

54. If you won't help, who will?

55. Remember, every day that goes by without our help,

56. Please find it in your heart to give. Even just a little gift will help!

57. _____ need[s] to know that someone cares.

58. Thanks to friends like you,

# Appendix G

# Fifteen Ways How *Not* to Get Results

**I CAN BEST APPROACH** the rules of copywriting through the back door, by advising you on how to avoid the most common errors I see. There are at least fifteen. They're described below, beginning with the five I believe cause the most trouble.

## Chaotic Thinking

Effective writing begins (and ends) with clear, disciplined thought. As William Strunk Jr. and E. B. White put it so elegantly in *The Elements of Style:* "Design informs even the simplest structure, whether of brick and steel or of prose. You raise a pup tent from one sort of vision, a cathedral from another. This does not mean that you must sit with a blueprint always in front of you, merely that you had best anticipate what you are getting into." So before you lay a finger on the keyboard or position your pen on paper, *make up your mind what it is you want to communicate.* Decide where you want to go and how you'll get there. If necessary, outline the steps you'll take along the way. If you don't decide in advance what the point is, it's unlikely you'll get it across.

## Hemming and Hawing

There may still be a place for slow and easy writing that meanders from point to point, but I think that approach went out of style with William Faulkner— and there is no room for such laziness when you're writing to achieve results. Get to the point—the quicker the better! Unless you can devise a clearly superior lead sentence, I suggest you start a letter with the words, "I'm writing to you today because . . ." That approach won't win a prize in a creative writing contest, but it does force you to communicate quickly and directly the result you're hoping to achieve with your letter. Creativity doesn't raise money, but directness does. If your writing doesn't get to the point, your readers' eyes and minds will wander off to more satisfying pursuits. Bluntness is usually a wiser and more productive course than subtlety.

## Boring Leads

If you're faced with the task of writing a six-page letter or a ten-page memo, you'd better be sure your opening paragraph—and especially the opening sentence—is intriguing enough to pique your readers' interest. And that goes double for a letter intended to secure a gift or sell a product.

Writing that engages the reader often begins with a question, a challenge, a human interest story, a bold assertion, a familiar phrase turned on its head—or straightforward, unalloyed directness. The special circumstances and conditions of your writing assignment (or simple inspiration) may suggest that one of these approaches is ideal. But it may be enough simply to sum up the points you're going to make—if you state them dramatically enough and set the proper tone for the audience you're addressing—for example:

> *I'm writing today to invite you to join me in launching a historic initiative with vast potential to improve the quality of life in our community.*

For a general audience, that pompous lead might guarantee your letter will quickly make its way into the proverbial circular file. But for a high-brow group with a demonstrated commitment to your community and a connection to the person who signs the memo or the letter, the boldness of your claim may be captivating.

## Run-On Sentences

Writing of any type suffers from overlong sentences; a letter to raise money or sell software can die a horrible death from this malady. If a sentence is longer than three typewritten lines, analyze it, looking for a way to break it down into two or three simpler and shorter sentences. Almost always, you'll get your point across more effectively if you do so.

Keep this in mind: a reader dedicated enough to tackle Proust or Joyce may be willing to concentrate hard enough to follow a tortured thought all the way to a long-overdue period. (Understandably, the period is sometimes known as a *full stop.*) But *your* readers aren't likely to pay that much attention. Long sentences will test readers' limited attention span, and you'll come up the loser.

## Failure to Use Visual Devices to Guide the Reader

A novelist who is highly skilled in moving the reader from one page to the next may be able to do so with the power of words alone. Most of us aren't so lucky, and our readers, who often have far more meager incentives to read on for page after page, are typically far less tolerant. To write effectively for impact, you'll probably need to make liberal use of subheads, bulleted or numbered series, boldfaced section headings, and other devices to break the monotony of gray, unbroken text. Only by providing your readers with clues that are visible at a glance can you make your writing actually *look* easy to read—and you'll substantially reinforce that impression by using short sentences and short paragraphs. Signals such as these send an important message to the reader: that you're writing for *her* benefit, not for your own.

## Inconclusive (and Uninteresting) Endings

A strong appeal requires a forceful ending as well as a thought-provoking lead. It's not enough to sum up and repeat the strongest points made along the way. A letter should end on a high note: affirming the relationship between the signer and the recipient and relating the appeal to the organization's mission and the values that inspire it. End with something readers will remember.

## Vague Language

Bad writing is full of excuses, qualifications, exceptions, and caveats. For example, a sales letter might begin:

*Most people agree, this product is one of the best things since the hula hoop.*

Well, is it the best—or isn't it? If "most people" agree, then why not write instead:

*This incredible product will knock your socks off! Take it from me— it's the best thing since the hula hoop!*

When a writer constantly relies on evasions, they signify fuzzy thinking. If you can't make your case in clear, unequivocal language, it's time to reexamine the reasoning that led you to conclude the case that you're presenting was defensible. Your readers won't become excited about helping you if your writing doesn't clearly convey what you want, and why, and when.

## Overwriting

Inexperienced and insecure writers frequently overuse adjectives and adverbs, robbing their writing of clarity and impact. As Strunk and White wrote in *The Elements of Style*, "The adjective hasn't been built that can pull a weak or inaccurate noun out of a tight place." If you want to write for results, try doing so without using any adjectives at all. You can go back later and insert an adjective or two for the sake of precision or honesty. To the extent you exercise restraint, your readers will thank you—and they'll reward you with the ultimate gift to a writer: they'll go on reading.

## Ten-Dollar Words

Like overwriting, the use of long, obscure, and highly technical language is a form of showing off. It's not necessary to write *cessation* when *end* will do, or use *communicate* when you can get the point across with *say* or *write*. Unfortunately, this sort of thing is all too common in writing today, and communication suffers as a result. Board chairs and chief executive officers are especially susceptible to this malady. Avoid it like any deadly (shall I say *communicable*?) disease.

## "Business English"

The tendency to use widely accepted but grammatically incorrect—and often abysmally wordy—constructions is one of the afflictions of contemporary writing, and it infects a great deal of advertising and fundraising copy. Stay clear of abominations such as the following; choose their equivalents in acceptable English—or shun them altogether:

| Avoid Using | What to Use Instead |
|---|---|
| accordingly | so |
| along the lines of | like |
| and/or | [*Leave this one to the lawyers!*] |
| as to whether | whether |
| at this point in time | now [*or*] today |
| dialogue | talk |
| enclosed herewith | I'm sending you |
| etc. | [*Use very sparingly*] |
| finalize | finish |
| for the purpose of | for |
| implementation | [*Just do it!*] |
| in order to | [*"To" will suffice*] |
| inasmuch as | because |
| in the event that | if |
| interface | work with [*or*] meet |
| make use of | use |
| owing to the fact that | because |
| per your request | as you asked |

| prioritize | set priorities |
| prior to | before |
| pursuant to | according to |
| quite [*or*] very | [*Lilies sell better without gilt!*] |
| results-wise | result is that |
| revert back | revert |
| the foreseeable future | [*How far away is that?*] |
| with a view to | to |

Then there are all those words wasted because writers insist on doubling up, presumably out of some deep, hidden fear that they'll otherwise fail to get the point across. For example:

| **Avoid Using** | **What to Use Instead** |
| --- | --- |
| exact opposites | [*"Opposites" will suffice*] |
| the reason is because | [*Which is it: "the reason is" or " because"? Choose one!*] |
| final conclusion | [*If it's the conclusion, isn't it final?*] |
| actual experience | [*As opposed to an unauthentic experience?*] |
| continue on | [*Is the alternative "continue off"?*] |
| end result | [*Give me a break!*] |

You get the point. From this time forward, I trust you'll be on guard against these boring and objectionable word wasters. While you're at it, please put the following words on your list of what to avoid:

| **Avoid Using** | **What to Use Instead** |
| --- | --- |
| hopefully | [*Do you really hope so? Given the way this word is so frequently misused, I think that's unlikely. But if you really hope so, then say it!*] |
| frankly | [*This word is commonly used when its opposite is intended. It puts the reader on guard. So does, "To be honest with you."*] |
| irregardless | [*The correct word is "regardless."*] |
| very unique | [*If something's unique, it's one of a kind. Drop the "very."*] |

Every one of these words and phrases is a violation of common sense. (Strunk and White comment, sometimes at greater length, about some of these examples in their *Elements of Style*.)

## Stilted Language

Just because a word is grammatically correct and properly spelled and precisely expresses the thought you want to convey, you shouldn't assume it's the *right* word. When you are seeking to achieve results, it's important to write as you speak, using familiar, everyday words. The best way to guard against problems of this sort is to give your writing a road test: read your letter aloud before you let anyone else see it. If you have trouble pronouncing a word or phrase, chances are it will trip up your reader too. Find another way to say what you've written.

## Lack of Agreement

One of the most common violations of the rules of grammar typically happens because the writer fails to decide in advance what point a sentence is to make. This confusion is often reflected in a mismatch between subject and verb or between a pronoun and its antecedent—for example:

*If members choose not to attend, you may obtain a discount instead.*

There's nothing wrong with this sentence that a little forethought wouldn't have cured. Here is one possible approach:

*Members who choose not to attend are eligible for discounts.*

This alternative wording is less likely to trip up the reader, who could easily do a double take on the original. The second version is also two words shorter, making it that much easier to read.

## Dangling Modifiers

Closely related to the preceding problem, this common error typically arises from the same source: foggy thinking. I know of no way to describe it other than to use the grating language of the grammarian or to give examples:

*An example of the very best the community had to offer, the mayor awarded her the prize last year.*

*Loaded with valuable benefits, I thought the product was the best I
could buy.*

To avoid the confusion caused by mismatches like these, try revising them. Usually, there are numerous acceptable alternatives. Here's one alternative for each example:

*The mayor awarded her the prize last year because she exemplified the
very best the community has to offer.*

*It was simply loaded with valuable benefits—the best product I could
buy, I thought.*

You don't need to know what a modifier is: all you have to do is remember when you near the end of the sentence what you were writing about when you started it.

## Overuse of the Passive Voice

There are times when the passive voice is unavoidable, or at least convenient—in the following, for instance:

*The snowfall was unprecedented, but the streets were plowed clean in
record time.*

In this example, which is about streets and snow, not people, it's not important *who* plowed the streets (although the members of the street-plowing crew might have a different opinion). The point of the sentence is clear. Nothing is lost by the use of the passive voice. The corresponding active-voice statement is no clearer or more elegant than the passive one:

*Snow accumulated to an unprecedented depth, but the crews plowed it
clean in record time.*

Usually, however, the passive voice detracts from the impact of a statement. The passive voice is frequently used to evade straightforward assertions of fact. Thus it rarely helps you sell products or obtain charitable gifts. Consider the following example:

*Voting members of the museum are required to attend one meeting per
year to preserve their status and receive all these discounts.*

That sentence reads like a passage from a rulebook, not a promise of benefits that might entice someone to join the museum. Try this instead:

*As a voting member of the museum, you'll receive all these discounts if
you attend just one meeting per year.*

Writing for results requires communicating conviction. The active voice helps the writer to be direct and permits the reader to grasp the point more quickly.

## Atrocious Spelling

My mother always said that respect for spelling died in the 1950s when educators decided there was a better way to teach reading than by using phonetics. I think she was right. I know few Americans younger than I who can spell worth a damn. Fortunately, most of us who live by the word are likely to use one of the popular word-processing programs, all of which feature spell-checking utilities. I heartily recommend these devices as a partial answer for the spelling-impaired (only partial, because they won't pick up words that are correctly spelled but wrong in context). Using such a program requires only a few seconds, yet it may rescue you from years of mortification. Perhaps you don't care whether there are spelling errors in your copy, *but I do!*

For example, I will cast a dark eye on you if I catch you committing all-too-common spelling errors such as any of the following egregious examples:

- *except* (meaning "to exclude") instead of *accept* (meaning "to receive" or "to acknowledge")

- *it's* instead of *its* (when used as the possessive form of *it*)

- *affect* (meaning "to act on" or change something) instead of *effect* (meaning "to do" or "to bring about as a result")

- *loose* (as in "loose screw" or "loose clothing") instead of *lose* (as in "lose your keys")

•  •  •

If you heed the fifteen points just outlined and if you're faithful to Strunk and White's rules of grammar and vocabulary in *The Elements of Style* and Rudolf Flesch's "25 Rules of Effective Writing," from *How to Write, Speak and Think More Effectively,* you'll avoid most of the common mistakes that can prevent you from communicating effectively. You'll also be more likely to achieve the results you intend from your fundraising letters.

# Appendix H

# Books and Other Resources to Help You Write Successful Fundraising Letters

**IF YOU'RE ONE** of those people who learns a lot by reading—and I certainly hope you are since you're reading this book!—you'll find it useful to explore other written materials that will deepen your understanding of copywriting, fundraising, direct mail, and direct marketing. In these final pages, I've listed several books and online resources that my colleagues and I have found especially helpful.

## Books

You might be surprised just how many books have been published on the subject of letter writing. Books about letters that are effective or powerful—or tried and tested. Books of "classic" or "all-time great" letters. Books of model letters. Books about sales letters. Books about business letters. Even several books specifically devoted to fundraising letters—including several volumes of sample letters.

I've found very few of those books to be useful. Most are dull. Some are dangerously misleading.

It's disappointing. The books by writers whose experience lies outside fundraising sometimes make suggestions inappropriate to this very peculiar field of ours. Some of the books written by people with extensive fundraising experience have fallen into the trap of dogmatism ("this worked for me once, so it's got to work for you," or "long letters always outpull short ones"). And the collections of letters pose problems of their own, since the implication is that a letter published in a book of "good" letters is a "good" model for any fundraiser to follow under any circumstances.

The following list, arranged in alphabetical order by author, includes only the books I genuinely believe you'll find useful. It's a short list, only ten titles.

• Burnett, K. *Relationship Fundraising: A Donor-Based Approach to the Business of Raising Money.* (2nd ed.) San Francisco: Jossey-Bass, 2002. Ken Burnett is one of the world's leading practitioners of the art of raising money by mail. Many of us in the fundraising field speak about "building relationships with donors," but Burnett has systematically developed the techniques to bring this ideal down to earth.

• Caples, J. *Tested Advertising Methods.* (4th ed.) Upper Saddle River, N.J.: Prentice Hall, 1974. Caples virtually invented the field of direct response copywriting. His classic 1920s ad, "They laughed when I sat down to play the piano," is so well known it's become what is probably the only certifiable cliché in direct marketing. Although Caples wrote space advertising in the main, not fundraising letters, the principles he developed through years of exhaustive testing are as applicable today—and in the writing of fundraising letters—as they were when he wrote his ads.

• Flesch, R. *How to Write, Speak and Think More Effectively.* New York: New American Library, 1963. Generations of Americans have turned to Rudolf Flesch for advice on effective writing and speaking. Much of his teaching is summed up in this wonderfully useful little volume, first copyrighted in 1946 but still readily available in paperback. Flesch's extensive and well-known findings on readability are threaded through the text, and it's chock-full of concrete and colorful examples. This book brims over with insight and useful advice—and it's a treasure chest of fascinating information for anyone intrigued by the dynamics of human language.

• Heath, C., and Heath, D. *Made to Stick: Why Some Ideas Survive and Others Die.* Random House: New York, 2007. The brothers Heath explore the endlessly fascinating topic of urban myths and emerge with insightful lessons for anyone who wishes to promote a product or a cause—including the writers of direct mail fundraising letters. This book is fun to read, too.

• Ogilvy, D. *Ogilvy on Advertising.* New York: Vintage Books, 1983. The late dean of the advertising industry was a direct marketer at heart and one of its most articulate and insightful writers. Reading Ogilvy's several useful books is one of the best possible ways for a fledgling copywriter to gain entry to the mysteries of writing fundraising letters.

• Sargeant, A., and Jay, E. *Building Donor Loyalty: The Fundraiser's Guide to Increasing Lifetime Value.* San Francisco: Jossey-Bass, 2004. Adrian Sargeant is one of the world's leading researchers on fundraising and philanthropy. His work is consistently rigorous and revealing. This is the best of his several books to date. It's jam-packed with chapter and verse from the results of his and Elaine Jay's extensive research into which techniques work (and which don't) to foster enduring relationships with donors.

- Smith, G. A*sking Properly: The Art of Creative Fundraising.* London: White Lion Press, 1996. Fundraising innovator George Smith is known around the world as one of the brightest lights in the business. This lively book, crammed with Smith's characteristic insight and wit, is an indispensable tool for the direct mail fundraising writer eager to learn how to think outside the box.
- Strunk, W., Jr., and White, E. B. *The Elements of Style.* (4th ed.) New York: Longman, 2000. If you write anything more than grocery lists and are intent on improving the quality of your work, read this book. I've commented on this indispensable little classic in Chapter Nine.
- Vögele, S. *Handbook of Direct Mail: The Dialogue Method of Direct Written Sales Communication.* Hemel Hempstead, U.K.: Verlag Moderne Industrie/Prentice Hall, 1992. I never thought I'd read, much less highly recommend, a dry direct marketing textbook translated from the German. But the German professor who wrote this insightful book was all the rage in European direct marketing circles for over a decade. Vögele is familiar to some Americans as the author of the eye-motion studies I wrote about in my earlier book, *999 Tips, Trends and Guidelines for Successful Direct Mail and Telephone Fundraising.* It's time now for Americans to start catching onto the wisdom of his dialogue method, which is a way of looking at direct mail that's based in large part on—but goes far beyond—the professor's eye-motion research. I've commented at length on Vögele's Dialogue Method in Chapter Two.
- Warwick, M. *Revolution in the Mailbox: Your Guide to Successful Direct Mail Fundraising.* (Rev. and updated ed.). San Francisco: Jossey-Bass, 2004. Originally published in 1990, this book is my attempt to place direct mail fundraising in a larger context, spelling out the strategic potential and long-range impact of launching a direct mail fundraising program. The novice copywriter will find this book useful not just because it explains how direct mail really works but also because it contains a great many sample fundraising letters, many of them reproduced in their entirety, as well as my illustrated analysis of the components of a successful fundraising appeal.

## Online Resources

No reading list compiled in the twenty-first century is complete without electronic newsletters, listservs, Web logs (*blogs*), Web sites, and perhaps other online resources as well. Like everything else on line, materials concerning fundraising and direct mail have multiplied ceaselessly.

You could drive yourself nuts just trying to keep up with all of them. However, precious few of these resources focus on the specific topic of writing fundraising appeals. And, truth to tell, aside from a handful of fundraising newsletters and blogs, I spend little time on line exploring the periodicals and sites related to my craft. I'm too busy working on my own. So, all modesty aside, let's start there:

• *Mal Warwick's Newsletter: Successful Direct Mail, Telephone & Online Fundraising*™. My free, monthly electronic newsletter, now in its third decade of publication, is the only online periodical I'm aware of that is devoted exclusively to direct response fundraising. Almost every issue contains at least one article on writing fundraising materials. Often, you'll find several. Best of all, the newsletter is available free at www.malwarwick.com. So are the archives of back issues from 2001 to the present.

• My company's Web site, www.malwarwick.com, dates to 1994, which has to qualify as the dark ages of the World Wide Web (which went public only in 1992). Because my colleagues and I have been loading up our site with articles, newsletters, book chapters, magazine columns, Q&As, case studies, and who-knows-what-all for nearly a decade and a half, I'm confident you'll find a wealth of useful material there on just about any topic related to direct response fundraising—writing appeals emphatically included. It's all free.

• My friends Deborah Block and Paul Karps, an able freelance copywriting team who collaborate with me on producing my newsletter, compiled a list of online resources for the newsletter and wrote about them in two articles. You can access them at http://www.malwarwick.com/assets/pdfs/9–06final.pdf and http://www.malwarwick.com/assets/pdfs/May07newsletter.pdf.

But don't stop there: explore the Web on your own using Google or another search engine to seek out the very newest fundraising resources. There's a whole world of wisdom out there in cyberspace, and it's there for the taking.

## A Final Word

You're unlikely to write a good fundraising appeal without understanding the dynamics of direct mail fundraising. If you're serious about this, you'll read up on the basics. For the grounding you need, I recommend three of the books listed above: Burnett's *Relationship Fundraising,* Sargeant and Jay's *Building Donor Loyalty,* and my own *Revolution in the Mailbox.* Read these three books cover to cover, understand them, apply the lessons they teach, use www.malwarwick.com to find answers to any specific questions you have, and you'll be off to a great start in your direct mail fundraising career.

# Index

# How to Use the CD

## System Requirements

PC with Microsoft Windows 98SE or later

Mac with Apple OS version 10.1 or later

## Using the CD With Windows

To view the items located on the CD, follow these steps:

1. Insert the CD into your computer's CD-ROM drive.

2. A window appears with the following options:

   Contents: Allows you to view the files included on the CD.

   Software: Allows you to install useful software from the CD.

   Links: Displays a hyperlinked page of websites.

   Author: Displays a page with information about the author(s).

   Contact Us: Displays a page with information on contacting the publisher or author.

   Help: Displays a page with information on using the CD.

   Exit: Closes the interface window.

If you do not have autorun enabled, or if the autorun window does not appear, follow these steps to access the CD:

1. Click Start → Run.

2. In the dialog box that appears, type d:\start.exe, where d is the letter of your CD-ROM drive. This brings up the autorun window described in the preceding set of steps.

3. Choose the desired option from the menu. (See Step 2 in the preceding list for a description of these options.)

## In Case of Trouble

If you experience difficulty using the CD, please follow these steps:

1. Make sure your hardware and systems configurations conform to the systems requirements noted under "System Requirements" above.

2. Review the installation procedure for your type of hardware and operating system. It is possible to reinstall the software if necessary.

To speak with someone in Product Technical Support, call 800-762-2974 or 317-572-3994 Monday through Friday from 8:30 A.M. to 5:00 P.M. EST. You can also contact Product Technical Support and get support information through our website at www.wiley.com/techsupport.

Before calling or writing, please have the following information available:

- Type of computer and operating system.

- Any error messages displayed.

- Complete description of the problem.

It is best if you are sitting at your computer when making the call.